The Articulate Mammal

The Articulate Mammal

An introduction to psycholinguistics

Third edition

Jean Aitchison

London

UNWIN HYMAN

Boston   Sydney   Wellington

Published by the Academic Division of

Unwin Hyman Ltd
15/17 Broadwick Street, London W1V 1FP, UK

Unwin Hyman Inc.,
8 Winchester Place, Winchester, Mass. 01890, USA

Allen & Unwin (Australia) Ltd,
8 Napier Street, North Sydney, NSW 2060, Australia

Allen & Unwin (New Zealand) Ltd in association with the
Port Nicholson Press Ltd,
Compusales Building, 75 Ghuznee Street, Wellington 1, New Zealand

First published in 1989

British Library Cataloguing in Publication Data

Aitchison, Jean
    The articulate mammal: an introduction to psycholinguistics. — 3rd ed.
    1. Language. Psychological aspects
    I. Title
    401'.9

    ISBN 0-04-445355-8

Library of Congress Cataloging-in-Publication Data

Aitchison, Jean, 1938-
    The articulate mammal: an introduction to psycholinguistics/
Jean Aitchison.—3rd ed.
    p. cm.
    Bibliography: p.
    Includes index.
    ISBN 0-04-445355-8
    1. Psycholinguistics. I. Title.
P37.A37   1989   89-30576 CIP
401'.9—dc19

Typeset in 10/12 Times by Fotographics (Bedford) Ltd
and printed in Great Britain by Billing and Sons, London and Worcester

Contents

Preface to the first edition

Some years ago, I gave an evening course entitled 'Psycholinguistics'. I was quite amazed at the response. A large, eager and intelligent group of people arrived, many of them with a serious reason for wanting to know about the subject. There were speech therapists, infant school teachers, an advertising executive, a librarian, an educational psychologist – to name just a few of those whose jobs I noted. There were also parents interested in understanding how children acquire language, and one student who wanted to know how she might help a relative who had lost her language as a result of a stroke. In addition, there were a number of men and women who said they 'just wanted to find out more about language'.

The Articulate Mammal was written for the members of that class, and for others like them: people like me who would like to know why we talk, how we acquire language, and what happens when we produce or comprehend sentences. The book is also intended for students at universities, polytechnics and colleges of education who need an introduction to the subject. It cannot, of course, provide all the answers. But I have tried to set out clearly and briefly what seem to me to have been the major topics of interest in psycholinguistics in recent years, together with an assessment of the 'state of play' in the field at the moment. I hope it will be useful.

I am extremely grateful to a number of scholars who made helpful comments on the manuscript. In particular, and in alphabetical order, Michael Banks of the London School of Economics, David Bennett of the School of Oriental and African Studies, Paul Fletcher of Reading University, Jerry Fodor of the Massachusetts Institute of Technology, Phil Johnson-Laird of the University of Sussex, Geoffrey Sampson of Lancaster University, and Deirdre Wilson of University College, London.

The book would probably have been better if I had taken more notice of their comments – but as the suggested improvements were often contradictory, it was difficult to decide whose opinion to accept. In cases of doubt, I preferred my own, so I am wholly responsible for any errors or over-simplifications that the text may still contain.

My thanks also go to Irene Fekete, the evening course student (and Hutchinson's executive) who persuaded me to write this book.

Let me add a brief note on style. In English, the so-called 'unmarked' or 'neutral between sexes' pronoun is *he*. Had I used this all the way through *The Articulate Mammal*, it might have given the misleading impression that only male mammals are articulate. I have therefore tried to use an equal number of *he*'s and *she*'s in passages where a 'neutral between sexes' pronoun is required.

Jean Aitchison
London, 1975

Preface to the third edition

In the ten or so years since this book was first published, psycholinguistics has increased considerably, both in popularity and in the amount written about it. It has expanded like a young cuckoo, and is in danger of pushing some more traditional areas of linguistics out of the nest. Luckily, many of the questions asked remain the same, though many more tentative answers have been put forward. It is clearly impossible to include all the new developments in this revised edition. I have, however, attempted to outline those which seem most relevant to the issues discussed in this book. In particular, I have added sections on Chomsky's recent views, which differ markedly from those of twenty years ago. Consequently substantial new portions have been added to Chapters 5, 7, and 10. In addition, Chapters 4 and 11 have been rearranged, and extra paragraphs and new references have been inserted all the way through. I hope this new edition will enable readers to keep up with what is happening in the field at the moment.

Jean Aitchison
London, 1988

I find my position as an articulate mammal
bewildering and awesome
Would to God I were a tender apple blawssom

OGDEN NASH

Introduction

Psycholinguistics is sometimes defined as the study of language and the mind. As the name suggests, it is a subject which links psychology and linguistics. The common aim of all who call themselves psycholinguists is to find out about the structures and processes which underlie a human's ability to speak and understand language. Psycholinguists are not necessarily interested in language interaction between people. They are trying above all to probe into what is happening within the individual.

Both psychologists and linguists are involved in studying psycholinguistics. Both types of people can be classified as social scientists, so in one way their approach is similar. All social scientists work by forming and testing hypotheses. For example, a psycholinguist might hypothesize that the speech of someone who is suffering from a progressive disease of the nervous system will disintegrate in a certain order, perhaps suggesting that the constructions the patient learned most recently will be the first to disappear. This hypothesis will then be tested against data collected from the speech of someone who is brain-damaged. This is where psychologists and linguists differ. Psychologists test their hypotheses mainly by means of carefully controlled experiments. Linguists, on the other hand, test their hypotheses mainly by checking them against spontaneous utterances. They feel that the rigidity of experimental situations sometimes falsifies the results. Neither way is right or wrong. Provided that each side is sympathetic to and interested in the work of the other, it can be a great advantage to have two approaches to the subject. And when the results of linguists and psychologists coincide, this is a sure sign of progress.

Most introductory books published so far have been written by psychologists. This is an attempt to provide an introduction to the subject from the linguist's point of view – although inevitably and rightly, it includes accounts of work done by psychologists. This book does not presuppose any knowledge of linguistics – though for those who become interested in the subject, a number of elementary books are suggested on p. 272.

Psycholinguistics is in many ways like the proverbial hydra – a monster with an endless number of heads: There seems no limit to the aspects of the subject which could be explored. This is a rather unsatisfactory state of affairs. As one researcher expressed it: 'When faced with the inevitable question, "What do psycholinguists do?" it is somehow quite unsatisfactory to have to reply, "Everything" ' (Maclay 1973, p. 574).* Or, as another psychologist put it: 'Trying to write a coherent view of psycholinguistics is a bit like trying to assemble a face out of a police identikit. You can't use all of the pieces, and no matter which ones you choose it doesn't look quite right' (Tanenhaus 1988, p. 1). In this situation, it is necessary to specialize fairly rigidly. And amidst the vast array of possible topics, *three* seem to be of particular interest:

1 *The acquisition problem* Do humans acquire language because they are born equipped with specific linguistic knowledge? Or are they able to learn language because they are highly intelligent animals who are skilled at solving problems of various types?

2 *The link between language knowledge and language usage* Linguists often claim to be describing a person's internal representation of language (language *knowledge*), rather than how that knowledge is actually *used*. How then does usage link up with knowledge? If we put this another way, we can say that anybody who has learned a language can do three things:

1 Understand sentences or 'decode' 2 Produce sentences or 'encode'	LANGUAGE USAGE
3 Store linguistic knowledge	LANGUAGE KNOWLEDGE

Many pure linguists claim to be interested in (3) rather than (1) or (2). What psycholinguists need to know is this: is it correct to assume that the type of grammar proposed by linguists really reflects a person's internalized knowledge of their language? And how is that knowledge actually *used* when someone encodes or decodes?

* A complete list of references quoted in the text is contained in the References at the back.

3 *Producing and comprehending speech* Assuming that language usage does differ from language knowledge, what actually happens when a person encodes or decodes?

These are the three questions which this book examines. It does so by considering four types of evidence:

(a) animal communication
(b) child language
(c) the language of normal adults
(d) the speech of dysphasics (people with speech disturbances).

As the diagram below shows, these are not watertight compartments. Each type of evidence is connected to the next by an intermediate link. Animal communication is linked to child language by the 'talking chimps' – apes who are being taught a language system. The link between child and adult language is seen in the

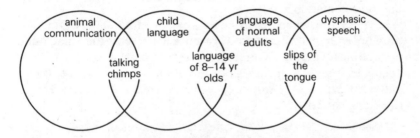

speech of 8-to-14-year-olds. The language of normal adults is linked to those with speech disturbances by 'slips of the tongue' which occur in the speech of all normal people, yet show certain similarities with the speech of dysphasics.

Before moving on to the first topic, the acquisition problem and the question of innate linguistic knowledge, we must make a few comments about the use of the word *grammar*.

We assume that, in order to speak, every person who knows a language has the grammar of that language internalized in their head. The linguist who writes a grammar is making a hypothesis about this internalized system, and is in effect saying, 'My guess as to the knowledge stored in the head of someone who knows a language is as follows . . . .' For this reason, the word *grammar* is used interchangeably to mean both the internal representation of

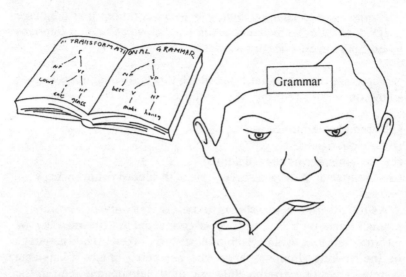

language within a person's head, and a linguist's 'model' or guess of that representation.

Furthermore, when we talk about a person's internalized grammar the word *grammar* is being used in a much wider sense than that found in some old textbooks. It refers to a person's total knowledge of their language. That is, it includes not just a knowledge of *syntax* (word patterns) but also *phonology* (sound patterns) and *semantics* (meaning patterns).

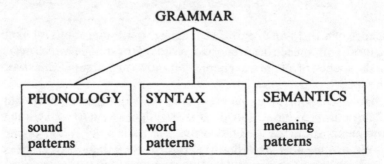

However, since syntax is in a sense the 'key' to language – it is the syntactic patterns which link the sounds and meaning together – the syntactic 'rules' of language will be the basic concern of this book. Phonology and semantics are, as far as possible, omitted, and only referred to where they illuminate syntactic problems.

Perhaps here we need to mention also a vast and woolly subject which is *not* the concern of this book – the relationship of language to thought. Although it is clear that thought is *possible* without language, it seems that people *normally* think in terms of their language. That is, a person's thoughts are 'pre-packaged' into words and grammatical categories. This means that when we are discussing encoding and decoding, we shall not spend time discussing an abstract layer of 'concepts' which some people have assumed to exist at a level 'above' language. When discussing, say, encoding, we shall take it for granted that the first thing a person tells herself to do is, 'Select the relevant words and syntax' rather than 'Package together concepts and see if they can be translated into language'. In other words, if it is necessary to take sides in the controversy as to which comes first, language or thought, we are more on the side of the nineteenth-century poet Shelley, who said 'He gave men speech, and speech created thought' than that of the eighteenth-century lexicographer Samuel Johnson, who claimed that 'Language is the dress of thought'.

Another voluminous topic which is not discussed in this book is that of 'communicative competence'. In recent years, a number of psychologists have made the rather obvious point that children do not merely acquire the structure of language, they also learn to use it appropriately within various social settings. Therefore, it is argued, psycholinguists should pay as much attention to social context as to language structure itself, particularly as children in the early stages of speech are heavily dependent on their surroundings. This work is interesting and important, and most people nowadays agree wholeheartedly that it is useless to consider child utterances in a vacuum. However, humans, if they so wish, are able to rely on structure alone when they communicate. They often manage to comprehend and produce quite unexpected and inappropriate utterances. In fact, it might even be claimed that the ultimate goal of language acquisition is to lie effectively, since 'real lying . . . is the deliberate use of language as a tool . . . with the content of the message unsupported by context to mislead the listener' (De Villiers and De Villiers 1978, p. 165). This book, therefore, takes more interest in the steps by which this mastery of structure is attained, than in the ways in which utterances fit into the surrounding context.

1 The great automatic grammatizator
Need anything be innate?

He reached up and pulled a switch on the panel. Immediately the room was filled with a loud humming noise, and a crackling of electric sparks . . . sheets of quarto paper began sliding out from a slot to the right of the control panel . . . . They grabbed the sheets and began to read. The first one they picked up started as follows: 'Aifkjmbsao-egweztpplnvoqudskigt, fuhpekanvbertyuiolkjhgfdsazxcvbnm, per-uitrehdjkgmvnb, wmsuy . . . .' They looked at the others. The style was roughly similar in all of them. Mr Bohlen began to shout. The younger man tried to calm him down.

'It's all right, sir, Really it is. We've got a connection wrong somewhere, that's all. You must remember, Mr Bohlen, there's over a million feet of wiring in this room.'

'It'll never work,' Mr Bohlen said.

ROALD DAHL
The Great Automatic Grammatizator

Every normal human being can talk. So the average person tends to think that there is little or nothing mysterious about language. As Chomsky has pointed out,

We lose sight of the need for explanation when phenomena are too familiar and 'obvious'. We tend too easily to assume that explanations must be transparent and close to the surface . . . . As native speakers, we have a vast amount of data available to us. For just this reason it is easy to fall into the trap of believing that there is nothing to be explained. Nothing could be further from the truth . . . . [CHOMSKY 1972, pp. 25–6]

But the mysterious nature of human language becomes more apparent when one realizes that no one has yet managed to simulate the language ability of a human being. Computers can play chess, sort bank statements, and even talk about limited topics such as cubes, squares and cones. But we are far from producing a 'great automatic grammatizator' which could unaided hold conversations on any topic. Why is this? Perhaps we should think about language more carefully.

Nature or nurture?

When people start thinking about language, the first question which often occurs to them is this: is language *natural* to man? – in the same way that grunting is natural to pigs, and barking comes naturally to dogs. Or is it just something we happen to have *learned*? – in the same way that dogs may learn to beg, or elephants may learn to waltz, or humans may learn to play the guitar.

Clearly, in one sense, children 'learn' whatever language they are exposed to, be it Chinese, Nootka or English. So no one would deny that 'learning' is very important. But the crucial question is whether children are born with 'blank sheets' in their head as far as language is concerned – or whether humans are 'programmed' with an outline knowledge of the structure of languages in general.

This question of whether language is partly due to *nature* or wholly due to learning or *nurture* is often referred to as the *nature–nurture* controversy, and has been discussed for centuries. For example, it was the topic of one of Plato's dialogues, the *Cratylus*. Controversies which have been going on for literally ages tend to behave in a characteristic fashion. They lie dormant for a while, then break out fiercely. This particular issue resurfaced in linguistics in 1959 when the linguist Noam Chomsky wrote a devastating and witty review of *Verbal Behavior*, a book by the Harvard psychologist B. F. Skinner (Chomsky 1959; Skinner 1957). This book claimed to 'explain' language as a set of habits gradually built up over the years. According to Skinner, no complicated innate or mental mechanisms are needed. All that is necessary is the systematic observation of the events in the external world which prompt the speaker to utter sounds.

Skinner's claim to understand language was based on his work with rats and pigeons. He had proved that, given time, rats and pigeons could be trained to perform an amazing variety of seemingly complex tasks, provided two basic principles were followed. Firstly, the tasks must be broken down into a number of carefully graduated steps. Secondly, the animals must be repeatedly rewarded.

In a typical experiment, a rat is put in a box containing a bar. If it presses the bar, it is rewarded with a pellet of food. Nothing forces it to press the bar. The first time it possibly does so accidentally. When the rat finds that food arrives, it presses the bar again. Eventually it learns that if it is hungry, it can obtain food by pressing the bar. Then the task is made more difficult. The rat only gets rewarded if it presses the bar while a light is flashing. At first the rat is puzzled. Eventually it learns the trick. Then the task is made more difficult again. This time the rat only receives food if it presses the bar a certain number of times. After initial confusion, it learns to do this also. And so on, and so on.

This type of 'trial-and-error' learning is called *operant conditioning* by Skinner, which can be translated as 'training by means of voluntary responses' (the word 'operant' means a voluntary response rather than an automatic one). Skinner suggests that it is by means of this mechanism that the vast majority of human learning takes place, including language learning:

The basic processes and relations which give verbal behaviour its special characteristics are now fairly well understood. Much of the experimental work responsible for this advance has been carried out on other species, but the results have proved to be surprisingly free of species restrictions. Recent work has shown that the methods can be extended to human behaviour without serious modification. [SKINNER 1957, p. 3]

All one needs to do in order to understand language, he says, is to identify the 'controlling variables', which will enable us to predict specific utterances. For example, in the same way as it is possible to say that a rat's bar-pressing behaviour is partly 'under the control' of a flashing light, so a feeling of hunger might 'control' or predict a human utterance such as 'Please pass the bread and butter'. Or the presence of a beautiful painting might call forth the exclamation, 'Oh how beautiful'. Or a bad smell might cause one to exclaim 'Oh what a terrible smell'. A French notice, such as *'Ne touchez pas'*, might result in one saying, 'That means "Don't touch".' And if a child said 'Hickory dickory dock', you are likely to continue 'The mouse ran up the clock'. In theory, Skinner sees no difficulty in linking up any particular set of words which a human might wish to produce with an identifiable external happening.

In practice, the matter is far from simple, as Chomsky points out. Chomsky makes two major criticisms of Skinner's work. Firstly, the behaviour of rats in boxes is irrelevant to human language. Secondly, Skinner fundamentally misunderstands the nature of language.

The irrelevance of rats

Chomsky points out that the simple and well-defined sequence of events observed in the boxes of rats is just not applicable to language.

And the terminology used in the rat experiments cannot be re-applied to human language without becoming hopelessly vague.

For example, how do you know that someone is likely to say 'Oh what a beautiful picture' when looking at a beautiful painting? They might say instead, 'It clashes with the wallpaper', 'It's hanging too low', 'It's hideous'. Skinner would say that instead of the utterance being 'controlled' by the beauty of the picture, it was 'controlled' by its clash with the wallpaper, its hanging too low, its hideousness. But this reduces the idea of 'control' to being meaningless, because you have to wait until you hear the utterance before you know what controlled it. This is quite unlike the predictable behaviour of rats, which could be relied upon to respond to certain stimuli such as a flashing light with a fixed response.

Another problem is that the rats were repeatedly rewarded. It is quite clear that children do not receive pellets of food when they make a correct utterance. However, the idea of reward or *reinforcement* (since it reinforces the behaviour that is being learned) can in humans be naturally extended to approval or disapproval. One might suppose that a parent smiles and says 'Yes dear, that's right' when a child makes a correct utterance. Even if this were so, what happens to this idea of approval when there is nobody around, since children are frequently observed to talk to themselves? Skinner suggests that in these cases children automatically 'reinforce' *themselves* because they know they are producing sounds which they have heard in the speech of others. Similarly, Skinner assumes that someone like a poet who is uttering words aloud in an empty room will be 'reinforced' by the knowledge that others will be influenced by the poetry in the future. So reinforcement seems a very woolly notion, since an actual reward need not exist, it need only be imagined or hoped for. Such a notion is certainly not comparable to the food pellets given to rats when they make a correct response.

Studies by Roger Brown and his associates provide even more problems for Skinner's notion of reinforcement (Brown, Cazden, Bellugi 1968). After observing mother–child interactions they have pointed out that parents tend to approve statements which are *true* rather than those which are grammatically correct. So a boy who said 'Teddy sock on' and showed his mother a teddy bear wearing a sock would probably meet with approval. But if the child said the grammatically correct utterance 'Look, Teddy is wearing a sock', and showed his mother a bear *without* a sock, he would meet with disapproval. In other words, if approval and disapproval worked in the way Skinner suggests, you would expect children to grow up telling the truth, but speaking ungrammatically. In fact the opposite seems to happen.

Another example of a problem which crops up in trying to match rat and human behaviour is that of defining the notion of *response strength*. When a rat has learned to respond to a particular external happening, the extent to which it has learned the lesson can be measured in terms of the speed, force and frequency of the bar-pressing. Skinner suggests that similar measures of response strength might be found in some human responses. For example, a person who is shown a prized work of art might, much to the gratification of the owner, instantly exclaim 'Beautiful!' in a loud voice. Chomsky points out:

It does not appear totally obvious that in this case the way to impress the owner is to shriek 'Beautiful' in a loud, high-pitched voice, repeatedly, and with no delay (high response strength). It may be equally effective to look at the picture silently (long delay), and then to murmur 'Beautiful' in a soft low-pitched voice (by definition, very low response strength). [CHOMSKY 1959, p. 35]

Chomsky used these and similar arguments to show the irrelevance of Skinner's experiments to the problem of understanding language. Perhaps 'irrelevance' is too strong a word, since there are areas of language where habit forming works. For example, some people invariably say 'Damn' if they drop a raw egg, or 'Good night' when they are going to bed, or 'London Transport gets worse every day' when standing at a bus-stop. And there is one sad character in a Beatles' song who only ever says 'Good morning':

> I've got nothing to say but it's OK
> Good morning, good morning, good morning.

But apart from trivial exceptions such as these, language is infinitely more complex and less predictable than Skinner's theory would suggest.

The nature of language

What is there about language that makes it so special? There are a large number of human activities such as learning to drive or learning to knit which seem to be learnt in the same way as bar pressing by rats. Why not language also?

Chomsky points out some of the special properties of language in his review of Skinner's book, where he suggested that Skinner was not in a position to talk about the causation of verbal behaviour, since he knew little about the character of such behaviour.

There is little point in speculating about the process of acquisition without a much better understanding of what is acquired. [CHOMSKY 1959, p. 55]

Chomsky has since discussed the nature of language in a number of places (e.g. Chomsky 1972, 1980, 1986, 1988). One point which he stresses is that language makes use of *structure-dependent operations*. By this he means that the composition and production of utterances is not merely a question of stringing together sequences of words. Every sentence has an inaudible internal structure which must be understood by the hearer.

In order to see more clearly what is meant by a *structure-dependent* operation, it is useful to look at *structure-independent* operations.

Suppose a martian had landed on earth, and was trying to learn English. She might hear the sentence:

AUNT JEMIMA HAS DROPPED HER FALSE TEETH DOWN THE DRAIN

as well as the related question:

HAS AUNT JEMIMA DROPPED HER FALSE TEETH DOWN THE DRAIN?

If she was an intelligent martian, she would immediately start trying to guess the rules for the formation of questions in English. Her first guess might be that English has a rule which says, 'In order to form a question, scan the sentence for the word *has* and bring it to the front.' Superficially, this strategy might occasionally work. For example, a sentence such as:

PETRONELLA HAS HURT HERSELF

would quite correctly become

HAS PETRONELLA HURT HERSELF?

But it is clearly a wrong strategy, because it would also mean that the martian would turn a statement such as:

THE MAN WHO HAS RUN AWAY SHOUTING WAS ATTACKED BY A WASP

into

*HAS THE MAN WHO RUN AWAY SHOUTING WAS ATTACKED BY A WASP?

which is not English. (An asterisk denotes an impossible sentence.)

Looking at the Aunt Jemima sentence again, the martian might make a second guess, 'In order to form a question, bring the third word to the front.' Once again, this might superficially appear to work because a sentence such as:

THE ALLIGATOR HAS ESCAPED

would correctly become

HAS THE ALLIGATOR ESCAPED?

But it is obviously accidental that this type of rule gets the right result, because it also produces a number of non-sentences:

SLUGS ARE SLIMY

would become

*SLIMY SLUGS ARE?

and

MARY HAS SWALLOWED A SAFETY PIN

turns into

*SWALLOWED MARY HAS A SAFETY PIN?

The martian went wrong in her guesses because she was trying out structure-independent operations – manoeuvres which relied solely on mechanical counting or simple recognition procedures without looking at the *internal* structure of the sentences concerned. In order to grasp the principles of question formation, the martian must first realize that

AUNT JEMIMA, THE MAN WHO HAS RUN AWAY SHOUTING, SLUGS, MARY

each behaves as a unit of structure. The number of words within each unit is irrelevant, so no amount of counting will produce the right result for question formation. In these sentences (though not in all English sentences) the solution is to take the word which follows the first unit and bring it to the front:

AUNT JEMIMA	HAS	DROPPED HER FALSE TEETH DOWN THE DRAIN
THE MAN WHO HAS RUN AWAY SHOUTING	WAS	ATTACKED BY A WASP
SLUGS	ARE	SLIMY
MARY	HAS	SWALLOWED A SAFETY PIN

This may seem an obvious solution to people who already know English – but it is not at all clear *why* language should behave in this way. As Chomsky points out:

The result is . . . surprising from a certain point of view. Notice that the structure-dependent operation has no advantages from the point of view of communicative efficiency or 'simplicity'. If we were, let us say, designing a language for formal manipulations by a computer, we would certainly prefer structure-independent operations. These are far simpler to carry out, since it is only necessary to scan the words of the sentence, paying no attention to the structures which they enter, structures that are not marked physically in the sentence at all. [CHOMSKY 1972a, p. 30]

Yet, amazingly, all children learning language seem to know automatically that language involves structure-dependent operations. On the face of it, one might expect them to go through a prolonged phase of testing out martian-like solutions – but they do not. This leads Chomsky to suggest that humans may have an innate knowledge of this phenomenon:

Given such facts, it is natural to postulate that the idea of 'structure-dependent operations' is part of the innate schematism applied by the mind to the data of experience. [CHOMSKY 1972a, p. 30]

This knowledge, he argues, 'is part of the child's biological endowment, part of the structure of the language faculty' (Chomsky 1988, p. 45).

The structure-dependent nature of the operations used in language is all the more remarkable because there are often no overt clues to the structure. Experiments carried out by psycholinguists have made it clear that listeners do not have to rely on auditory clues for interpreting the main structural divisions. For example, Garrett, Bever and Fodor (1966) constructed two sentences which each contained the words:

GEORGE DROVE FURIOUSLY TO THE STATION:

1 IN ORDER TO CATCH HIS TRAIN GEORGE DROVE FURIOUSLY TO
   THE STATION
2 THE REPORTERS ASSIGNED TO GEORGE DROVE FURIOUSLY TO
   THE STATION.

In the first sentence, it is GEORGE who is driving furiously. In the second, it is the REPORTERS. In order to understand the sentence, the listener must (mentally) put the structural break in the correct place:

IN ORDER TO CATCH HIS TRAIN	GEORGE DROVE FURIOUSLY TO THE STATION
THE REPORTERS ASSIGNED TO GEORGE	DROVE FURIOUSLY TO THE STATION.

Just to check that the listeners were *not* using auditory clues, the experimenters recorded both these sentences on to tapes. Then they cut the words GEORGE DROVE FURIOUSLY TO THE STATION off each tape, and spliced them to the *other* sentence:

IN ORDER TO CATCH HIS TRAIN	GEORGE DROVE FURIOUSLY TO THE STATION
THE REPORTERS ASSIGNED TO	GEORGE DROVE FURIOUSLY TO THE STATION.

They then played the newly spliced tapes to students – but into one ear only. In the other ear the students heard a click, which was placed in the middle of a word, for example, GEORGE. The students were then asked whereabouts in the sentence the click had occurred. The interesting result was that in their reports students tended to move the location of the click in the direction of the structural break:

IN ORDER TO CATCH HIS TRAIN GEORGE DROVE FURIOUSLY TO THE
STATION

THE REPORTERS ASSIGNED TO GEORGE DROVE FURIOUSLY TO THE
STATION.

This indicates clearly that listeners impose a structure on what they hear for which there is often *no* physical evidence.

   Another point which has been made by Chomsky (1959) and a number of other writers (e.g. Bever, Fodor and Weksel 1965) is that simple slot-filling operations are inadequate as explanations of language. It has sometimes been suggested that anyone learning language allocates to each sentence a number of 'slots' and then fits units of structure into each hole:

For example:

1	2	3
BEES	LOVE	HONEY
I	WANT	MY TEA
MY BROTHER	HAS HIT	ME

No one would deny the existence of such substitutions and their value in language learning. But the problem is that there is a lot more going on besides, which cannot be accounted for by the 'slot' idea: 'It is evident that more is involved in sentence structure than insertion of lexical items in grammatical frames' (Chomsky 1959, p. 54). For example, look at the following sentences:

PERFORMING FLEAS	CAN BE	AMUSING
PLAYING TIDDLYWINKS	CAN BE	AMUSING

As soon as we try to find other words to fit into the slot occupied by *can be*, we run into problems. *Are* fits in with the first sentence but not the second, whereas *is* fits in with the second but not the first:

PERFORMING FLEAS	ARE	AMUSING
*PERFORMING FLEAS	IS	AMUSING
*PLAYING TIDDLYWINKS	ARE	AMUSING
PLAYING TIDDLYWINKS	IS	AMUSING

If slot-filling was the sole principle on which language worked, one would not expect this result. In fact, slot-filling makes it quite impossible to explain how the listener knows, in the sentences where the centre slot is filled by *can be*, that it is the fleas who are performing, but that it is not the tiddlywinks who are playing. But examples of 'constructional homonymity' (as Chomsky calls such superficially similar utterances) are by no means rare.

Even more inexplicable from a slot-filling point of view are sentences which can be interpreted in two different ways:

CLEANING LADIES CAN BE DELIGHTFUL:
1 LADIES WHO CLEAN CAN BE DELIGHTFUL
2 TO CLEAN LADIES CAN BE DELIGHTFUL

THE MISSIONARY WAS READY TO EAT:
1 THE MISSIONARY WAS ABOUT TO EAT
2 THE MISSIONARY WAS ABOUT TO BE EATEN.

Sentences such as these indicate that merely filling a grammatical frame may be only part of what is happening when we speak.

It would be possible to proliferate slot-filling problems. But one interesting one to which much attention has been paid involves the behaviour of a word such as PUT. Consider the sentence:

JOSHUA	PUT	A SNAIL	INTO MAVIS'S SOUP

The verb PUT requires two types of slot after it: a slot for what you put (A SNAIL) and another for where you put it (INTO MAVIS'S SOUP). Both slots are necessary, because you can't say:

*JOSHUA PUT
*JOSHUA PUT A SNAIL
*JOSHUA PUT INTO MAVIS'S SOUP.

But then how are we to explain the sentences:

WHAT DID JOSHUA PUT INTO MAVIS'S SOUP?
WHAT DID I HEAR THAT JOSHUA PUT INTO MAVIS'S SOUP?
WHAT DID I HEAR YOU SAY THAT JOSHUA PUT INTO MAVIS'S SOUP?

Here, the 'what you put' slot has apparently been moved away from its 'proper' place, and placed at the beginning of the sentence, in some cases quite a long way from the word PUT. But the matter gets even more complicated with sentences such as:

DID YOU SEE WHAT JOSHUA PUT INTO MAVIS'S SOUP?
IT WAS IMPOSSIBLE TO SEE WHAT PETER THOUGHT HE SAW JOSHUA
   PUT INTO MAVIS'S SOUP.

Here, the 'what you put' slot is not in its 'proper place', nor is it in some easily identifiable location, such as the beginning of the sentence. So what is happening?

This type of example has led Chomsky to suggest that language is organized on two levels: a *surface* level, in which words are in the place where they actually occur, and a *deep* level, in which words are located in their 'proper' place in the slot structure. So, in the sentences above, the 'what you put' slot would always appear after PUT in the deep structure:

JOSHUA	PUT	WHAT	INTO MAVIS'S SOUP

(Although the words in the deep structure would occur in this order, the deep structure, or D-structure, as Chomsky now calls it, is considerably more complicated.)

Chomsky's arguments that a 'deeper' level of syntax underlies the surface level are persuasive – but not necessarily right. Other explanations are possible. The important point to note is that the type of phenomena found in sentences containing words such as PUT can *not* be explained by means of the bar-pressing antics of rats, nor by means of simple slot-filling operations. Some more complex mechanism is involved.

So far, then, language can be said to be structure-dependent – and the types of structure-dependent operations involved seem to be complex.

Creativity is another fundamental aspect of language which is stressed repeatedly by Chomsky. By this, he seems to mean two things. Firstly, and primarily he means the fact that humans have the ability to understand and produce novel utterances. Even quite strange sentences, which are unlikely to have been uttered before, cause no problems for speakers and hearers:

THE ELEPHANT DRANK SEVENTEEN BOTTLES OF SHAMPOO, THEN
    SKIPPED DRUNKENLY ROUND THE ROOM.
THE AARDVARK CLEANED ITS TEETH WITH A PURPLE TOOTHBRUSH.

This means that it is quite impossible to assume that a person gradually accumulates strings of utterances throughout their life and stores them ready for use on an appropriate occasion. And as well as producing new grammatical sequences, anyone who has mastered a language is automatically able to discard deviant utterances which they may never have met before. Sequences such as:

*HE WILL HAD BEEN SINGING

or:

*GIRAFFE UNDER IN WALKS GORILLA THE

will be rejected instantaneously.

Chomsky also uses 'creativity' in a second, subsidiary sense to mean that utterances are not controlled by external happenings. The appearance of a daffodil does not force humans to shriek 'Daffodil'. They can say whatever they like: 'What a lovely colour', 'It's spring, I must remember to clean my car', or 'Why do flowers always give me hay fever?'

Most humans are so used to these properties of language that they no longer seem odd – but they have not yet been fully explained. Chomsky speaks of 'this still mysterious ability' when referring to the creative nature of man's speech:

Having mastered a language, one is able to understand an indefinite number of expressions that are new to one's experience, that bear no simple physical resemblance and are in no simple way analogous to the expressions that constitute one's linguistic experience; and one is able with greater or less facility to produce such expressions on an appropriate occasion, despite their novelty and independently of detachable stimulus configurations, and to be understood by others who share this still mysterious ability. The normal use of language is, in this sense, a creative activity. This creative aspect of normal language is one fundamental factor that distinguishes human language from any known system of animal communication. [CHOMSKY 1972, p. 100]

Chomsky stresses that the creative aspect of language is *normal*. Humans produce novel utterances all the time, and anybody who does not is likely to be brain damaged:

It is important to bear in mind that the creation of linguistic expressions that are novel but appropriate is the normal mode of language use. If some individual were to restrict himself largely to a definite set of linguistic patterns, to a set of habitual responses to stimulus configurations . . . we would regard him as mentally defective, as being less human than animal. He would immediately be set apart from normal humans by his inability to understand normal discourse, or to take part in it in the normal way – the normal way being innovative, free from control by external stimuli, and appropriate to a new and ever-changing situation. [CHOMSKY 1972, p. 100]

It becomes clear that there is much more to language than merely stringing together words. In order to speak, a human possesses a highly complex internalized set of rules which enables him to utter any of (and only) the permissible sequences of English – though he is unlikely to have any conscious knowledge of the rules. The rules are both complex and stringent, as Mr Knipe discovered (a character in a short story by Roald Dahl):

Then suddenly he was struck by a powerful but simple little truth, and it was this: that English grammar is governed by rules that are almost mathematical in their strictness! . . . Therefore, it stands to reason that an engine built along the lines of the electric computer could be adjusted to arrange words in their right order according to the rules of grammar . . . . There was no stopping Knipe now. He went to work immediately. After fifteen days of continuous labour, Knipe had finished building his 'Great Automatic Grammatizator'.

But Mr Knipe is a character in a science-fiction story. As already noted, in real life no linguist, no computer expert has yet managed to build an 'automatic grammatizator' – a device which will account for all and only the permissible sequences of English.

Yet children do it all the time: in a remarkably short period, they acquire a complex set of internalized rules. And children have considerably less data to work from than the linguists who have failed to produce 'automatic grammatizators'. They are often restricted to hearing their parents and relatives talking – and, according to Chomsky, this speech is likely to be full of unfinished sentences, mistakes and slips of the tongue. We must therefore 'explain how we know so much, given that the evidence available to us is so sparse' (Chomsky 1986, p. xxvii). Furthermore, according to him, the acquisition of one's native language seems to be largely independent of intelligence. The language ability of dim children is not noticeably inferior to that of bright children – yet in most other areas of human activity – such as roller-skating or playing the piano – the gap between different children is enormous.

Although Chomsky is now generally thought to exaggerate the rapidity of acquisition, the sub-standard nature of the data, and the uniformity of ability, the great mystery remains: how do children construct 'automatic grammatizators' for themselves?

At the moment, the issue is an open one. Two possibilities exist:

Possibility 1 Human infants 'know' in advance what languages are like. This is the possibility preferred by Chomsky:

Given the richness and complexity of the system of grammar for a human language and the uniformity of its acquisition on the basis of limited and often degenerate evidence, there can be little doubt that highly restrictive universal principles must exist determining the general framework of each human language and perhaps much of its specific structure as well. [CHOMSKY 1980, p. 232]

Possibility 2 No special advance knowledge is needed, because children are highly efficient puzzle-solvers in all areas of human behaviour. Language is just one type of puzzle which their high level of general intelligence enables them to solve fast and well. In the words of the linguist Geoffrey Sampson:

Individual humans inherit no 'knowledge of language' . . . they succeed in mastering the language spoken in their environment only by applying the same general intelligence which they use to grapple with all the other diverse and unpredictable problems that come their way. [SAMPSON 1980, p. 178]

It may not be necessary to choose between these possibilities. As the book will suggest, the answer may well lie somewhere between these two extremes. In this controversy, it is important to keep an open mind, and not be swayed by the fashion of the moment. In the 1960s, it was fashionable to follow Chomsky. In the 1970s it was equally fashionable to hold the view of his opponents. Yet Chomsky's claim that children are 'pre-programmed' to speak is a serious and interesting one which cannot easily be dismissed. As the nineteenth-century American philosopher C. S. Peirce pointed out: 'If men had not come . . . with special aptitudes for guessing right, it may well be doubted whether . . . the greatest mind would have attained the amount of knowledge which is actually possessed by the lowest idiot' (Peirce 1932, p. 476).

Chomsky's belief that humans are genetically imprinted with knowledge about language is often referred to as 'the innateness hypothesis'. Unfortunately, the word 'innate' has given rise to a considerable amount of confusion. Misunderstandings have arisen in two ways. First, to call Chomsky an 'innatist' wrongly implies that those who disagree with him are 'non-innatists'. Yet his opponents have never asserted that *nothing* is innate. All human skills, even apparently unnatural ones, make use of innate predispositions. For example, driving a car is an 'unnatural' acquired skill, yet it makes use of innate propensities, such as the ability to see, or to co-ordinate arm and leg movements (Sampson 1975, p. 12). The issue under discussion is whether an innate language ability exists independently of other innate abilities. The point is expressed well by two philosophers: 'It is beyond dispute that some innate equipment figures in the acquisition of language (otherwise the baby's rattle would learn language as well as the baby, since they have comparable linguistic environments). The only question at issue is whether this innate structure has significant components that subserve the development of no other faculty than language' (Osherson and Wasow 1976, p. 208). Chomsky claims that the mind is 'constituted of "mental organs" just as specialized and differentiated as those of the body' (1979, p. 83), and that 'Language is a system . . . easy to isolate among the various mental faculties' (1979, p. 46). This is the claim which we are trying to evaluate.

The second misunderstanding involves a mistaken belief by some people that 'innate' means 'ready-made for use'. By innate, Chomsky simply means 'genetically programmed'. He does not literally think that children are born with language in their heads ready to be spoken. He merely claims that a 'blueprint' is there, which is brought into use when the child reaches a certain point in her general development. With the help of this blueprint, she analyses the language she hears around her more readily than she would if she were totally unprepared for the strange gabbling sounds which emerge from human mouths.

Or perhaps a better metaphor would be that of a seed, which contains within itself the intrinsic ability to become a dahlia or rose, provided it is planted and tended. Chomsky argues that 'language grows in the mind/brain' (Chomsky 1988, p. 55). He explains the situation by quoting the eighteenth-century thinker James Harris: 'The growth of knowledge . . . [rather resembles] . . . the growth of Fruit; however external causes may in some degree cooperate, it is the internal vigour, and virtue of the tree, that must ripen the juices to their maturity' (Chomsky 1986, p. 2).

In the next few chapters, we will examine the suggestion that language is a special, pre-programmed activity in more depth. As Chomsky notes:

No one finds it outlandish to ask the question: what genetic information accounts for the growth of arms instead of wings? Why should it be shocking to raise similar questions with regard to the brain and mental faculties? [1979, p. 84]

2 Animals that try to talk
Is language restricted to humans?

An ant who can speak
French, Javanese and Greek
Doesn't exist.
Why ever not?
ROBERT DESNOS

Judging by newspapers and popular books, there appear to be a vast number of animals which 'talk' – talking budgerigars, talking dolphins – even a talking fish:

Anne, Anne, come quick as you can
There's a fish that talks in the frying pan.
[WALTER DE LA MARE]

Clearly, the word 'talk' can be used in two totally different senses. On the one hand, it can mean simply 'to utter words', as in 'Archibald's got a talking parrot which says *Damn* if you poke it'. On the other hand, it can mean 'to use language in a meaningful way'. We already know that animals such as budgerigars can 'talk' in the first sense of the word. Psycholinguists would like to find out whether animals can 'talk' in the second sense also. They are interested in this problem because they want to know the answer to the following question: are we the only species which possesses language? If so, are we the only species capable of acquiring it?

These are the topics examined in this chapter. First of all animal communication systems are compared with human language to see if animals can be said to 'talk' in any real sense. Secondly, various attempts to teach language to animals are considered. The overall purpose behind such inquiries is to find out whether humans alone have the power of speech. Are we biologically singled out as 'articulate mammals' or not?

Of course, if we discover that animals *do* talk, then we shall not have learned anything useful, just as the fact that we can do the breast stroke does not tell us anything about a frog's innate swimming ability. Or, as Fodor, Bever and Garrett acidly note, 'The fact that a dog can be trained to walk on its hind legs does not prejudice the claim that bipedal gait is genetically coded in humans. The fact that we can learn to whistle like a lark does not prejudice the species-specificity of birdsong' (Fodor, Bever and Garrett 1974, p. 451). If, on the other hand, we find that animals do *not* talk, this will provide some support for the claim that language is restricted to the human race. We are not merely indulging in a neurotic desire to verify that humans are still superior to other species, as has sometimes been suggested. The purpose of this chapter is a more serious one. Some animals, such as dolphins and chimpanzees, have a high level of intelligence. If, in spite of this, we find that language is beyond their capability, then we may have found some indication that language is a genetically-programmed activity which is largely separate from general intelligence.

Do animals talk naturally?

Our first task is to find out whether any animals naturally have a true 'language'. In order to answer this question, we must compare human language with animal communication. But such a comparison presents a number of perhaps unsolvable problems. Two in particular need to be discussed before we can give a coherent reply to the query, 'Do animals talk naturally?'

The first problem we must consider is this: are we comparing systems which differ quantitatively or qualitatively? On the one hand, human language may have gradually evolved from a more primitive animal means of communication in a continuous line of growth – a viewpoint sometimes known as a 'continuity' theory. On the other hand, human language may be something quite different from our basic animal heritage, and superimposed on it. This is a 'discontinuity' theory.

Supporters of continuity theories suggest that language grew out of a primate call system, like the ones used by apes today. They assume that humans started out with a simple set of cries in which each one meant something different, such as, 'Danger!' or 'Follow me!' or 'Don't touch that female, she's mine!' These cries gradually became more elaborate, and eventually evolved into language. A possible intermediate stage is seen in the cries of the vervet monkey. This monkey has several alarm calls which distinguish between different types of danger (Struhsaker 1967). The *chutter* announces that a puff adder or cobra is around. The *rraup* gives warning of an eagle. A *chirp* is used for lions and leopards. A less panic-stricken utterance, the *uh!*, signals the presence of a spotted hyena or Masai tribesman. According to some, it is a very short step from an alarm call warning of a poisonous snake to using the *chutter* as a 'word' symbolizing a poisonous snake.

But another interpretation of these signals is possible. The monkeys could merely be distinguishing between the *intensity* of different types of danger. They may be more frightened of puff adders than eagles – or vice versa. This plausible explanation has been ruled out by an experiment in which a concealed loudspeaker played recordings of the various alarm calls. When they heard a *chutter*, the vervets stood on their hind legs and looked around for a snake. At the sound of a *rraup* they dived into the vegetation as if hiding from an eagle. And at the lion-leopard *chirp*, they hastily climbed up a tree (Seyfarth, Cheney and Marler 1980, 1980a). So the monkeys clearly have a special signal for each type of enemy.

But the call systems of moneys are still so far from human language that many people argue for a discontinuity theory. Proponents of discontinuity theories claim that humans still retain their basic set of animal cries, which exist alongside language. Yelps of pain, shrieks of fear, and the different types of crying observed in babies may be closely related to the call systems of monkeys. If this view is correct, then it is fairly difficult to compare human and animal means of communication. It may be like comparing two things as different as the Chinese language and a set of traffic lights. But at the moment the question is an open one. We do not yet know whether the continuity or the discontinuity theorists are correct. But we must keep both possibilities in mind when discussing the main topic of this chapter.

The second major problem we face is that it is not always easy to decide what counts as communication in animals. As one researcher notes:

Students of animal behaviour have often noted the extreme difficulty of restricting the notion of communication to anything less than every potential interaction between an organism and its environment. [MARSHALL 1970, p. 231]

So that, at the very least, sticklebacks mating, cats spitting, and rabbits thumping their back legs must be taken into consideration – and it isn't at all clear where to stop. It is sometimes suggested that this problem could be solved by concentrating on examples where the animal is *intentionally* trying to convey information. But such distinctions are difficult to draw, both in humans and animals. If a man smoothes down his hair when an attractive woman walks into the room, is this an unconscious response? Or is he doing it intentionally in the hope of catching her attention? In the sea, so-called 'snapping shrimps' can produce loud cracks by closing their claws sharply. Since the cracks can upset naval sonar devices, marine biologists have attempted to discover the circumstances which lead the shrimps to produce them. But no one has yet discovered the significance of the snaps. They may be informative – but they may not. There is no way in which we can be sure about making the right decision when it comes to interpreting such a phenomenon.

Having outlined these fundamental problems – which show that any conclusions we draw are only tentative – we can now return to our main theme: a comparison of human language and animal communication. How should we set about this?

A useful first step might be to attempt to define 'language'. This is not as easy as it sounds. Many definitions found in elementary textbooks are too wide. For example: 'A language is a system of arbitrary vocal symbols by means of which a social group cooperates' (Bloch and Trager 1942, p. 5). This definition might equally well apply to a pack of wolves howling in chorus.

Perhaps the most promising approach is that suggested by the linguist Charles Hockett. In a series of articles stretching over ten years he has attempted to itemize out the various 'design features' which characterize language. For example: '*Interchangeability*: Adult members of any speech community are interchangeably transmitters and receivers of linguistic signals'; '*Complete Feedback*: The transmitter of a linguistic signal himself receives the message' (Hockett 1963, p. 9). Of course, such an approach is not perfect. A list of features may even be misleading, since it represents a random set of observations which do not cohere in any obvious way. To use this list to define language is like trying to define a man by noting that he has two arms, two legs, a head, a belly button, he bleeds if you scratch him, and shrieks if you tread on his toe. But in spite of this, a definition of language based on design features or 'essential characteristics' seems to be the most useful proposed so far.

But how many characteristics should be considered? Two? Ten? A hundred? The number of design features Hockett considers important has changed over the years. His longest list contains sixteen (Hockett and Altmann 1968). Perhaps most people would consider that ten features capture the essential nature of language, not all of which are mentioned by Hockett. These are: *use of the vocal-auditory channel, arbitrariness, semanticity, cultural trans-mission, spontaneous usage, turn-taking, duality, displacement, structure-dependence,* and *creativity.* Some of these features are fairly general, and occur widely in the animal world. Others are more specialized, and concern the way in which language is organized.

Let us discuss each of these features in turn, and see whether it is present in animal communication. If any animal naturally possesses *all* the design features of human language, then clearly that animal can talk.

The use of the *vocal-auditory channel* is perhaps the most obvious characteristic of language. Sounds are made with the vocal organs, and a hearing mechanism receives them – a phenomenon which is neither rare nor particularly surprising. The use of sound is widespread as a means of animal communication. One obvious advantage is that messages can be sent or received in the dark or in a dense forest. Not all sound signals are vocal – woodpeckers tap on wood, and rattlesnakes have a rattle apparatus on their tail. But vocal-auditory signals are common and are used by birds, cows, apes and foxes, to name just a few. The advantages of this method of producing the sound are that it leaves the body free to carry on other activities at the same time, and also requires relatively little physical energy. But this design feature is clearly neither unique to humans, nor all-important, since language can arguably be transferred without loss to visual symbols (as in sign language, or writing) and to tactile symbols (as in Braille). Patients who have had their vocal cords removed, and communicate mainly by writing, have not lost their language ability. It follows that this characteristic is of little use in an attempt to distinguish animal from human communication. So let us proceed to the second feature, arbitrariness.

Arbitrariness means that human languages use neutral symbols. There is no connection between the word DOG and the four-legged animal it symbolizes. It can equally be called UN CHIEN (French), EIN HUND (German), or CANIS (Latin). GÜL (Turkish) and RHODON (Greek) are equally satisfactory names for a 'rose'. As Juliet notes:

> What's in a name? that which we call a rose
> By any other name would smell as sweet.
> [SHAKESPEARE]

Onomatopoeic words such as CUCKOO, POP, BANG, SLURP, and SQUISH are exceptions to this. But there are relatively few of these in any language. On the other hand, it is normal for animals to have a strong link between the message they are sending and the signal they use to convey it. A crab which wishes to convey extreme aggression will extend a large claw. A less angry crab will merely raise a leg: 'Extending a major chaliped is more effective than raising a single ambulatory leg in causing the second crab to retreat or duck back into its shell' (Marshall 1970). However, arbitrary symbols are not unique to man. Gulls, for example, sometimes indicate aggression by turning away from their opponent and uprooting beakfuls of grass. So we are forced to conclude that arbitrariness cannot be regarded as a critical distinction between human and animal communication.

Semanticity, the third suggested test for language ability, is the use of symbols to 'mean' or refer to objects and actions. To a human, a CHAIR 'means' a four-legged contraption you can sit on. Humans can generalize by applying this name to all types of chairs, not just one in particular. Furthermore, semanticity applies to actions as well as objects. For example, to JUMP 'means' the act of leaping in the air. Some writers have claimed that semanticity is exclusively human. Animals may be able to communicate only about a total situation. A hen who utters 'danger' cries when a fox is nearby is possibly conveying the message 'Beware! Beware! There is terrible danger about!' rather than using the sound to 'mean' FOX. But, as was shown by the call of the vervet monkey who might mean 'snake' when it *chutters*, it is difficult to be certain. We must remain agnostic about whether this feature is present in animal communication.

Cultural transmission or *tradition* indicates that human beings hand their languages down from one generation to another. The role played by teaching in animal communication is unclear and varies from animal to animal – and even with species. Among birds it is claimed that the song-thrush's song is largely innate, but can be slightly modified by learning, whereas the skylark's song is almost wholly learned. Birds such as the chaffinch are particularly interesting: the basic pattern of the song seems to be innate, but all the finer detail and much of the pitch and rhythm have to be acquired by learning (Thorpe 1961, 1963). However, although the distinction between man and animals is not clear-cut as regards this feature, it seems that a far greater proportion of communication is genetically inbuilt in animals than in humans. A child brought up in isolation, away from human beings, does not acquire language. In contrast, birds reared in isolation sing songs that are sometimes recognizable (though almost always abnormal).

The fifth and sixth features are social ones, in that they relate to the way in which language is used. *Spontaneous usage* indicates that humans initiate speech freely. Speaking is not something which they do under duress, like a dog which will stand on its hind legs only when a biscuit is held above its nose. This feature is certainly not restricted to humans, and many animals use their natural communication systems freely. The other social feature, *turn-taking*, means exactly what it says: we take it in turns to speak. In the majority of conversations, we do not talk while other people are talking, nor do we compete with them. Instead, we politely wait our turn, as shown in a brief conversation between two characters in P. G. Wodehouse's *Carry on Jeeves*:

> 'What ho!' I said
> 'What ho!' said Motty.
> 'What ho! What ho!'
> 'What ho! What ho! What ho!'

As we can see, Motty and the narrator have no idea what to say to one another. Nevertheless, they know that they have to take it in turns to talk. Such turn-taking begins at a very early age. Even mothers and babies alternate as they mouth nonsense syllables at each other. Once again, this is not an exclusively human characteristic, since birds sometimes sing duets together. One bird sings a few phrases, then pauses while the other has its turn, a phenomenon known as antiphonal singing.

The seventh property, *duality* or *double-articulation*, means that language is organized into two 'layers': the basic sound units of speech, such as P, I, G, are normally meaningless by themselves. They only become meaningful when combined into sequences such as P-I-G PIG. This property is sometimes claimed to be unique to humans. But this is not so. Duality is also present in bird song, where each individual note is itself meaningless – it is the combinations of notes which convey meaningful messages. So once again we have not found a critical difference between animals and humans in their use of this feature.

A more important characteristic of language is *displacement*, the ability to refer to things far removed in time and place. Humans frequently say things such as 'My Aunt Matilda, who lives in Australia, cracked her knee-cap last week'. It may be impossible for an animal to convey a similar item of information. However, as in the case of other design features, it is sometimes difficult to decide whether displacement is present in an animal's communication system. A bird frequently continues to give alarm cries long after the disappearance of a cat which was stalking it. Is this displacement or not? The answer is unclear. Definite examples of displacement are hard to find. But it is undoubtedly found in bee communication (von Frisch 1950, 1954, 1967). When a worker bee finds a source of nectar she returns to the hive to perform a complex dance which informs the other bees of its location. She does a 'round dance', which involves turning round in circles if the nectar is close to the hive, and a 'waggle dance' in which she wiggles her tail from side to side if it is far away. The other bees work out the distance by noting the tempo of her waggles, and discover what kind of flower to look for by smelling its scent on her body. After the dance, they unerringly fly to the right place, even if it is several miles away, with a hill intervening.

This is an unusual ability – but even this degree of displacement is considerably less than that found in human speech. The bee cannot inform other bees about anything further removed than the nectar patch she has just visited. She cannot say 'The day before yesterday we visited a lovely clump of flowers, let's go and see if they are still there' – she can only say, 'Come to the nectar I have just visited'. Nor can she communicate about anything further away in place. She could not say 'I wonder whether there's good nectar in Siberia'. So displacement in bee communication is strictly limited to the number of miles a bee can easily fly, and the time it takes to do this. At last, it seems we may have found a feature which seems to be of importance in human language, and only partially present in non-human communication.

The ninth feature, *structure-dependence*, was discussed in Chapter 1. Humans do not just apply simple recognition or counting techniques when they speak to one another. They automatically recognize the patterned nature of language, and manipulate 'structured chunks'. For example, they understand that a group of words can sometimes be the structural equivalent of one:

SHE	
THE OLD LADY WHO WAS WEARING A WHITE BONNET	GAVE THE DONKEY A CARROT

and they can arrange these chunks according to strict rules:

A CARROT	WAS GIVEN TO THE DONKEY	BY THE OLD LADY WHO WAS WEARING A WHITE BONNET

As far as we know, animals do not use structure-dependent operations. We do not know enough about the communication of all animals to be sure, but no definite example has yet been found.

Finally, there is one feature that seems to be of overwhelming importance, and unique to humans – the ability to produce and understand an indefinite number of novel utterances. This property of language has several different names. Chomsky calls it *creativity* (Chapter 1), others call it *openness* or *productivity*. Humans can talk about anything they like – even a platypus falling backwards downstairs – without causing any linguistic problems to themselves or the hearers. They can say *what* they want *when* they want. If it thunders, they do not automatically utter a set phrase, such as 'It's thundering, run for cover'. They can say 'Isn't the lightning pretty?' or 'Better get the dog in' or 'Thunder is two dragons colliding in tin tubs, according to a Chinese legend'.

In contrast, most animals have a fixed number of signals which convey a set number of messages, sent in clearly definable circumstances. A North American cicada can give four signals only. It emits a 'disturbance squawk' when it is seized, picked up or eaten. A 'congregation call' seems to mean 'Let's all get together and sing in chorus!' A preliminary courtship call (an invitation?) is uttered when a female is several inches away. An advanced courtship call (a buzz of triumph?) occurs when the female is almost within grasp (Alexander and Moore, quoted in McNeill 1970). Even the impressive vervet monkey has only thirty-six distinct vocal sounds in its repertoire. And as this includes sneezing and vomiting, the actual number used for communication is several fewer. Within this range, choice is limited, since circumstances generally dictate which call to use. An infant separated from its mother gives the lost *rrah* cry. A female who wishes to deter an amorous male gives the 'anti-copulatory squeal-scream' (Struhsaker 1967).

But perhaps it is unfair to concentrate on cicadas and monkeys. Compared with these, bees, dolphins and birds have extremely sophisticated communication systems. Yet researchers have reluctantly concluded that even they seem unable to say anything new. The bees were investigated by the famous 'bee-man', Karl von Frisch (1954). He noted that worker bees normally give information about the *horizontal* distance and direction of a source of nectar. If bee communication is in any sense 'open', then a worker bee should be able to inform the other bees about *vertical* distance and direction if necessary. He tested this idea by placing a hive of bees at the foot of a radio beacon, and a supply of sugar water at the top. But the bees who were shown the sugar water were unable to tell the other bees where to find it. They duly performed a 'round dance', indicating that a source of nectar was in the vicinity of the hive – and then for several hours their comrades flew in all directions *except* upwards, looking for the honey source. Eventually, they gave up the search. As von Frisch noted, 'The bees have no words for "up" in their language. There are no flowers in the clouds' (von Frisch 1954, p. 139). Failure to communicate this extra item of information means that bee communication cannot be regarded as 'open-ended' in the same way that human language is open-ended.

The dolphin experiments carried out by Dr Jarvis Bastian were considerably more exciting – though in the long run equally disappointing. Bastian tried to teach a male dolphin, Buzz, and a female, Doris, to communicate across an opaque barrier.

First of all, while they were still together, Bastian taught the dolphins to press paddles when they saw a light. If the light was kept steady, they had to press the right-hand paddle first. If it flashed, the left-hand one. When they did this correctly they were rewarded with fish.

As soon as they had learned this manoeuvre, he separated them. They could now hear one another, but they could not see one another. The paddles and light were set up in the same way, except that the light which indicated which paddle to press first was seen only by Doris. But in order to get fish both dolphins had to press the levers in the correct order. Doris had to *tell* Buzz which this was, as only she could see the light. Amazingly, the dolphins 'demonstrated essentially perfect success over thousands of trials at this task' (Evans and Bastian 1969, p. 432). It seemed that dolphins could *talk*! Doris was conveying novel information through an opaque barrier!

But it later became clear that the achievement was considerably less clever. Even while the dolphins were together Doris had become accustomed to making certain sounds when the light was flashing and different sounds when it was continuous. When the dolphins were separated she continued the habit. And Buzz had, of course, already learnt which sounds of Doris's to associate with which light. Doris was therefore not 'talking creatively'.

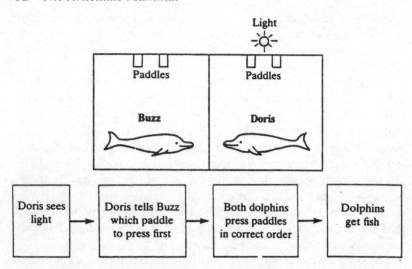

So not even dolphins have a 'creative' communication system, it seems – though it is always possible that more is known of 'delphinese' than has been made public. The high intelligence of dolphins has obvious implications for naval warfare, and so has attracted the attention of military authorities, with the result that much research is shrouded in official secrecy. But on the whole it seems unlikely that there exist hidden tanks of 'talking dolphins' (as was suggested in a well-known film). Most researchers would agree with the comment of the psychologist John Morton:

On the question as to whether dolphins have a language, I would like to comment parenthetically from the evidence I have seen, if they do have a language they are going to extraordinary lengths to conceal the fact from us. [MORTON 1971, p. 83]

Finally, we come to birds. They also have failed to give any evidence of creativity. We might expect them to communicate about a multiplicity of situations, since the individual notes of a bird's song can be combined in an indefinite number of ways. But as far as researchers can judge, bird song deals above all with just two aspects of life: courting a mate, and the marking of territory (Nottebohm 1975). A bird who appears to humans to be indulging in an operatic aria on the pleasures of life is more likely to be warning other birds not to encroach on its own particular area of woodland.

It seems, then, that animals cannot send truly novel messages, and that Ogden Nash encapsulates a modicum of truth in his comment.

The song of canaries
never varies.

And so does Alice in her complaint about kittens:

It is a very inconvenient habit of kittens that, whatever you say to them, they always purr. If they would only purr for 'yes' and mew for 'no', or any rule of that sort, so that one could keep up a conversation! But how *can* you talk with a person if they *always* say the same thing? [LEWIS CARROLL]

It is now possible to answer the question, can animals talk? If, in order to qualify as 'talkers' they have to utilize all the design characteristics of human language 'naturally', the answer is clearly 'no'. Some animals possess some of the features. Bird song has duality, and bee dancing has some degree of displacement. But, as far as we know, no animal communication system has duality *and* displacement. No animal system can be proved to have semanticity or to use structure-dependent operations. Above all, no animal can communicate creatively with another animal.

But although animals do not 'naturally' talk, this does not mean that they are *incapable* of talking. Perhaps they have just never had the chance to learn language. The next section examines the results obtained with animals which have had this opportunity.

Teaching animals to talk: Washoe and Sarah

In discussing attempts to teach language to animals it is important (as we have already noted) to distinguish mimicry from 'true' language. Parrots and mynah birds can imitate humans with uncanny accuracy. But it is unlikely that they ever understand what people are saying. There are reports of a grey parrot which could say 'Good morning' and 'Good evening' at the right times, and 'Good-bye' when guests left (Brown 1958). But most talking birds are merely 'parrotting' back what they hear. For example, a budgerigar I knew heard a puppy being trained with words such as 'Sit!' 'Naughty boy!' and used to shriek 'Sit!' 'Naughty boy!' whenever anyone went near its cage, whether or not the dog was present.

Although psychologists have spent considerable time experimenting with mynah birds, it is perhaps not surprising that the results have been disappointing. Apes seem more promising candidates. Over the past fifty or so years several attempts have been made to teach human language to chimpanzees.

The first experiment was a failure. An animal named Gua was

acquired by Professor and Mrs Kellogg in 1931, when she was seven months old (Brown 1958; Kellogg and Kellogg 1933). She was brought up as if she was a human baby, and was fed with a spoon, bathed, pinned up in nappies, and continuously exposed to speech. Although she eventually managed to understand the meaning of over seventy single words, she never spoke. Gua showed clearly that it was *not* just lack of opportunity which prevents a chimp from learning language. The Kelloggs' son Donald, who was brought up alongside Gua, and was approximately the same age, grew up speaking normally.

A second chimp acquired by Keith and Cathy Hayes in 1947 also proved disappointing (Brown 1958; Hayes 1951). Viki was given intensive coaching in English. She eventually learnt four words: PAPA, MAMA, CUP, UP. But these were very unclearly articulated, and remained the sum total of Viki's utterances after three years of hard training.

It is now clear why these attempts failed. Chimps are not physiologically capable of uttering human sounds. More recent experiments have avoided this trap and used sign language, the manipulation of tokens, or button pressing. Let us consider some of this later research.

Over the past twenty years, teaching language to apes has become a popular pastime among American psychologists. There was a minor population explosion of 'talking chimps' in the 1970s. We shall begin our discussion with Washoe and Sarah. These were the first two chimps to acquire a significant amount of language. (References to the numerous books and articles written about them are in the notes on p. 273). After outlining their achievements, we shall then go on to discuss whether their ability has been surpassed by any of the more recently trained chimps.

Washoe's exact age is unknown. She is a female chimp acquired by Professor and Mrs Gardner in 1966, when she was though to be approximately a year old. She has been taught to use modified American sign language (ASL). In this system signs stand for words. For example, Washoe's word for 'sweet' is made by putting her finger on the top of her tongue, while wagging the tongue. Her word for 'funny' is signalled by pressing the tip of her finger on to her nose, and uttering a snort.

Washoe acquired her language in a fairly 'natural' way. The Gardners kept her continuously surrounded by humans who communicated with her and each other by signs. They hoped that some of this would 'rub off' on her. Sometimes they asked her to imitate them, or tried to correct her. But there were no rigorous training schedules.

Even so, teaching a wild chimpanzee can be quite a problem: 'Washoe can become completely diverted from her original object, she may ask for something entirely different, run away, go into a tantrum, or even bite her tutor' (Gardner and Gardner 1969, p. 666). But her progress was impressive and, at least in the early stages, her language development was not unlike that of a human child.

First, she acquired a number of single words, for example, COME, GIMME, HURRY, SWEET, TICKLE – which amounted to thirty-four after twenty-one months, but later crept up to well over one hundred. The number is accurate because a rota of students and researchers made sure that Washoe, who lived in a caravan in the Gardners' garden, was never alone when she was awake. And a sign was assumed to be acquired only after Washoe had used it spontaneously and appropriately on consecutive days.

Washoe's speech clearly had 'semanticity'. She had no difficulty in understanding that a sign 'means' a certain object or action, as was shown by her acquisition of the word for 'toothbrush' (index finger rubbed against teeth). She was forced, at first against her will, to have her teeth brushed after every meal. Consequently, she had seen the sign for 'toothbrush' on numerous occasions, though she had never used it herself. One day, when she was visiting the Gardners' home she found a mug of toothbrushes in the bathroom. Spontaneously, she made the sign for 'toothbrush'. She was not asking for a toothbrush, as they were within reach. Nor was she asking to have her teeth brushed, a procedure she hated. She appeared simply to be 'naming' the object. Similarly, Washoe made the sign for 'flower' (holding the fingertips of one hand together and touching the nostrils with them) when she was walking towards a flower garden, and another time when she was shown a picture of flowers.

Washoe could also generalize from one situation to another, as was clear from her use of the sign meaning 'more'. Like all chimps, she loved being tickled, and she would pester any companion to continue tickling her by using the 'more' sign. At first the sign was specific to the tickling situation. Later, she used it to request continuation of another favourite activity – being pushed across the floor in a laundry basket. Eventually, she extended the 'more' sign to feeding and other activities. Similarly the word for 'key' referred originally only to the key used to unlock the doors and cupboards in Washoe's caravan. Later, she used the sign spontaneously to refer to a wide variety of keys, including car ignition keys. Her 'speech' also incorporated a limited amount of displacement, since she could ask for absent objects and people.

But most impressive of all was Washoe's creativity – her apparently spontaneous use of combinations of signs. She produced two- and three-word sequences of her own invention, such as GIMME TICKLE 'Come and tickle me', GO SWEET 'Take me to the raspberry bushes', OPEN FOOD DRINK 'Open the fridge', LISTEN EAT 'Listen to the dinner gong', HURRY GIMME TOOTHBRUSH, and ROGER WASHOE TICKLE. Washoe's signs were not just accidental juxtapositions. During a sequence of signs Washoe kept her hands up in the 'signing area'. After each sequence she let them drop. This is comparable to the use of intonation by humans to signal that words are meant to be joined together in a construction. Does this mean that Washoe can actually 'talk'? At least superficially, her sequences seem parallel to the utterances of a human child. Washoe's requests for MORE SWEET, MORE TICKLE seem similar to requests for MORE MILK or MORE SWING recorded from children. But there is one important difference. Children normally preserve a fixed word order. English children put the subject or agent of a sentence before the action word, as in MUMMY COME, EVE READ, ADAM PUT, CAR GONE. But Washoe did not always seem to care in what order she gave her signs. She was as likely to say SWEET GO as GO SWEET to mean 'Take me to the raspberry bushes'.

There are a number of possible explanations. Firstly, the overeagerness of the researchers who worked with Washoe. They were so anxious to encourage her that they rushed to gratify every whim. Since SWEET GO and GO SWEET have only one possible interpretation – Washoe wants some raspberries – they immediately understood and took her there. The idea that word ordering was necessary may never have occurred to her. Perhaps if she had ever experienced difficulty in making herself understood she might have been more careful about structuring her sequences.

Another possibility is that it may be easier to utter vocal sounds in sequence than it is to maintain a fixed order with signs. Some studies have suggested that deaf adults are inconsistent in their ordering of sign language.

A third possibility is that the fluctuating order in Washoe's signing was merely a temporary intermediate stage which occurred before Washoe eventually learnt to keep to a fixed sequence. This is the point of view supported by the Gardners. They claim that Washoe eventually settled down to a standard sign order which was based on the order of adult English (since, of course, Washoe's companions had used an English word order when they used sign language with her).

Yet another possible explanation of Washoe's unreliable sign order is that she did not, and cannot, understand the essentially patterned nature of language. In this case, she certainly did not understand or use structure-dependent operations – one of the key tests for determining whether she can 'talk'. But it is difficult to be sure. And we may never know for certain as she is no longer in the situation where she is continually surrounded by humans whose main task is to hold conversations with her. She grew so large and potentially dangerous that the Gardners were obliged to send her to live at a primate station. But although though her period of intensive exposure to sign language is over, research assistants still come to talk to her. After leaving the Gardners, she continued to use signs creatively, as when she spontaneously signed WATERBIRD to mean 'swan'. However, since she was beside a river when she produced this combination, it is possible that she made two separate signs, one referring to the water, the other to the swan. In her new home, she was given an infant chimp, Loulis, to adopt, and tried to teach him some signs. On one occasion, Washoe put a chair in front of Loulis, and then demonstrated the CHAIR-SIT sign to him five times. And now, both through imitating Washoe and other signing chimps, Loulis has his own repertoire of signs (Fouts, Hirsch and Fouts 1982; Fouts 1983). Now the fact that Washoe spontaneously transmitted signs to another chimp is interesting and important, but it does not magically turn these signs into 'language'. In brief, we have to conclude that although Washoe's speech is creative, and shows semanticity and displacement, it has not been shown to be structure-dependent.

Let us now consider Sarah. Sarah began her training in 1966 under Dr David Premack at the University of California, Santa Barbara. Unlike Washoe, whose life was one continuous game, Sarah was strictly trained by methods not unlike those used by Skinner with his rats. She lived in a cage, and was taught to manipulate plastic tokens on a magnetic board. Each token represented a word. A mauve triangle meant 'apple', and a red square meant 'banana'. A black T-shaped token denoted the colour 'yellow', and a pale blue star meant 'insert'. Sarah understood over one hundred words, including complicated ideas such as 'colour of', 'same', 'different', and 'if . . . then'. For example, if she was given a choice of an apple or banana, and told IF APPLE, THEN CHOCOLATE, she would correctly take the apple in order to get a reward of chocolate, her favourite food. Sarah could clearly cope with arbitrary symbols and semanticity. However, the fact that Sarah could understand the logical notion 'if . . . then' does not prove that she had language. The relationship of language to logic is still very unclear.

But Sarah's communication was rather odd. She did not hold conversations, as Washoe did. She sat in her cage and was tested at intervals by her trainers. Most of the tests were comprehension ones. She could obey orders such as SARAH INSERT APPLE DISH. And when told to put GREEN ON RED she could place a symbol for green on top of the red one. If she was asked QUERY CUP EQUAL SPOON ('Is the cup the same thing as the spoon'?) she could respond appropriately with the token for NO. Whenever she got a response right, she was rewarded, usually with chocolate. She was trained to use a fixed word order, so did not get her chocolate if she got the order wrong. Some people have suggested that Sarah did not really understand what she was doing. They suggest that she may have been responding to cues in the questioner's behaviour. Animals, like people, frequently guess from the look on someone's face what answer they are required to give (Sebeok and Rosenthal 1981). It is difficult to be sure how much Sarah actually comprehends. But her achievements seem too complex to be completely explained away by the 'behavioural cue' theory.

Perhaps we cannot fully assess Sarah's achievements because in her six years of training she never learned to initiate conversations, something which all normal humans do.

The results of the Washoe and Sarah experiments are not clear cut. On the one hand, the systems they are learning are less complicated than human language. This is proved by the fact that severely mentally handicapped children who are unable to acquire normal language can be taught Sarah's system with considerable success (Premack and Premack 1974). On the other hand, between them, the two chimps show a possible grasp of some basic design characteristics of language previously thought to be restricted to humans.

More recent experiments

As we noted earlier, Washoe and Sarah can be regarded as the pioneers in this field. More recently, a whole new generation of 'talking apes' has grown up, whose trainers were able to draw on the experience gained from Washoe and Sarah. The most famous of the more recent ones are Lana, Koko, a gorilla, and Nim Chimpsky. (References to detailed accounts of their abilities are in the notes on p. 273.) Do the achievements of these animals go further than those of Washoe and Sarah? Let us briefly consider each in turn.

Lana, like Sarah, is undergoing rigorous training in a highly controlled environment, though her surroundings are considerably more sophisticated than Sarah's, as befits an animal whose project is partly funded by the Coca-Cola company. Lana's 'cage' at the Yerkes Regional Primate Research Centre in Atlanta, Georgia, is a room of which one side is a huge keyboard linked up to a computer. Beginning in 1971, she has been taught to communicate by pressing the keys, each one of which is marked with a symbol standing for a word. A vending device is attached to the keyboard, so that if Lana correctly requests some item of food or drink, she is able to obtain it immediately.

Like Sarah, Lana has over 100 symbols in her repertoire, which mainly involve items and actions around her, such as 'give', 'banana', 'Coke', and so on. She can cope well with arbitrary symbols, since the symbols on her keyboard are formed by combinations of geometric figures on different coloured backgrounds. For example, a small solid circle inside a larger diamond on a purple background is the symbol for 'Lana', the animal's name. A diamond super-imposed on a circle inside a rectangle on a blue background is the symbol for 'eat'.

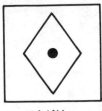

LANA

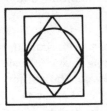

EAT

Moreover, Lana's ability to generalize shows that her system has semanticity, that is, she understands that a symbol refers to a certain *type* of object, or colour, not just one particular thing. For example, she was taught the word MORE in connection with an extra ration of fruit-juice. Within a few days, she was reliably attaching the symbol for MORE to other types of food and drink whenever she wanted an additional helping, as in MORE BREAD, MORE MILK. Lana also shows some evidence of creativity. For example, she was taught the words PUT and IN in connection with putting a ball into a bowl or box. Soon after, Tim, one of her trainers, was late with her morning drink of milk. Lana spontaneously made the request TIM PUT MILK IN MACHINE. This shows not only creativity, but also displacement – the ability to talk about absent objects and events. In addition, Lana coined the descriptive phrases APPLE WHICH-IS ORANGE for 'orange', and BANANA WHICH-IS GREEN for 'cucumber'.

So far, then, Lana's language ability seems similar to that of Washoe and Sarah in that she shows semanticity, displacement, and creativity. Let us now look at the way in which she combines symbols. Is she able to cope with structure-dependent operations? Clearly, Lana realizes that symbols cannot be jumbled together randomly. She has learned to follow a set sequence in accordance with her trainer's instructions. Like Sarah, she can carry out simple slot-filling exercises, helped by the fact that in her symbol system, each type of word has a different background colour.

Yellow	Purple	Blue	Purple	Red
QUERY	TIM	GIVE	LANA	COFFEE
QUERY	TIM	GIVE	LANA	JUICE
PLEASE	MACHINE	GIVE		COKE
PLEASE	MACHINE	GIVE		MILK

It is possible, though unlikely, that she understands the notion of hierarchical structure: the idea that a group of symbols can be substituted for a single one without altering the basic sentence pattern. Her colour-coding system probably hinders her from drawing such conclusions, since in a phrase such as THIS BOWL each word would be a different colour. Furthermore, there is no concrete evidence that she manipulates slots in the way humans do.

To be fair to Lana, however, we perhaps need to consider a conversation which she had with her trainer Tim one Christmas day. On that day, she produced two similar strings of symbols (Stahlke 1980):

QUERY YOU GIVE COKE TO LANA IN CUP
QUERY YOU GIVE COKE IN CUP TO LANA.

This looks remarkably like the kind of structure-dependent operation performed by humans, in which they manipulate groups of words to produce different effects. But a closer look at Lana's behaviour on that Christmas day suggests that she was not as clever as one might at first suspect. She had begun by demanding Coke, using the first of the sentences listed above: QUERY YOU GIVE COKE TO LANA IN CUP. She repeated this demand seven times, with no success. Then in desperation, and once only, she tried another variant: QUERY YOU GIVE COKE IN CUP TO LANA. It seems, then, that such structural manipulations are not characteristic of Lana's output, and this one probably occurred by chance. Normally, she adheres rigidly to the sequence she has been taught in order to get her reward, so she has little scope for stylistic modifications. On the basis of this one example, then, it would be premature to conclude that she can cope with structure-dependent operations, which are a crucial characteristic of human language.

Lana's trainers, incidentally, confidently claim that she has 'language', but they define 'language' in a much broader way than we have done. To them, a language is any communication system which refers consistently to the outside world by means of a set of arbitrary symbols which are combined together in accordance with conventional rules (Rumbaugh 1977, p. 66), a definition which might bring even a set of traffic lights within its scope!

Austin and Sherman also deserve a mention. These are two young male chimpanzees who have been taught the same system as Lana (Savage-Rumbaugh 1986). They have surpassed her in one way, in that they are able to communicate with one another. If Austin presses a symbol for a banana, then Sherman can go into the next room, select the banana from a tray of food, and take it back to Austin. This impressive piece of cooperation does not, however, make the whole system any more language-like.

Let us now move on to Koko and Nim Chimpsky. To many psycholinguists the achievements – or non-achievements – of these animals are more interesting, since they were taught to communicate under conditions which were far more like those experienced by human children. Like Washoe, they learnt adaptations of American Sign Language.

Koko is a female gorilla who was trained by Penny Patterson at Stanford University in California. Koko is of interest partly because she is a gorilla, but mainly because she is reputed to have an IQ only marginally below that of an average human. In a standard intelligence test (Stanford-Binet), her score fluctuated between eight-five and ninety-five, compared with an average human total of 100.

Patterson claims that even this underestimates her ability, since the test was inevitably biased towards humans. For example, at one point, Koko was shown drawings of a hat, a spoon, a tree and house, and asked where one might shelter in case of rain. Koko selected the tree, which had to be counted as wrong under the conventional marking system, even though it might be more natural for gorillas to shelter in trees than in houses. Since human children within Koko's IQ range learn language without difficulty, Koko may be able to reveal to us the extent to which language in humans is dependent on general intelligence (though some people are sceptical about Penny's claims over Koko's intelligence).

Koko is undoubtedly the star performer among apes in the number of vocabulary items in her repertoire. After five and a half years of training, she is reported to have acquired a total of 645 lexical items, with her working vocabulary estimated at approximately 375 words. A sign was considered acquired if she used it once a day for at least fifteen days in a month, and was noted by two separate observers. Like the chimps, she can generalize, using the sign for 'straw' first to refer to a drinking straw, then extending it to include cigarettes, plastic tubing, and car radio antennae. Patterson also claims that Koko generalized the sign for 'tree' to asparagus and green onions, on the grounds that she was using it to mean 'tall, thick green objects presented vertically'. To those of us not so impressed by gesticulating gorillas, it seems that Koko may simply have made a mistake: it is tempting for a trainer to behave like a fond parent and imagine that her charge is cleverer than is in fact the case.

Koko is also creative: she spontaneously used the sequences EYE HAT for 'mask', WHITE TIGER for 'zebra', and COOKIE ROCK for a sweet, stale roll. She signed ME CRY THERE when she saw a picture of a gorilla in a bath, apparently a cry of sympathy, since she herself hates being bathed. And in a flurry of fury, she once signed PENNY TOILET DIRTY DEVIL when she was angry with Penny, her trainer. Her most impressive conversation is one in which she supposedly apologized for a biting incident which had taken place three days previously. When shown a bite mark on Penny's arm she allegedly signed SORRY BITE SCRATCH. WRONG BITE. 'Why bite?' queried Penny. BECAUSE MAD, Koko replied. 'Why mad?' asked Penny. DON'T KNOW, responded Koko.

Even allowing for a certain amount of exaggeration on the part of Koko's trainers, it seems that she is capable of creativity and a certain amount of displacement. There is little evidence, however, that her utterances are structured. Koko does not keep to any strict sequences, and the problems of analysing her utterances are compounded by the fact that she often makes two signs simultaneously, one with each hand.

Let us now turn to Nim Chimpsky, a male chimpanzee who was for several years under the care of Herbert Terrace at Columbia University, New York. Somewhat ironically, Nim's achievements began to interest psycholinguists mainly after the project ran out of money, and Nim was returned to a chimpanzee colony in Oklahoma. Without Nim around, Terrace found that he had much more time to analyse the material he had collected so far. The data from Project Nim, therefore, have been examined much more carefully than those from any of the other animals. With Nim out of the way, Herbert Terrace was able to sort out and classify the data he had accumulated over the previous four years.

At first sight, Nim's sign sequences were impressive. Of the 20,000 recorded, approximately half were two-sign combinations, and 1378 were different. A superficial look at the signs suggested to Terrace that they were structured (Terrace 1979a, p. 72). For example, of the two-sign utterances which included the word MORE, 78 per cent had MORE at the beginning as in MORE TICKLE, MORE DRINK, and of the two-sign utterances involving a transitive verb (a verb which takes an object), 83 per cent had the verb before the object, as in TICKLE NIM, HUG NIM. But a closer analysis showed that the appearance of structure was an illusion. Nim simply had a statistical preference for putting certain words in certain places, while other words showed no such preference. He preferred to put the word MORE at the beginning of a sequence, the word NIM at the end, and any foods he was requesting at the beginning also. But many other words had a random distribution. Take the word EAT, a high frequency item in his vocabulary. It occurred in the two- three- and four-sign sequences set out in the tables.

Two-sign sequences	
EAT NIM	302
MORE EAT	287
ME EAT	237
NIM EAT	209
EAT DRINK	98
GUM EAT	79
GRAPE EAT	74

Three-sign sequences

EAT ME NIM	48	YOGHURT NIM EAT	20
EAT NIM EAT	46	ME MORE EAT	19
GRAPE EAT NIM	37	MORE EAT NIM	19
BANANA NIM EAT	33	BANANA ME EAT	17
NIM ME EAT	27	NIM EAT NIM	17
BANANA EAT NIM	26	APPLE ME EAT	15
EAT ME EAT	22	EAT NIM ME	15
ME NIM EAT	21	GIVE ME EAT	15

Four-sign sequences

EAT DRINK EAT DRINK	15	DRINK EAT ME NIM	3
EAT NIM EAT NIM	7	EAT GRAPE EAT NIM	3
BANANA EAT ME NIM	4	EAT ME NIM DRINK	3
BANANA ME EAT BANANA	4	ME EAT DRINK MORE	3
GRAPE EAT NIM EAT	4	ME EAT ME EAT	3
DRINK EAT DRINK EAT	4	ME NIM EAT ME	3
NIM EAT NIM EAT	4		

It would require a considerable amount of imagination and wishful thinking to detect a coherent structure in such a collection. Looking at the two-sign sequences, we note that EAT NIM, NIM EAT, and ME EAT are all very common, making it impossible to claim that there is a firm subject-verb, or verb-subject order. A similar pattern occurs in the three-sign sequences, with EAT ME NIM, NIM ME EAT, ME NIM EAT, and EAT NIM ME all occurring a significant number of times. It is particularly noticeable that Nim's longer utterances were not in any way more interesting and sophisticated than his shorter ones – they were simply more repetitive. Of the thirteen four-sign sequences noted above, ten of them involved repeated items, and five of them were simply a doubling up of two-sign utterances: EAT DRINK EAT DRINK, EAT NIM EAT NIM, DRINK EAT DRINK EAT, NIM EAT NIM EAT, ME EAT ME EAT. Nim's longest recorded utterance was a sixteen sign sequence which involved only five different signs: GIVE ORANGE ME GIVE EAT ORANGE ME EAT ORANGE GIVE ME EAT ORANGE GIVE ME YOU. On this evidence, it seems incontestable that 'Repetitive, inconsistently structured strings are in fact characteristic of ape signing' (Pettito and Seidenberg 1979, p. 186).

Terrace found a number of other differences between Nim's signing and true language. For example, when Nim was just over two-years-old, 38 per cent of his utterances were full or partial imitations. Almost two years later, the number of imitations had gone up to 54 per cent. Nim was producing more imitations as he got older, the reverse of what happens with human children. Nim was also unable to grasp the give-and-take of conversation, and his signing showed no evidence of turn-taking. Furthermore, he rarely initiated conversations. Only 12 per cent of his utterances were truly spontaneous, and the remaining 88 per cent were in response to his teachers. We may conclude, therefore, that Nim did not use his signs in the structured, creative, social way that is characteristic of human children. It seems reasonable to agree with Terrace that 'It would be premature to conclude that a chimpanzee's combinations show the same structure evident in the sentences of a child' (1979, p. 221) and that 'Nim's signing with his teachers bore only a superficial resemblance to a child's conversations with his or her parents' (Terrace 1983, p. 57).

Somewhat surprisingly, this conclusion has been fiercely challenged. Terrace's critics point out that Nim was a highly disturbed young chimp. Due to frequent changes in those who taught him, Nim was insecure and maladjusted. They claim that his achievements are considerably lower than one might expect from a 'normal' animal. Others have argued that a computer analysis of chimp utterances which takes no account of the actual situation is bound to give an odd result. Negative results are to be expected if one chooses to

lump together four years' worth of recorded utterances, remove all verbal and nonverbal context and grind the result through a computer to look for statistical regularities. [GARDNER AND GARDNER 1980, p. 357]

The battle still rages, and provokes fierce responses on either side (e.g. de Luce and Wilder 1983). And there is competition between trainers of different species, who each tend to claim that their own animal is the brightest. An orang-utan called Chantek shows slow, more deliberate and spontaneous signing than Nim, which, according to his trainer, 'may indicate superior linguistic and cognitive abilities' of orang-utans when compared to African apes (Miles 1983, p. 56).

Meanwhile, primates may eventually fade from the centre of attention. Reports are coming in of two dolphins, Phoenix and Akeakamai, who can respond to language-like commands (Herman, Richards and Wolz 1984). Phoenix copes with whistle signals which stand for words, and Akeakamai (Hawaiian for 'lover of wisdom') understands gestures. They can each obey a wide range of instructions, including novel ones. For example, PHOENIX AKEAKAMAI OVER instructs Phoenix to swim up to her playmate and jump over her. SURFBOARD FETCH SPEAKER means 'take the surfboard to the speaker', and HOOP FETCH BOTTOM PIPE means 'get the hoop and take it to the pipe at the bottom of the pool'. The dolphins' achievements are fairly similar to those of the ape Sarah, since they do not, as yet, initiate language – though this is a hope for the future (Richards, Wolz and Herman 1984).

Apes, however, are still the 'stars' among the 'talking animals'. Let us now summarize our conclusions on these primates. We need to recognize, perhaps, that having language is not an 'all or nothing' matter. It is misleading to 'treat language like virginity – you either have it or you don't' (Miles 1983, p. 44). All the apes we have discussed can cope with arbitrary symbols and semanticity, and display some displacement and creativity in their 'speech'. They therefore have a grasp of some design characteristics of language which hitherto had been regarded as specifically human. However, their ability does not extend much further. The caged animals can carry out simple slot filling manoeuvres, providing they are adequately rewarded. The naturalistically trained ones show no evidence of structure, they merely display a preference for placing certain signs first or last in a sequence. Chomsky may be right, therefore, when he points out that the higher apes 'apparently lack the capacity to develop even the rudiments of the computational structure of human language' (1980, p. 57).

We cannot, therefore, agree with Koko's trainer, who proclaims that 'language is no longer the exclusive domain of man' (Patterson 1978, p. 95), nor with Lana's trainers who assert that 'neither tool-using skills nor language serve qualitatively to separate man and beast any more' (Rumbaugh 1977, p. 307).

Note finally that even though intelligent animals seem *capable* of coping with some of the rudimentary characteristics of human language, they do not seem *predisposed* to cope with them. As one commentator noted: 'As with watching a circus horse walk on its hind legs, I could not escape the feeling that a species ill-adapted to symbolic communication was struggling with an unnatural task' (Marshall 1987, p. 310). The situation is parallel to that found among birds (Thorpe 1963). Some birds are able to learn the songs of a different species. But they find the task a difficult one. When the birds are removed from the alien species, and placed among their own kind, they learn their normal song with extreme rapidity. They seem to have an innate predisposition towards one kind of song rather than another.

The apparent ease with which humans acquire language, compared with apes, supports the suggestion that they are innately programmed to do so. The next chapter examines whether there is any biological evidence for this apparently unique adaptation to language.

3 Grandmama's teeth
Is there biological evidence for innate language capacity?

'O grandmama, what big teeth you have!' said Little Red Riding
Hood.
'All the better to *eat* you with, my dear,' replied the wolf.

If an animal is innately programmed for some type of behaviour, then
there are likely to be biological clues. It is no accident that fish have
bodies which are streamlined and smooth, with fins and a powerful
tail. Their bodies are structurally adapted for moving fast through
the water. The same is true of whales and dolphins, even though they
evolved quite separately from fish. Similarly, if you found a dead bird
or mosquito, you could guess by looking at its wings that flying was
its normal mode of transport.

However, we must not be over-optimistic. Biological clues are not
essential. The extent to which they are found varies from animal to
animal and from activity to activity. For example, it is impossible to
guess from their bodies that birds make nests, and, sometimes,
animals behave in a way quite contrary to what might be expected
from their physical form: ghost spiders have tremendously long legs,
yet they weave webs out of very short strands. To a human observer,
their legs seem a great hindrance as they spin and move about the
web. On the other hand, the orb spider, who has short legs, makes
its web out of very long cables, and seems to put a disproportionate
amount of effort into walking from one side of the web to another
(Duncan 1949, quoted in Lenneberg 1967, p. 75). In addition, there
are often inexplicable divergences between species which do not
correlate with any obvious differences in behaviour. The visible
sections of the ear differ in chimps, baboons and men – but there is
no discernible reason behind this. However, such unpredictability is
not universal, and need not discourage us from looking for biological
clues connected with speech – though we must realize that we are
unlikely to find the equivalent of a large box labelled 'language'.

Changes in the form of the body or *structural* changes are the most
direct indications of innate programming. But we must also take into
consideration *physiological* adaptations – change in the bodily

functions such as rate of heart-beat, and breathing. The first part of this chapter looks at parts of the human body where adaptations related to language are likely to be found. The organs used to produce and plan it are examined – the mouth, vocal cords, lungs and the brain.

The second part of the chapter is slightly different. It considers aspects of language where complex neuromuscular sequencing is involved. It becomes clear that the co-ordination required is perhaps impossible without biological adaptations.

Mouth, lungs and grey matter

If we look at the organs used in speech, humans seem to be somewhere in the middle between the obvious structural adaptation of birds to flying, and the apparent lack of correlation between birds and nest-building. That is, the human brain and vocal tract have a number of slightly unusual features. By themselves, these features are not sufficient to indicate that people can talk. But if we first assume that all humans speak a language, then a number of puzzling biological facts fall into place. They can be viewed as *partial* adaptations of the body to the production of language (Lenneberg 1967; Lieberman 1975, 1984).

For example, human teeth are unusual compared with those of other animals. They are even in height, and form an unbroken barrier. They are upright, not slanting outwards, and the top and bottom set meet. Such regularity is surprising – it is certainly not needed for *eating*. Yet evenly spaced, equal-sized teeth which touch one another are valuable for the articulation of a number of sounds, s, F, and v, for example, as well as SH (as in *shut*), TH (as in *thin*) and several others. Human lips have muscles which are considerably more developed, and show more intricate interlacing than those in the lips of other primates. The mouth is relatively small, and can be opened and shut rapidly. This makes it simple to pronounce sounds such as *p* and *b*, which require a total stoppage of the airstream with the lips, followed by a sudden release of pressure as the mouth is opened. The human tongue is thick, muscular, and mobile, as opposed to the long thin tongues of monkeys. The advantage of a thick tongue is that the size of the mouth cavity can be varied, allowing a range of vowels to be pronounced.

It seems, then, that humans are naturally geared to produce a number of different sounds rapidly and in a controlled manner.

Their mouths possess features which either differ from, or appear to be missing in the great apes. In all one cannot help agreeing with the comment of a nineteenth-century writer:

What a curious thing speech is! The tongue is so serviceable a member (taking all sorts of shapes just as it is wanted) – the teeth, the lips, the roof of the mouth, all ready to help; and so heap up the sound of the voice into the solid bits which we call consonants, and make room for the curiously shaped breathings which we call words! [OLIVER WENDELL HOLMES, quoted in *Critchley 1970*]

Another important difference between humans and monkeys concerns the larynx, which contains the 'voice box' or 'vocal cords'. Strangely, it is simpler in structure than that of other primates. But this is an advantage. Air can move freely past and then out through the nose and mouth without being hindered by other appendages. Biologically, streamlining and simplification are often indications of specialization for a given purpose. For example, hooved animals have a reduced number of toes, and fish do not have limbs. So the streamlining of the human larynx may be a sign of adaptation to speech. But we pay a price for our specialized larynx. A monkey can seal its mouth off from its windpipe and breath while it is eating. Humans cannot do this, so food can get lodged in the windpipe, sometimes causing them to choke to death (Lieberman 1972).

We now come to the lungs. Although there is no apparent peculiarity in the structure of our lungs, our breathing seems to be remarkably adapted to speech. In most animals the respiratory system is a very finely balanced mechanism. A human submerged under water for more than two minutes will possibly drown. Anyone who pants rapidly and continuously for any length of time faints and sometimes dies. Yet during speech the breathing rhythm is altered quite noticeably without apparent discomfort to the speaker. The number of breaths per minute is reduced. Breathing-in is considerably accelerated, breathing-out is slowed down. Yet people frequently talk for an hour or more with no ill-effects. A child learning to play the flute or trumpet has to be carefully instructed in breathing techniques – but no-one has to instruct a two-year-old in the breathing adaptations required for talking. It is impossible to tell which came first – speech or breathing adaptations. As Lenneberg inquires (1967, p. 81), do donkeys say *hee-haw* on inspired and expired air so efficiently because of the way their breathing mechanisms were organized, or did the *hee-haw* come first? The answer is irrelevant. All that matters to us is that any child born in the twentieth century has a breathing mechanism apparently 'biologically organized' for speech.

It seems, then, that there are clear indications in the mouth, larynx and lungs that we speak 'naturally'. However, let us now consider the human brain. To what extent is this programmed for speech? The answer is unclear. Our brain is very different in appearance from that of other animals. It is heavier, with more surface folding of the *cortex*, the outer layer of 'grey matter' which surrounds the inner core of nerve fibres. Of course, size alone is not particularly important. Elephants and whales have bigger brains than humans, but they do not talk. But elephants and whales also have bigger bodies, so some people have suggested that it is the brain–body ratio which matters. At first sight, this seems a promising approach. It appears quite reasonable to suggest that a high brain–body ratio means high intelligence, which in turn might be a prerequisite for language – especially when we find that the brain of an adult human is more than 2 per cent of his or her total weight, while that of an adult chimp is less than 1 per cent. But such ratios can be very misleading. Some animals are designed to carry around large reserves of energy which makes their bodies enormously heavy. Camels, for example, are not necessarily stupider than horses just because they have huge humps.

But even apart from problems such as this, brain–body ratio cannot be a decisive factor as far as language is concerned, since it is possible to find young chimpanzees and human children who have similar brain–body ratios – yet the child can talk and the chimp cannot. Even more convincing is a comparison between a 3-year-old chimp and a 12-year-old nanocephalic dwarf – a human who because of a genetic defect grows to a height of around 760 mm (or two foot six inches). Although the chimp and the dwarf have exactly the same brain and body weights (and so, of course, the same brain–body ratio), the dwarfs speak, in a somewhat limited fashion, but the chimps do not.

	Brain (kg)	*Body* (kg)	*Ratio*
Human, age 13½	1.35	45	1 : 34
Human dwarf, age 12	0.4	13.5	1 : 34
Chimp, age 3	0.4	13.5	1 : 34

(Lenneberg 1967, p. 70)

These figures show conclusively that the difference between human and chimp brains is a *qualitative*, not a *quantitative* one.

Superficially, the brains of a chimp and a human have certain similarities. As in a number of animals, the human brain is divided into a lower section, the *brain stem*, and a higher section, the *cerebrum*. The brain stem keeps the body alive by controlling breathing, heart beats and so on. A cat with the upper section of its brain removed but with the brain stem intact could still swallow milk, purr, and pull its paw away from a thorn when pricked. The higher section, the cerebrum, is not essential for life. Its purpose seems to be to integrate an animal with its environment. This is the part of the brain where language is likely to be organized.

The cerebrum is divided into two halves, the *cerebral hemispheres*, which are linked to one another by a series of bridges. The left hemisphere controls the right side of the body, and the right hemisphere the left side.

But the two hemispheres do not function identically. This was first discovered over a hundred years ago. A Frenchman, Marc Dax,

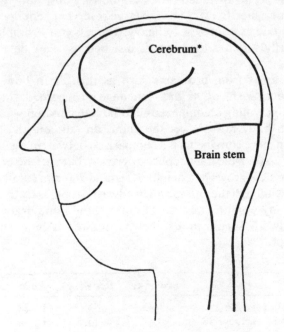

* The cerebrum actually occupies a slightly larger area than that shown in the diagram.

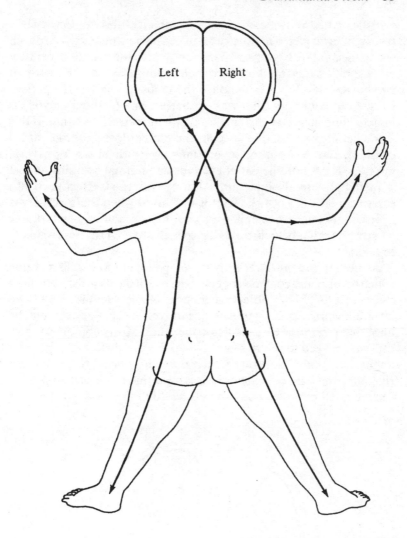

read a paper at Montpellier in 1836, pointing out that paralysis of the right side of the body was often associated with loss of speech, while patients whose left side was paralysed could usually talk normally. This suggested that the left hemisphere controlled not only the right side of the body, but *speech* also. Dax's hypothesis turned out to be correct. Speech in the majority of humans is the concern of the *left*, not the right hemisphere. But it was a long time before this was reliably confirmed. Until relatively recently, statistics could only be drawn up by chance observations, when researchers managed to note cases of people in whom loss of speech was associated with right side paralysis. But in the twentieth century more sophisticated methods have been adopted. One is the 'sodium amytal' test developed by Wada in the 1940s. In this test the patient is asked to count out loud while a barbiturate (sodium amytal) is injected into an artery carrying blood to one side of the brain. If this is the hemisphere used in speech, the patient loses all track of his counting and experiences severe language difficulties for several minutes. If it is not, the patient can resume normal counting almost immediately after the injection. Although this test is effective, it also carries an element of risk. So it is only used when brain surgery is advisable (as in severe epilepsy) and the surgeon wishes to know whether he is likely to disturb vital speech areas. If so, he is unlikely to operate.

A simpler and more recently developed method for discovering which hemisphere controls speech is the use of dichotic listening tests (Kimura 1967). The subject wears headphones, and is played two different words simultaneously, one into each ear. For example, he might hear *six* in one ear, and *two* in the other. Most people can report the word played to the right ear (which is directly linked to the left hemisphere) more accurately than the word played to the left ear (linked to the right hemisphere). It is clear that this is not simply due to an overall preference for sounds heard in the right ear, because

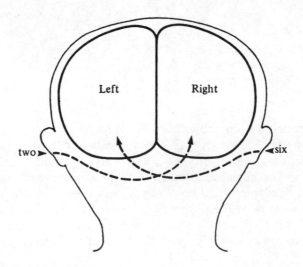

for non-linguistic sounds the left ear is better. If different tunes are played simultaneously into each ear, subjects will identify the tune played into the left ear better than the one directed into the right ear. We conclude that the left hemisphere is better at processing linguistic signals – and so is normally the dominant one for speech.

A further technique which is still being developed is electro-diagnosis (Rosenfield 1978). Electrodes are attached to the skull in order to measure the amount of electrical activity in the area beneath. Various experimenters have shown that spoken words produce a greater response in the left hemisphere, whereas noises, such as mechanical clicks, arouse a greater response in the right.

The results of the observations and tests described above are surprisingly consistent. The majority of normal human beings – perhaps as many as 90 per cent – have speech located primarily in the left hemisphere. This cannot be due to chance.

A further interesting and related discovery is that the location of speech centres in the left hemisphere seems to be linked to right-handedness. That is, most humans are right-handed, and most people's speech is controlled by the left hemisphere. In the nineteenth century it was commonly assumed that left-handers must have speech located in the right hemisphere, and this seemed to be confirmed by a report in 1868 by the influential neurologist John Hughlings Jackson that he had discovered loss of speech in a left-hander who had sustained injury to the right side of the brain. But this viewpoint turns out to be false. Surprisingly, most left-handers also have language controlled predominantly by the left hemisphere, though the picture is not completely straightforward. Of the relatively few people who do not have their speech centres located in the right hemisphere, more are left-handed than right-handed.

Location of speech centres	Right-handers	Left-handers
Left hemisphere	90% or more	70–90%
Right hemisphere	10% or less	10–30%

Figures averaged from Penfield and Roberts 1959; Zangwill 1973; Milner, Branch and Rasmussen 1964.

These figures indicate two things: firstly, it is normal for speech and handedness to be controlled by the same hemisphere (and it has been suggested that speech and writing problems are found more frequently in children where the two are not linked). Secondly, there is a strong tendency for speech to be located in the left hemisphere even when this appears to disrupt the standard linking of speech and handedness.

More recent work has been directed at finding out if *all* speech processing must be located in one hemisphere or whether subsidiary linguistic abilities remain in the non-dominant hemisphere. One group of researchers at Montreal, Canada, claim to have found ten patients who had speech abilities in both halves of the brain. The sodium amytal test disturbed speech whichever side of the brain it was injected. Interestingly enough, all these patients were either left-handed or ambidextrous (Milner, Branch and Rasmussen 1964).

Other studies suggest that the right hemisphere contains a limited potential for language which is normally latent, but which can be activated if needed. Patients who have had the whole of the left hemisphere removed are at first without speech. But after a while, they are likely to acquire a limited vocabulary, and be able to comprehend a certain amount, though they always have difficulty in producing speech (Kinsbourne 1975). The right hemisphere is not useless, however. Patients with right hemisphere damage have difficulty with intonation, and in understanding jokes and metaphors (Moscovitch 1983; Caplan 1987).

Perhaps the most widely reported experiments on this topic are those involving 'split brain' patients (Gazzaniga 1970, 1983; Levy 1979). In cases of severe epilepsy it is sometimes necessary to sever the major links between the two hemispheres. This means that a patient has virtually two separate brains, each coping with one half of the body independently. A patient's language can be tested by dealing with each hemisphere separately. An object shown to the *left* visual field is relayed only to the *right* (non-language hemisphere). Yet sometimes the patient is able to name such an object. This indicates that the right hemisphere may be able to cope with simple naming problems – but it seems unable to cope with syntax. However, the results of these experiments are disputed. Some people have suggested that the information is being transferred from one hemisphere to the other by a 'back route' after the major links have been severed.

This lateralization or localization of language in one half of the brain, then, is a definite, biological characteristic of the human race. At one time, it was thought to develop gradually (e.g. Lenneberg 1967). But recent research indicates that it may be present at birth (Kinsbourne and Hiscock 1987). Even foetuses have been claimed to show traces of it, with some areas of the left hemisphere being bigger than the right (Buffery 1978). The issue is an important one for psycholinguists, since it is sometimes argued that the period of lateralization coincides with a 'critical period' for language acquisition (to be discussed in Chapter 4).

Although most neurologists agree that language is mainly restricted to one hemisphere, further localization of speech is still the centre of a raging controversy. The basic difficulty is that all the evidence available is derived from brain-damaged patients. And injured brains may not be representative of normal ones. After a stroke or other injury the damage is rarely localized. A wound usually creates a blockage, causing a shortage of blood in the area beyond it, and a build-up of pressure behind it. So detailed correlations of wounds with speech defects cannot often be made, especially as a wound in one place may trigger off severe speech problems in one person, but only marginally affect the speech of another. This suggests to some neurologists that speech can be 're-located' away from the damaged area – it has (controversially) been suggested that there are 'reserve' speech areas which are kept for use in emergencies. This creates an extremely complex picture – like a ghost, speech drifts away to another area just as you think you have located it. But these problems have not deterred neurologists – and some progress has been made.

There are two main methods of investigation – observation and experiment. Observation depends on unfortunate accidents and post-mortems. A man called Phineas Gage had an accident in 1847 in which a four-foot iron bar became embedded in the front left-hand section of his head. The bar remained there until his death, twenty years later, and bar and skull are now preserved in a museum at the Harvard Medical School. Although Gage's personality changed for the worse – he became unreliable and unpredictable – his language was unaffected. This suggests that the front part of the brain is not involved in language. Conversely, a French surgeon named Broca noted at a post-mortem in 1861 that two patients who had had severe speech defects (one could only say *tan* and *sacré nom de Dieu*) had significant damage to an area just in front of, and slightly above, the left ear – which suggests that this area, now named 'Broca's area', is important for speech.

The experimental method was pioneered by two Canadian surgeons, Penfield and Roberts (1959). They were primarily concerned with removing abnormally functioning cells from the brains of epileptics. But before doing this they had to check that they were not destroying cells involved in speech. So, with the patients fully conscious, they carefully opened the skull, and applied a minute electric current to different parts of the exposed brain. Electrical stimulation of this type normally causes temporary interference. So if the area which controls leg movement is stimulated, the patient is unable to move his or her leg. If the area controlling speech production is involved, the patient is briefly unable to speak.

There are obvious disadvantages in this method. Only the surface of the brain was examined, and no attempt was made to probe what was happening at a deeper level. The brain is not normally exposed to air or electric shocks, so the results may be quite unrepresentative. But in spite of the problems involved, certain outline facts have become clear.

First of all, it is possible to distinguish the area of the brain which is involved in the actual articulation of speech. The so-called 'primary somatic motor area' controls all voluntary bodily movements and is situated just in front of a deep crack or 'fissure' running down from the top of the brain. The control for different parts of the body works upside down: control of the feet and legs is near the top of the head, and control of the face and mouth is further down.

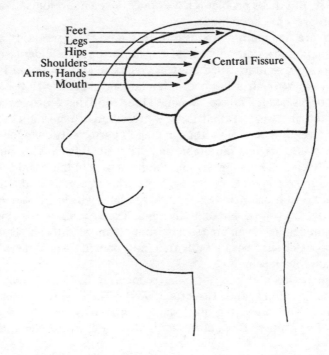

The bodily control system in animals works in much the same way – but there is one major difference. In humans, a disproportionate amount of space is allotted to the area controlling the hands and mouth.

But the sections of the brain involved in the actual articulation of speech seem to be fairly distinct from those involved in its planning and comprehension. Where are these planning and comprehension areas? This is where experts disagree, often fundamentally (Caplan 1987, 1988). Nevertheless, perhaps the majority of neurologists agree that some areas of the brain are statistically likely to be involved in speech planning and comprehension. Two areas seem to be particularly relevant: the neighbourhood of *Broca's area* (in front of and just above the left ear), and the region around and under the left ear, which is sometimes called *Wernicke's area* after the neurologist who first suggested this area was important for speech (in 1874). Damage to Wernicke's area often destroys speech comprehension, and damage to Broca's frequently hinders speech production – though this is something of an over-simplification, since serious damage to either area usually harms all aspects of speech (Mackay *et al.* 1987).

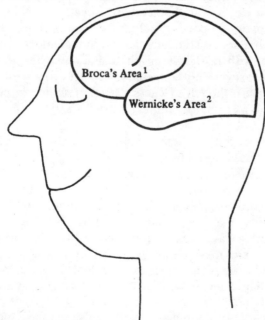

[1] Broca's Area covers approximately the space under the *s* of *Broca's* and the *A* of *Area*.
[2] Wernicke's Area is roughly the space directly above the word *Wernicke's*.

Particularly puzzling are cases of damage to Broca's or Wernicke's area where the patient suffers no language disorder. Conversely, someone's speech may be badly affected by a brain injury, even though this does not apparently involve the 'language areas'. There may simply be more variation in the location of brain areas than in the position of the heart or liver. A particular function may be 'narrowly localized in an individual in a particular area . . ., localized equally narrowly in another area in another individual, and carried out in a much larger area . . . in the third. The only constraint seems to be that core language processes are accomplished in this area of neocortex' (Caplan 1988, p. 248).

In addition there are likely to be deeper interconnections about which little is known. Some neurologists have suggested that the interconnections are as important as the areas themselves, and claim that major speech defects occur when these connections are severed (Geschwind 1979; Penfield and Roberts 1959).

Can studies of the brain clarify the relationship between language and intelligence? Not very much, it seems. The notion of intelligence involves a complex interweaving of different types of skill, and exactly where (if anywhere) each is located is highly controversial. The most we can say is that certain aspects of intelligence, in particular spatio-temporal intelligence (intelligence involving judgements of space and time) are largely independent of language, and associated with the right hemisphere. Patients with major speech problems due to severe left-hemisphere damage can still solve spatio-temporal puzzles, though to a lesser level of skill than previously (Zangwill 1964). In all, the whole question is a tricky one on which further work needs to be done.

Another unsolved problem is that of heredity. Can language defects be handed down from generation to generation? At the moment, the evidence is fragmentary. Perhaps the likeliest candidate is dyslexia or 'word blindness' which does seem to run in families. But, again, more research needs to be done on this topic.

In conclusion, then, the lungs, teeth, lips and vocal cords have evolved in such a way as to facilitate speech. More importantly, the human brain seems to be pre-programmed for language. Lateralization – the localization of language to one half of the brain – is a natural biologically-based phenomenon. Further localization within this hemisphere is a matter of controversy, although the sections of the brain known as Broca's area and Wernicke's area seem more likely to be involved than other areas.

But whatever the outcome of the various arguments connected with speech and the brain, it is clear that the human brain is 'wired' for language in a way that the brains of chimps and grasshoppers are not.

Patting one's head and rubbing the stomach

Another type of biological adaptation which is not so immediately obvious – but which is on second sight quite amazing – is the 'multiplicity of integrative processes' (Lashley 1951) which are taking place in speech production and comprehension.

In some areas of activity it is extremely difficult to do more than one thing at once. As schoolchildren discover, it is extraordinarily difficult to pat one's head and rub one's stomach at the same time. If you also try to swing your tongue from side to side, and cross and uncross your legs, as well as patting your head and rubbing your stomach, the whole exercise becomes impossible. The occasional juggler might be able to balance a beer bottle on his nose, twizzle a hoop on his ankle and keep seven plates aloft with his hands – but he is likely to have spent a lifetime practising such antics. And the exceptional nature of these activities is shown by the fact that he can earn vast sums of money displaying his skills.

Yet speech depends on the simultaneous integration of a remarkable number of processes, and in many respects what is going on is considerably more complex than the juggler's manoeuvres with his beer bottle, plates and hoop.

In speech, three processes, at the very least, are taking place simultaneously: firstly, sounds are actually being uttered; secondly, phrases are being activated in their phonetic form ready for use; thirdly, the rest of the sentence is being planned. And each of these processes is possibly more complicated than appears at first sight. The complexities involved in actually pronouncing words are not immediately apparent. One might assume that in uttering a word such as GEESE one first utters a G-sound, the an EE-sound, then an S-sound in that order. But the process is much more involved.

Firstly, the G-sound in GEESE differs quite considerably from the G in GOOSE. This is because of the difference in the following vowel. The speaker appears to anticipate (subconsciously) the EE or OO and alter the G accordingly. Secondly, the vowel in GEESE is shorter than in a word such as GEEZER. The speaker is anticipating the voiceless hissing sound of S in GOOSE rather than the voiced, buzzing sound of

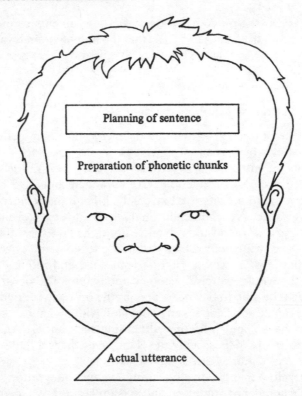

z in GEEZER, since in English (and some other languages) vowels are shortened before voiceless sounds (sounds which do not involve vibration of the vocal cords).

Therefore a speaker does not just utter a sequence of separate elements:

    1 2 3
    G . EE . SE

Instead he executes a series of overlapping actions in which the preceding sound is significantly influenced by the sound which follows it:

    G . . .
       EE . . .
         SE . . .

Such overlapping requires considerable neuro muscular co-ordination, particularly as the rate of speech is often quite fast. A normal person often utters over 200 syllables a minute. Meanwhile, simultaneously with actually uttering the sounds a speaker is activating phrases of two or three words in advance in their phonetic form. This is shown by slips of the tongue, in which a sound several words away is sometimes accidentally activated before it is needed. The linguist who once said PISS AND STRETCH in a lecture for 'pitch and stress' was already thinking of the final -SS of 'stress' when he started to say the first word. And the person who said ON THE NERVE OF A VERGEOUS BREAKDOWN has also activated the syllable 'nerve' before she needed it.

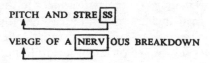

If humans only spoke in three or four word bursts, perhaps the prior activation of phrases would not be very surprising. What *is* surprising is that this activation is going on at the same time as the planning of much longer utterances. Lenneberg (1967, p. 107) likens the planning of an utterance to laying down a mosaic:

The sequence of speech sounds that constitute a string of words is a sound pattern somewhat analogous to a mosaic; the latter is put together stone after stone, yet the picture as a whole must have come into being in the artist's mind before he began to lay down the pieces.

Sometimes, sentences are structurally quite easy to process as in THE BABY FELL DOWNSTAIRS, THE CAT WAS SICK, AND I'VE RESIGNED. At other times they are considerably more complex, requiring the speaker and the hearer to remember quite intricate inter-dependencies between clauses. Take the sentence IF EITHER THE BABY FALLS DOWNSTAIRS OR THE CAT IS SICK, THEN I SHALL EITHER

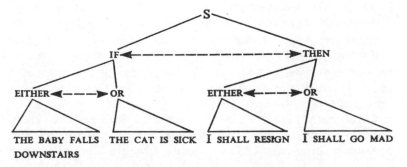

RESIGN OR GO MAD. Here, IF requires a dependent THEN, EITHER requires a partner OR. In addition, FALLS must have the right ending to go with BABY, and IS must 'agree' with CAT – otherwise we would get *IF EITHER THE BABY FALLS DOWNSTAIRS OR THE CAT ARE SICK. . . . This whole sentence with its 'mirror-image' properties must have been planned considerably in advance.

These examples show that in most human utterances, the amount of simultaneous planning and activity is so great that it seems likely that humans are specially constructed to deal with this type of co-ordination. But what type of mechanism is involved? In particular, how do humans manage to keep utterances in the right order, and not utter them in an incoherent jumble, as they think of them? How do most people manage to say RABBIT quite coherently, instead of BARIT or TIRAB – examples of misordering found in the speech of brain-damaged patients?

Lenneberg (1967) suggests that correct sequencing is based on an underlying rhythmic principle. Everybody knows that poetry is much easier to remember than prose because of the underlying 'pulse' which keeps going like the ticking of a clock:

> I WANDERED LONELY AS A CLOUD
> (ti-tum-ti-tum-ti-tum-ti-tum)
> THAT FLOATS ON HIGH O'ER VALES AND HILLS.
> (ti-tum-ti-tum-ti-tum-ti-tum)
> [WORDSWORTH]

There may be some underlying biological 'beat' which enables humans to organize language into a temporal sequence. Breakdown of this beat might also account for the uncontrollable acceleration of speech found in some illnesses such as Parkinson's disease. Lenneberg suggests that one-sixth of a second may be a basic time unit in speech production. He bases his proposals on a number of highly technical experiments, and partly on the fact that around six syllables per second seems to be the normal rate of uttering syllables. However, some people have queried the notion of a fixed 'pace-maker', and suggested that the internal beat can be re-set at different speeds (Keele 1987). This may be correct, since with practice speech can be speeded up, though the relative length of the various words remains the same (Mackay 1987).

We do not yet know the details, but the overall picture is clear. Humans are physically adapted to language in a way which snails, apes and sheep are not. Their vocal organs, lungs and brains are 'pre-set' to cope with the intricacies of speech in much the same way that monkeys are pre-set to climb trees, or bats to squeak. The next chapter gives further evidence of this biological programming by showing that language follows an inner 'time-clock' as it emerges and develops.

4 Predestinate grooves
Is there a pre-ordained language 'programme'?

There once was a man who said, 'Damn!'
It is born in upon me I am
An engine that moves
In predestinate grooves,
I'm not even a bus, I'm a tram

MAURICE EVAN HARE

Language emerges at about the same time in children all over the world. 'Why do children normally begin to speak between their eighteenth and twenty-eighth month?' asks one researcher. 'Surely it is not because all mothers on earth initiate language training at that time. There is, in fact, no evidence that any conscious and systematic teaching of language takes place, just as there is no special training for stance or gait.' (Lenneberg 1967, p. 125)

This regularity of onset suggests that language may be set in motion by a biological time-clock, similar to the one which causes kittens to open their eyes when they are a few days old, chrysalises to change into butterflies after several weeks, and humans to become sexually mature at around 13 years of age. However, until relatively recently, few people had considered language within the framework of biological maturation. But in 1967 E. H. Lenneberg, then a biologist at the Harvard Medical School, published an important book, entitled *The Biological Foundations of Language*. Much of what is said in this chapter is based on his pioneering work.

The characteristics of biologically triggered behaviour

Behaviour which is triggered off biologically has a number of special characteristics. In the following pages we shall list these features, and see to what extent they are present in language. If it can be shown that speech, like sexual activities and the ability to walk, falls into the category of biologically scheduled behaviour, then we shall be rather clearer about what is meant by the claim that language is 'innate'.

Exactly how many 'hallmarks' of biologically controlled behaviour
we should itemize is not clear. Lenneberg lists four. The six listed
below were obtained mainly by subdividing Lenneberg's four:

1 The behaviour emerges before it is necessary.
2 Its appearance is not the result of a conscious decision.
3 Its emergence is not triggered by external events (though the
  surrounding environment must be sufficiently 'rich' for it to
  develop adequately).
4 Direct teaching and intensive practice have relatively little effect.
5 There is a regular sequence of 'milestones' as the behaviour
  develops, and these can usually be correlated with age and other
  aspects of development.
6 There may be a 'critical period' for the acquisition of the
  behaviour.

Let us discuss these features in turn. Some of them seem fairly
obvious. We hardly need to set about testing the first one, that 'the
behaviour emerges before it is necessary' – a phenomenon sometimes pompously labelled the 'law of anticipatory maturation'.
Language develops long before children need to communicate in
order to survive. Their parents still feed them, clothe them, and look
after them. Without some type of inborn mechanism, language might
develop only when parents left children to fend for themselves. It
would emerge at different times in different cultures, and this would
lead to vastly different levels of language skills. Although children
differ enormously in their ability to knit or play the violin, their
language proficiency varies to a much lesser extent.

Again, little explanation is needed for the second characteristic of
biologically triggered behaviour: 'Its appearance is not the result of
a conscious decision'. Clearly, a child does not suddenly think to
herself, 'Tomorrow I am going to start to learn to talk'. Children
acquire language without making any conscious decision about it.
This is quite unlike a decision to learn to jump a four-foot height, or
hit a tennis ball, when a child sets herself a target, then organizes
strenuous practice sessions as she strives towards her goal.

The first part of feature (3) also seems straightforward: 'The
emergence of the behaviour is not triggered by external events'.
Children begin to talk even when their surroundings remain
unchanged. Most of them live in the same house, eat the same food,
have the same parents, and follow the same routine. No specific

event or feature in their surroundings suddenly starts them off talking. An inner biological clock is ticking away, set for the right time.

We know for certain that language cannot emerge before it is programmed to emerge. Nobody has ever made a young baby talk – though it seems that there is nothing much wrong with the vocal cords of a new-born infant, and from five or six months onwards it can 'babble' a number of the sounds needed in speech. Yet children utter few words before the age of eighteen months. It is clear that they have to wait for some biological trigger. The 'trigger' appears to be connected with brain growth. Two-word utterances, which are usually regarded as the beginning of 'true language', begin just as a massive spurt in brain growth slows down. Children do not manufacture any new brain cells after birth. They are born with millions, perhaps billions. At first the cells are not all interconnected, and the brain is relatively light (about 300 g). From birth to around two years, many more cells interconnect, and brain weight increases rapidly. By the age of two, it weighs nearly 1000 g (Lenneberg 1967).

However, there is one aspect of biologically scheduled behaviour that is sometimes misunderstood: although no external event *causes* the behaviour, the surrounding environment must be sufficiently 'rich' for it to develop adequately. Biologically programmed behaviour does not develop properly in impoverished or unnatural surroundings. We have the apparent paradox that some types of 'natural' behaviour require careful 'nurturing'. Just as Chris and Susie, two gorillas reared away from other gorillas in Sacramento Zoo, are unable to mate satisfactorily (according to an item in the *Evening Standard*) – so an impoverished linguistic environment is likely to retard language acquisition. Children brought up in institutions, for example, tend to be backward in speech development. Lenneberg notes that a child raised in an orphanage will begin to talk at the same time as other non-institutionalized children. But his speech will gradually lag behind the norm, being less intelligible, and showing less variety of construction. A less obvious example of linguistic impoverishment has been suggested by Basil Bernstein, a sociologist at London University's Institute of Education. He claims (somewhat controversially) that children from certain types of family may be language deprived (Bernstein 1972). They may be unable to learn language adequately because they do not have sufficient data at their disposal. He claims that such families use informal and elliptical speech, in contrast to the more formal and explicit language of households where children learn more quickly. For example, 'Hop it' in one family may correspond to 'Go outside and play, and stop worrying me, I'm busy' in another. As one man described it;

The words may be limited in number . . . there is a perpetual exchange of pebbled phrases: 'Ah well, some folk are like that; she's nowt but mutton dressed as lamb.' For most of what is said is not said by words but by tone of voice, by silences, by look, gesture and most keenly by touching.

The same man describes the cultural shock of school, where he was faced with 'an unending rush of words, multitudinous, fresh, and ordered in different ways' (Brian Jackson in the *Daily Telegraph* colour supplement). Children seem to need this 'unending rush of words', and those who are deprived of it may lag behind in their development. Luckily, the problem is usually only temporary. Language impoverished children tend to catch up quickly once their verbal environment is enriched: the biological factor takes over as soon as the environment enables it to do so.

Let us now turn to the fourth characteristic of biologically triggered behaviour, 'Direct teaching and intensive practice have relatively little effect.' In activities such as typing or playing tennis, a person's achievement is often directly related to the amount of teaching they receive and the hours of practice they put in. Even people who are not 'naturally' superb athletes can sometimes win tennis tournaments through sheer hard work and good coaching. But the same is not true of language, where direct teaching seems to be a failure. Let us consider the evidence for this.

When one says that 'direct teaching is a failure', people smile and say, 'Of course – whoever tries to *teach* a child to speak?' Yet many parents, often without realizing it, try to persuade their children to imitate them. They do this in two ways: firstly, by means of overt correction, secondly, by means of unconscious 'expansions'.

The pointlessness of overt correction has been noted by numerous researchers. One psychologist attempted over a period of several weeks to persuade his daughter to say OTHER + noun instead of OTHER ONE + noun. The interchanges went somewhat as follows:

Child: WANT OTHER ONE SPOON, DADDY.
Father: YOU MEAN, YOU WANT THE OTHER SPOON.
Child: YES, I WANT OTHER ONE SPOON, PLEASE DADDY.
Father: CAN YOU SAY 'THE OTHER SPOON'?
Child: OTHER . . . ONE . . . SPOON.

Father: SAY 'OTHER'.
Child: OTHER.
Father: 'SPOON.'
Child: SPOON.
Father: 'OTHER SPOON.'
Child: OTHER . . . SPOON. NOW GIVE ME OTHER ONE SPOON?

[BRAINE 1971, p. 161]

Another researcher tried vainly to coax a child into saying the past tense form HELD:

Child: MY TEACHER HOLDED THE BABY RABBITS AND WE PATTED THEM.
Adult: DID YOU SAY YOUR TEACHER HELD THE BABY RABBITS?
Child: YES.
Adult: WHAT DID YOU SAY SHE DID?
Child: SHE HOLDED THE BABY RABBITS AND WE PATTED THEM.
Adult: DID YOU SAY SHE HELD THEM TIGHTLY?
Child: NO, SHE HOLDED THEM LOOSELY.

[CAZDEN 1972, p. 92]

In fact, repeated corrections are not merely pointless: they may even hinder a child's progress. The mother of seventeen-month-old Paul had high expectations, and repeatedly corrected his attempts at speech. He lacked confidence, and his progress was slow. But the mother of fourteen-month-old Jane was an accepting person who responded uncritically to everything Jane said. Jane made exceptionally fast progress, and knew eighty words by the age of fifteen months (Nelson 1973, p. 105).

So forcing children to imitate is a dismal failure. Children cannot be trained like parrots. Equally unsuccessful is the second type of coaching often unconsciously adopted by parents – the use of 'expansions'. When talking to a child an adult continuously 'expands' the youngster's utterances. If the child says, THERE GO ONE, a mother is likely to expand this to 'Yes, there goes one'. MOMMY EGGNOG becomes 'Mommy had her eggnog', and THROW DADDY is expanded to 'Throw it to Daddy'. Children are exposed to an enormous number of these expansions. They account for perhaps a third of parental responses. Brown and Bellugi note:

The mothers of Adam and Eve responded to the speech of their children with expansions about 30 per cent of the time. We did it ourselves when we talked with the children. Indeed, we found it very difficult to withhold expansions. A reduced or incomplete English sentence seems to constrain the English-speaking adult to expand it into the nearest properly formed complete sentence. [BROWN AND BELLUGI 1964, p. 144]

At first researchers were uncertain about the role of expansions. Then Courtney Cazden carried out an ingenious experiment using two groups of children, all under three and a half (Cazden 1972). She exposed one group to intensive and deliberate expansions, and the other group to well-formed sentences which were *not* expansions. For example, if a child said, DOG BARK, an expanding adult would say, 'Yes, the dog is barking'. An adult who replied with a non-expanded sentence might say 'Yes, he's trying to frighten the cat' or 'Yes, but he won't bite', or 'Yes, tell him to be quiet'. After three months the rate of progress of each group was measured. Amazingly, the expansion group were *less advanced* than the other group, both in average length of utterance and grammatical complexity.

Several explanations of this unexpected result have been put forward. Perhaps adults misinterpret the child's intended meaning when they expand. Erroneous expansions could hinder his learning. Several 'wrong' expansions have been noted. For example:

Child: WHAT TIME IT IS?
Adult: UH HUH, IT TELLS WHAT TIME IT IS.

Alternatively, a certain degree of novelty may be needed in order to capture children's attention, since they may not listen to apparent repetitions of their own utterances. Or it may be that expansions over-restrict the data children hear. Their speech may be impoverished because of an insufficiently rich verbal environment. As we noted earlier, a child *needs* copious and varied samples of speech.

The last two explanations seem to be supported by a Russian experiment (Slobin 1966, p. 144). One group of infants was shown a doll, and three phrases were repeatedly uttered, 'Here is a doll . . . Take the doll . . . Give me the doll.' Another group of infants was shown the doll, but instead, *thirty* different phrases were uttered, such as 'Rock the doll . . . Look for the doll.' The total number of words heard by both groups was the same, only the composition differed. Then the experimenters showed the children a selection of toys, and asked them to pick out the dolls. To their surprise, the children in the second group, the ones who had heard a richer variety of speech, were considerably better at this task.

We may conclude then that parents who consciously try to 'coach' their children by simplifying and repeating may be actually *interfering* with their progress. It does not pay to talk to children as if one was telling a foreign tourist how to get to the zoo. Language that is impoverished is harder to learn, not simpler. Children appear to be naturally 'set' to extract a grammar for themselves, provided they have sufficient data at their disposal. Direct teaching is irrelevant, and those who get on best are those who are exposed to a rich variety of language – in other words, those whose parents talk to them in a normal way.

But what does 'talk in a normal way' mean? Here we need to clear up a misunderstanding which seems to have originated with Chomsky. He claims that what children hear 'consists to a large extent of utterances that break rules, since a good deal of normal speech consists of false starts, disconnected phrases and other deviations' (Chomsky 1967, p. 441). Certainly, children are likely to hear *some* deviant sentences. But recent research indicates that the speech children are exposed to is not particularly sub-standard. Adults tend to speak in shorter sentences and make fewer mistakes when they address children. There is a considerable difference between the way a mother talks to another adult, and the way she talks to her child. One researcher recorded a mother talking to an adult friend. Her sentences were on average fourteen to fifteen words long, and she used several polysyllabic medical terms:

'I was on a inhalation series routine. We wen' aroun' from ward to ward. People, are, y'know, that get all this mucus in their chest, and it's very important to breathe properly an' to be able to cough this mucus up and out an' through your chest, y'know as soon as possible. And we couldn't sterilize the instruments 'cause they were plastic.'

But when she spoke to her child the same mother used five- or six-word sentences. The words were shorter, and referred to things the child could see or do:

COME LOOK AT MOMMA'S COLORIN' BOOK.
YOU WANNA SEE MY COLORING BOOK?
LOOK AT MY COLORING BOOK.
LOOKIT, THAT'S AN INDIAN, HUH?
IS THAT AN INDIAN?
CAN YOU SAY INDIAN?
TALK TO ME.

[DRACH, quoted in *Ervin-Tripp* 1971]

Most parents automatically simplify both the content and syntax when they talk to children. This is not particularly surprising – after all, we do not address bus conductors and boy friends in the same way. The use of language appropriate to the circumstances is a normal part of a human's language ability.

Speech to children in different cultures is so similar that it might even 'have an innate basis in pan-human child-care behavior', according to the controversial claim of one researcher (Ferguson 1978, p. 215). 'Motherese', as it is sometimes called, tends to consist of short, well-formed sentences spoken slowly and clearly. We shall discuss the relationship between the structure of adult speech and children's progress in Chapter 7. Here we have simply pointed out that direct teaching, in the sense of correction and imitation, does not accelerate the speed of learning and might even be a hindrance.

Let us now return to the question of practice. What is being claimed here is that practice alone cannot account for language acquisition. Children do not learn language simply by repetition and imitation. Two types of evidence support this view.

The first concerns the development of 'inflections' or word endings. English has a number of very common verbs which have an 'irregular' past tense form (e.g. CAME, SAW, WENT) as opposed to the 'regular' forms such as LOVED, WORKED, PLAYED. It also has a number of irregular plurals such as FEET and MICE, as well as the far more numerous plurals ending in -s such as CATS, GIRAFFES and PYTHONS. Quite early on, children learn correct past tense and plural forms for common words such as CAME, SAW and FEET. Later, they abandon these correct forms and replace them with overgeneralized 'regular' forms such as COMED, SEED and FOOTS (Ervin 1964). The significance of this apparent regression is immense. It means that language acquisition cannot possibly be a straightforward case of 'practice makes perfect' or of simple imitation. If it were, children would never replace common forms such as CAME and SAW, which they hear and use all the time, with odd forms such as COMED, SEED and FOOTS which they are unlikely to have come across.

The second type of practice which turns out to be unimportant for language acquisition is spontaneous imitation. Just as adults subconsciously imitate and expand their children's utterances, so children appear to imitate and 'reduce' sentences uttered by their parents. If an adult says 'I shall take an umbrella', a child is likely to say TAKE 'RELLA. Or 'Put the strap under her chin' is likely to be repeated and reduced to STRAP CHIN. At first sight, it looks as if this might be an important mechanism in the development of language. But Susan Ervin of the University of California at Berkeley came to the opposite conclusion when she recorded the spontaneous utterances of a small group of toddlers (Ervin 1964). To her surprise she found that when a child spontaneously imitates an adult, her imitations are not any more advanced than her normal speech. She shortens the adult utterance to fit in with her current average length of sentence and includes the same number of endings and 'little' words as in her non-imitated utterances. Not a single child produced imitations which were more advanced. And one child, Holly, actually produced imitations that were less complex than her spontaneous sentences! Susan Ervin notes:

There is not a shred of evidence supporting a view that progress toward adult norms of grammar arises merely from practice in overt imitation of adult sentences. [ERVIN 1964, p. 172]

We may conclude, then, that mere practice – in the sense of direct repetition and imitation – does not affect the acquisition of language in a significant way. However, we must be careful that such a statement does not lead to misunderstandings. What is being said is that practice alone cannot account for language acquisition: children do not learn merely by constant repetition of items. In another sense, they do need to 'practise' talking but even this requirement is not as extensive as might be expected. They can learn a surprising amount by just listening. It has been shown that the amount of talking a child needs to do in order to learn language varies considerably. Some children seem to speak very little. Others are constantly chattering, and playing with words. One researcher wrote a whole book on the pre-sleep monologues of her first child Anthony, who murmured paradigms to himself as he prepared for sleep:

GO FOR GLASSES
GO FOR THEM
GO TO THE TOP
GO THROW
GO FOR BLOUSE
PANTS
GO FOR SHOES
   [WEIR 1962]

To her disappointment, her second child David, was nowhere near as talkative although he eventually learned to speak just as well.

These repetitious murmurs do not seem to be essential. Children vary enormously in the amount of 'language drills' they engage in (Kuczaj II 1983).

So far, then, we have considered four of the six characteristics of biologically triggered behaviour which we listed at the beginning of this chapter. All these features seem to be present in language. We now come to the fifth feature, 'There is a regular sequence of "milestones" as the behaviour develops, and these can usually be correlated with age and other aspects of development.' We shall deal with this in a section by itself.

The pre-ordained programme

All children seem to pass through a series of more or less fixed 'stages' as they acquire language. The age at which different children reach each stage or 'milestone' varies considerably, but the relative chronology remains the same. The milestones are normally reached in the same order, though they may be nearer together for some children and farther apart for others.

Consequently, we can divide language development up into a number of approximate phases. The diagram overleaf is highly oversimplified. The stages overlap, and the ages given are only a very rough guide – but it does give some idea of a child's likely progress.

In order to illustrate this progression we shall describe the successive phases which a typical (and non-existent) English child is likely to go through as she learns to speak. Let us call this child

Language stage	Beginning age
Crying	Birth
Cooing	6 weeks
Babbling	6 months
Intonation patterns	8 months
1-word utterances	1 year
2-word utterances	18 months
Word inflections	2 years
Questions, negatives	2¼ years
Rare or complex constructions	5 years
Mature speech	10 years

Barbara – a name derived from the Greek word for 'foreigner' and meaning literally 'someone who says bar-bar, who talks gibberish'.

Barbara's first recognizable vocal activity was *crying*. During the first four weeks of her life, she was truly:

> An infant crying in the night:
> An infant crying for the light:
> And with no language but a cry.
> [TENNYSON]

A number of different types of cry could be detected. She cried with hunger when she wanted to be fed. She cried with pain, when she had a tummy ache, and she cried with pleasure when she was fed, comfortable and lying in her mother's arms. However, strictly speaking, it is perhaps inaccurate to speak of crying as a 'language phase', because crying seems to be instinctive communication and may be more like an animal call system than a true language. This seems to be confirmed by some research which suggests that the different 'messages' contained in the crying of babies may be universal, since English parents could identify the 'messages' of a foreign baby as easily as those of English babies (Ricks 1975). So although crying may help to strengthen the lungs and vocal cords (both of which are needed for speech), crying itself perhaps should not be regarded as part of true language development.

Barbara then passed through two reasonably distinct pre-language phases, a *cooing* phase and a *babbling* phase. Early researchers confused these stages and sometimes likened them to bird song. The nineteenth-century scholar Taine noted of his daughter:

She takes delight in her twitter like a bird, she seems to smile with joy over it, but as yet it is only the twittering of a bird, for she attaches no meaning to the sounds she utters. [TAINE 1877, cited in Bar-Adon and Leopold 1971, p. 21]

The first of these two phases, *cooing*, began when Barbara was approximately six weeks old. To a casual observer, she sounded as if she was saying, GOO GOO. But cooing is difficult to describe. Some textbooks call it 'gurgling' or 'mewing'. The sound is superficially vowel-like, but the tracings produced on a sound spectrogram show that it is quite unlike the vowels produced by adults. Cooing seems to be universal. It may be the vocal equivalent of arm and leg waving. That is, just as babies automatically strengthen their muscles by kicking their legs and moving their arms about, so cooing may help them to gain control over their vocal apparatus.

Gradually, consonant-type sounds become interspersed in the cooing. By around six months, Barbara had reached the *babbling* stage. She gave the impression of uttering consonants and vowels together, at first as single syllables – but later strung together. The consonants were often made with the lips, or the teeth, so that the sequences sounded like MAMA, DIDIDI, or PAPAPA. On hearing these sounds, Barbara's parents confidently but wrongly assumed that she was addressing them. Such wishful thinking accounts for the fact that MAMA, PAPA and DADA are found as nursery words for mother and father all over the world (Jakobson 1962). Barbara soon learned that a cry of MAMA meant immediate attention – though she often used it to mean, 'I am hungry' rather than to refer to a parent. This phenomenon has been noted by numerous researchers. Charles Darwin, for example, remarked that at the age of one year his son 'made the great step forward of inventing a word for food, namely, *mum* but what led him to it I did not discover' (Darwin 1877, cited in Bar-Adon and Leopold 1971, p. 28). Another investigator observed that his child called MAMA as a request for a piece of bread being buttered by himself, the father.

Throughout the babbling period Barbara seemed to enjoy experimenting with her mouth and tongue. She not only babbled, she blew bubbles, gurgled and spluttered. Superficially, she appeared to be uttering an enormous variety of exotic sounds. At one time, researchers wrongly assumed that children are naturally capable of producing every possible speech sound. A Canadian psychologist once commented:

During this period that peculiarly charming infantile babble begins which, though only an 'awkward twittering', yet contains in rudimentary form nearly all the sounds which afterwards by combination, yield the potent instrument of speech. A wonderful variety of sounds, some of which afterwards give the child difficulty when he tries to produce them, are now produced automatically, by purely impulsive exercise of the vocal muscles. [TRACY 1909, cited in Bar-Adon and Leopold 1971, p. 32]

More recent investigators have noted that the variety of sounds used in babbling is not particularly great. But because the child does not yet have complete control over his vocal organs, the noises are often unlike adult sounds, and seem exotic to an untrained observer. In general, babbling seems to be a period when a child experiments and gradually gains muscular control over his vocal organs. Many people claim that babbling is universal. But there are a few puzzling records of children who did not babble, which provide problems for this point of view. All we can say at the moment is that babbling is sufficiently widespread to be regarded as a normal stage of development.

Some investigators have tried to compare babbling babies who have been exposed to different languages. For example, Chinese babbles seem to be easily distinguishable from American, Russian and Arabic ones (Weir 1966). Because Chinese is a language which distinguishes words by means of a change in 'tone' or 'pitch', Chinese babies tend to produce monosyllabic utterances with much tonal variation. American babies produce polysyllabic babbles with intonation spread over the whole sequence. The non-tone babies sound superficially similar – though American mothers could often pick out the American baby, Russians the Russian baby, and Arabs the Arab baby. But the mothers could not distinguish between the babies babbling the other two languages. This research indicates that there may be a 'babbling drift', in which children's babbling gradually moves in the direction of the sounds they hear around them. These findings have been confirmed by several later studies (e.g. Cruttenden 1970; Vihmann *et al.* 1985). For example, French adults can pick out French baby-babbles from non-French ones (de Boysson-Bardies *et al.* 1984). In this respect babbling is clearly distinct from crying, which has no discernible relationship with any one language.

A question which perhaps should be asked at this stage is the following: how much can children actually distinguish of their parents' speech? It is sometimes assumed that babies hear merely a general mish-mash of sound, and only gradually notice the difference between say P and B. However, recent research indicates that infants are capable of discriminating a lot more than we realize. They seem to be specially pre-set to notice the rhythms and sounds of speech, and probably begin to 'tune in' before birth. French infants as young as four days old can distinguish French from other languages, according to one group of researchers (Mehler *et al.* 1988). They found this out by giving babies pacifiers (dummies) to suck. It is well known that infants suck more strongly when they are aroused and interested in what they hear. These French newborns sucked at significantly higher rates when exposed to French, than to English or Italian. So they had possibly become acclimatized to the rhythm and intonation of French while still in the womb.

Using the same sucking technique, Eimas and his colleagues (1971, 1984, 1985) showed that babies between one and four months old can distinguish between P and B. The investigators started by playing a repeated B sound, then they switched to P. The babies suddenly increased their sucking rate, showing that they had noticed the alteration. So even though infants may not listen carefully to everything their parents say, they may well be capable of hearing a considerable amount from a very young age. Somewhat surprisingly, these results of Eimas have been replicated with rhesus and chinchilla monkeys (Morse 1976; Kuhl and Miller 1974, 1975), and so may be due to the hearing mechanisms in certain types of mammals, and not just humans alone. In brief, a child's perception may be much sharper than had previously been supposed, even though it may not be equivalent to an adult's for some time (Fourcin 1978).

Simultaneously with babbling, and from around eight or nine months, Barbara began to imitate *intonation patterns*. These made her output sound so like speech that her mother sometimes said, 'I'm sure she's talking, I just can't catch what she's saying.' An eighteenth-century German researcher observed of this stage: 'He attempted to imitate conversations, to which end he produced a profusion of incomprehensible sounds' (Tiedemann 1782, cited in Bar-Adon and Leopold 1971, p. 15). English mothers have noted that their children often use a 'question' intonation, with a rise in tone at the end of the sentence. This may be due to a normal parent's tendency to bend over the child, asking, 'What are your trying to say then?,' 'Do you want some milk?' 'Do you know who this is?' and so on.

Somewhere between one year and eighteen months Barbara began to utter *single words*. She continued to babble as well, though her babbling gradually diminished as true language developed (Stoel-Gammon and Cooper 1984). The number of single words acquired at around this time varies from child to child. Some have only four or five, others have around fifty. As an average child Barbara acquired about fifteen. Many of them were names of people and things, such as UF (woof) 'dog', DABA 'grandma', DA 'doll'. Then as she neared her second birthday, she reached the more impressive *two-word stage*.

From the time Barbara started to put words together she seemed to be in a state of 'language readiness', and mopped up language like a sponge. The most noticeable feature of this process was a dramatic increase in her vocabulary. By the time she was 2½-years-old, she knew several hundred words. Meanwhile, there was a gradual but steady increase in her average or mean length of utterance – usually abbreviated to MLU. MLU is calculated in terms of grammatical items or 'morphemes': plural -s and past tense -D, for example, each count as one item and so do ordinary words such as MUMMY and BATH.

Compound words such as BIRTHDAY and QUACK-QUACK also count as a single item (Brown 1973, p. 54). Many (but not all) researchers accept this as a useful guage of progress – though the child with the longest utterances does not necessarily have the most grammatically advanced, or even the most grammatically correct utterances (Bennett-Kastor 1988, Bates *et al* 1988)

The fact that a steady increase in MLU occurs from the age of around 2 onwards has been shown by Roger Brown of Harvard University, who carried out a detailed study of the speech development of three unacquainted children. Adam, Eve and Sarah – though he found that the chronological age at which different children reached an MLU stage differed considerably (Brown, Cazden and Bellugi 1968; Brown 1973). A comparison of Adam and Eve showed that Eve outstripped Adam by far. Eve's MLU was two items at around twenty months, three at twenty-two months and four at twenty-eight months. Adam was over twenty-six months old before he achieved an MLU of two items. He was nearly 3-years-old before his MLU reached three items and 3½ before it reached four items – a whole year behind Eve.

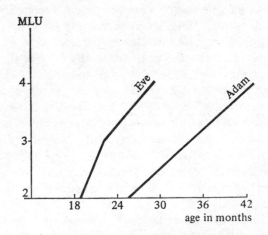

If we assume that Barbara is not as advanced as Eve, but ahead of Adam, she possibly had an MLU of two items a little before her second birthday, an MLU of three items at 2½, and four items around her third birthday.

In the early part of the two-word stage, when she was around 2 years old, Barbara's speech was 'telegraphic'. She sounded as if she was sending urgent telegrams to her mother: WANT MILK, WHERE

DUCK? As in a real telegram, she tended to preserve the nouns and verbs in the correct order, but omitted the 'little' words such as THE, A, HAS, HIS, AND. She also left out word endings, such as the plural -S or past tense -D, as in TWO SHOE and MILK SPILL.

Then, gradually, the 'little' words and *inflections* were added. 'All these, like an intricate work of ivy, begin to grow up between and upon the major construction blocks, the nouns and verbs' (Brown 1973, p. 249).

In this aspect of language, Barbara is following the same path of development as the Harvard child Adam, but at a slightly earlier age (Brown 1973, p. 271). Between the ages of 2 and 3½, Barbara acquired the following grammatical forms:

Age 2	Progressive -ING	I SINGING
	Plural -S	BLUE SHOES
	Copula AM, IS, ARE	HE IS ASLEEP
	Articles A, THE	HE IS A DOCTOR
Age 3	3rd person singular -S	HE WANTS AN APPLE
	Past tense -D	I HELPED MUMMY
	Full progressive AM, IS, ARE + -ING	I AM SINGING
	Shortened copula	HE'S A DOCTOR
	Shortened progressive	I'M SINGING

It is important to distinguish between the *emergence*, or first appearance of an ending, and its *acquisition*, its reliable use in the places where an adult would expect to find it. An ending can be considered acquired if it occurs in at least 90 per cent of the contexts where it is needed (Brown 1973, p. 258).

The actual age at which Barbara acquired each form is not significant because it varies widely from child to child. What is important and interesting is the *order* of acquisition. The sequence seems surprisingly similar among English-speaking children. Roger Brown notes that in the unacquainted Harvard children, the developmental order of these grammatical forms was 'amazingly consistent'. There were one or two minor variations: Sarah, for example, acquired the progressive -ING after the plural, whereas Adam and Eve acquired it before. But in all the children, both the progressive -ING and the plural -S occurred before the past tense, the third person singular -S, and the copula AM, IS, ARE.

Perhaps even more surprising, is the fact that in all the Harvard children the copula AM, IS, ARE as in I AM A DOCTOR developed before AM, IS, ARE when it was part of the progressive construction, for example, I AM SINGING. And the shortened copula as in HE'S A BEAR came before the shortened progressive, for example HE'S WALKING. This is quite an astonishing discovery. Although we might expect children to go through similar general lines of development, there seems to be no obvious reason why a variety of English children should correspond so closely in their acquisition of specific items. Possible reasons for this phenomenon will be discussed in Chapter 7.

A similar consistency of order is found in the acquisition of more complicated constructions, such as *questions* and *negatives*. For example, in the acquisition of WH-questions (questions beginning with WHAT, WHY, WHERE, WHO, etc.), we can safely assume that Barbara, like Adam, Eve and Sarah, went through three intermediate stages before she acquired them perfectly (Klima and Bellugi 1966). First of all, soon after her second birthday, she placed the WH-word in front of the rest of the sentence:

WHAT	MUMMY DOING?
WHY	YOU SINGING?
WHERE	DADDY GO?

A second stage occurred three or four months later when she added an auxiliary verb such as CAN or WILL to the main verb:

WHERE	YOU	WILL GO?
WHY	KITTY	CAN'T SEE?
WHY	YOU	DON'T KNOW?

Finally, before she was 3, she realized that the subject noun must change places with the auxiliary and produced correct sentences such as:

WHERE	WILL YOU	GO?
WHY	CAN'T KITTY	SEE?
WHY	DON'T YOU	KNOW?

Once again, the rather surprising finding that all English children tend to follow the same pattern will be discussed later. As already noted, the actual *age* at which each stage is reached is irrelevant. It is the order which matters.

By the age of 3½, Barbara, like most children, was able to form most grammatical constructions – and her speech was reasonably intelligible to strangers. Her constructions were, however, less varied than those of an adult. For example, she tended not to use the 'full' passive such as THE MAN WAS HIT BY A BUS. But she was able to converse quite adequately on most topics.

By 5, she gave the superficial impression of having acquired language more or less perfectly. But this was an illusion. Language acquisition was still continuing, though more slowly. The grammar of a child of 5 differs to a perhaps surprising degree from adult grammar. But the 5-year-old is not usually aware of his short-comings. In comprehension tests, children readily assign inter-pretations to the structures presented to them – but they are often the wrong ones. 'They do not, as they see it, fail to understand our sentences. They understand them, but they understand them wrongly' (Carol Chomsky 1969, p. 2). To demonstrate this point, the researcher showed a group of 5- to 8-year-olds a blindfolded doll, and said: 'Is this doll hard to see or easy to see?' All the 5- and 6-year-olds said HARD TO SEE, and so did some of the 7- and 8-year-olds. The response of 6-year-old Lisa was typical:

Chomsky: IS THIS DOLL EASY TO SEE OR HARD TO SEE?
Lisa: HARD TO SEE.
Chomsky: WILL YOU MAKE HER EASY TO SEE?
Lisa: IF I CAN GET THIS UNTIED.
Chomsky: WILL YOU EXPLAIN WHY SHE WAS HARD TO SEE?
Lisa: (to doll) BECAUSE YOU HAD A BLINDFOLD OVER YOUR EYES.

Some psychologists have criticized this particular test. A child sometimes believes, ostrich-fashion, that if his own eyes are covered, others will not be able to see him. And he may be partly switching to the doll's viewpoint when he says a blindfolded doll is hard to see. But a re-run of this experiment using wolf and duck puppets, and sentences such as:

THE WOLF IS HARD TO BITE
THE DUCK IS ANXIOUS TO BITE

confirmed the original results (Cromer 1970). Children of 5 and 6 just do not realize that pairs of sentences such as THE RABBIT IS NICE

TO EAT and THE RABBIT IS EAGER TO EAT have completely different underlying meanings.

In fact, the gap between child and adult speech lasts longer than was once realized. More recently, detailed experiments on French children's understanding and use of the articles LE/LA 'the' and UN/UNE 'a' have shown quite surprising differences between child and adult usage, which remained in some cases up till the age of 12 (Karmiloff-Smith 1979).

But the discrepancies between Barbara's speech and that of the adults around her gradually disappeared over the next few years. By the age of about 11, Barbara exhibited a command of the structure of her language comparable to that of an adult. At the age of puberty, her language development was essentially complete, apart from vocabulary. She would continue to accumulate lexical items throughout her life (Aitchison 1987a).

The language milestones we have outlined tend to run parallel with physical development. Clearly, there is no essential correlation between language and motor development, since there are numerous examples of children who learn to talk, but never walk, and vice versa. However, researchers are agreed that in normal children the two often go together. Language stages are often loosely linked to physical milestones. The gradual change of cooing to babbling occurs around the time an infant begins to sit up. Children utter single words just before they start to walk. Grammar becomes complex as hand and finger co-ordination develops.

We now need to discuss one final point. Is it crucial for children to develop language at the age they normally do? According to the sixth and final characteristic of maturationally controlled behaviour, there may be a 'critical period' for its acquisition – though this is not essential. Is this true of language? Let us consider this matter.

Is there a 'critical period'?

Are humans like chaffinches? Or like canaries? Both these birds have to partially learn their songs. But a chaffinch's song becomes fixed and unalterable when it is around fifteen-months old. If the young bird has not heard any chaffinch song before that time, it never learns to sing normally (Thorpe 1972). But canaries can continue to alter their song for years (Nottebohm 1984; Marler 1988). Lenneberg argued that humans, like chaffinches, have a narrow 'critical period'

set aside by nature for the acquisition of language. In his view, it lasts
from toddler time to adolescence:

Between the ages of two and three years language emerges by an interaction
of maturation and self-programmed learning. Between the ages of three and
the early teens the possibility for primary language acquisition continues to
be good; the individual appears to be most sensitive to stimuli at this time
and to preserve some innate flexibility for the organization of brain functions
to carry out the complex integration of sub-processes necessary for the
smooth elaboration of speech and language. After puberty, the ability for
self-organization and adjustment to the physiological demands of verbal
behaviour quickly declines. The brain behaves as if it had become set in its
ways and primary, basic skills not acquired by that time usually remain
deficient for life. [Lenneberg 1967, p. 158]

Twenty years ago, Lenneberg's views were widely accepted.
Children clearly start talking at about the age of two. And it seemed
plausible that language ability ceased at around 13. Almost
everybody can remember how difficult it was to learn French at
school. Even the best pupils had a slightly odd accent, and made
numerous grammatical mistakes. It was comforting to believe that
there was a biological explanation for this. On closer inspection,
however, the matter is not so clear cut.

Five strands of argument have been put forward in favour of the
notion of a 'critical period': first, the speech of humans who acquired
language late. Second, the development of children with Down's
syndrome. Third, the fate of youngsters with brain damage. Fourth,
the difficulties involved in learning a second language. Fifth, the
supposed synchrony of the critical period with lateralization. Let us
examine these claims.

The cases of three socially isolated children, Isabelle, Genie and
Chelsea provide superficial support for the existence of a critical period.
All three were cut off from language until long after the time they would
have acquired it, had they been brought up in normal circumstances.

Isabelle was the illegitimate child of a deaf mute. She had no
speech, and made only a croaking sound when she was found in Ohio
in the 1930s at the age of 6½. Mother and child had spent most of the
time alone in a darkened room. But once found, Isabelle's progress
was remarkable: 'Isabelle passed through the usual stages of
linguistic development at a greatly accelerated rate. She covered in
two years the learning that ordinarily occupies six years. By the age
of eight and one half Isabelle was not easily distinguishable from
ordinary children of her age' (Brown 1958, p. 192).

Genie, however, was not so lucky. She was not found until she was nearly 14. Born in April 1957, she had lived most of her life in bizarre and inhuman conditions. 'From the age of twenty months, Genie had been confined to a small room . . . She was physically punished by her father if she made any sounds. Most of the time she was kept harnessed into an infant's potty chair; otherwise she was confined in a home-made sleeping bag in an infant's crib covered with wire mesh' (Curtiss *et al.* 1974, p. 529). When found, she was totally without language. She began acquiring speech well after the onset of adolescence – after the proposed 'critical period'.

Although she learnt to speak in a rudimentary fashion, she progressed more slowly than normal children (Curtiss 1977). For example, ordinary children go through a stage in which they utter two words at a time(WANT MILK, MUMMY PLAY), which normally lasts a matter of weeks.

Genie's two-word stage lasted for more than five months. Again, ordinary children briefly pass through a phase in which they form negative sentences by putting the word NO in front of the rest of the utterance, as in NO MUMMY GO, NO WANT APPLE. Genie used this primitive form of negation for over two years. Normal children start asking questions beginning with words such as WHERE, WHAT, at the two-word stage (WHERE TEDDY?). Genie finds this kind of question impossible to grasp, occasionally making inappropriate attempts such as WHERE IS STOP SPITTING? The only aspect of speech in which Genie outstripped normal children was her ability to learn vocabulary. She knew many more words than ordinary children at a comparable stage of grammatical development. However, the ability to memorize lists of items is not evidence of language capacity – even the chimps Washoe and Sarah found this relatively easy. It is the rules of grammar which are the important part, and this is what Genie finds difficult. Her slow progress compared with that of Isabelle seems to provide evidence in favour of there being a 'cut-off' point for language acquisition. We must be cautious however. Two individual cases cannot provide firm proof, especially as each is problematical. Isabelle was not studied by linguists, so her speech may have been more deficient than was reported. Genie, on the other hand, shows some evidence of brain damage. Tests suggest that her left hemisphere is atrophied, which means that she may be functioning with only one half of her brain, the half not usually associated with language (Curtiss 1977; Curtiss *et al.* 1974).

Chelsea is a recently reported case of another late starter (Curtiss

1988). She is an adult with hearing problems who started learning language in her early thirties. Like Genie, her vocabulary is good, but her syntax is poor. She says things such as: THE WOMAN IS BUS THE GOING, ORANGE TIM CAR IN, BANANA THE EAT. Chelsea's strange syntax could be due to her late start. But it might also be because of her defective hearing. So neither Genie nor Chelsea provides convincing proof of a 'cut-off' point for language acquisition. Each of them has severe non-linguistic problems, which could account for their rudimentary language.

According to Lenneberg, further evidence in favour of a critical period is provided by mentally handicapped children, such as 'mongols' (Down's syndrome cases) (Lenneberg 1967). These follow the same general path of development as normal children, but much more slowly. Lenneberg claims that they never catch up because their ability to learn language slows down dramatically at puberty. But some researchers have disputed this claim, arguing that the children's language ceases to develop through lack of stimulation. Moreover, recent work suggests that Down's syndrome children have a built-in endpoint to their ability. They may reach this ceiling at any age, though often quite a long time before adolescence (Gleitman 1984).

The recovery possibilities of brain-damaged patients were another strand in Lenneberg's argument. He claimed that if a child under the age of 2 sustained severe damage to the left (language) hemisphere of the brain, speech would develop normally, though it would be controlled by the right hemisphere. The 'critical period' had in his view not yet begun. But the older the child, the greater the likelihood that left hemisphere damage would cause permanent impairment. In an adolescent or adult, he argued, such harm would result in lifelong speech disturbance. The 'critical period' would be over.

Lenneberg's claim that the language of younger children is less severely impaired by brain damage than the speech of older ones appears to be true (Vargha-Khadem *et al.* 1985). This is not surprising. Young brains have greater powers of recovery. Infant monkeys with brain damage recover faster than older ones (Goldman-Rakic 1982). But there is no good evidence for the sudden onset of a critical period at age 2, nor of a shuddering halt to language ability at adolescence.

Over the onset time, Lenneberg seems to be wrong in assuming that children under 2 will not be affected by left hemisphere damage. On the contrary, babies who have had this half of their brain removed in the first year of life have considerable language problems (Dennis 1983). Severe left hemisphere injury usually results in permanent linguistic impairments, whatever the age of the patient.

As for Lenneberg's presumed adolescent full-stop, teenagers in the western world alter their language considerably (e.g. Cheshire 1982). Adults often complain that they cannot bear the 'sloppy' speech of their children, or even comprehend it, in some cases. This is inconsistent with the notion of language which becomes fixed and unalterable at adolescence.

But isn't the struggle we all had to acquire extra languages at school clear evidence of some 'cut-off' point? Controversy rages around this matter (Hatch 1983). Youngsters are better at acquiring sound patterns, though the situation over syntax is much less clear. Older learners progress faster initially (e.g. Harley 1986), but younger children win out in the long run, according to some researchers (e.g. Asher and Price 1967).

However, many older learners may be inefficient because they have let their language learning skills become rusty. Those who keep in practice may never lose the knack. This is a plausible explanation for our difficulty with languages at school. Bever (1981) points out that there is a discrepancy between what infants perceive, and what they produce. As long as this imbalance exists, a special channel may be available which links the two types of activity. Eventually, perception and production become aligned, and there is a gradual loss of the mechanism which works out how they correlate. However, if languages continue to be learned, the linking mechanism never fully fades away – though, as we get older, our brains like our bodies slowly lose flexibility.

Finally, let us consider Lenneberg's claim that the supposed critical period coincides with the period of lateralization, the specialization of language to one side of the brain (Chapter 3). This process, in his view, occurs between the ages of 2 and 14. Lenneberg is probably wrong about this. Lateralization appears to take place much earlier than he suggests. Even babies under a year old show some evidence of it. In one experiment, five- and six-month old infants were presented with sounds and lip movements which were sometimes synchronized, sometimes not. They seemed to notice the synchrony only when the direction of their gaze showed that they were using their left hemisphere (MacKain *et al.* 1983). So lateralization is apparently under way in the first few months of life. And as soon as young children can be tested with dichotic listening

(Chapter 3), around age 2½ or 3, they seem to be using their left hemisphere for language (Kinsbourne and Hiscock 1987). So lateralization may even be complete at this age, and most people assume it has occurred by the age of 5 (e.g. Krashen 1973–4).

To summarize, all the arguments for a well-defined critical period are unconvincing. Genie's brain-damage and Chelsea's deafness may account for their language problems. The language 'ceiling' in Down's syndrome children is unrelated to adolescence. Severe left hemisphere damage causes problems at any age. Keeping in practice may preserve people's ability to learn languages. Lateralization is complete well before adolescence. There is no evidence of a sudden onset, or final endpoint of the supposed critical period. Instead, we are dealing with a phenomenon well known in animals, the fact that young brains are more flexible than older ones.

In this chapter, therefore, we have shown that language seems to have the characteristics of biologically programmed behaviour. It emerges before it is necessary, and its emergence cannot be accounted for either by an external event, or by a sudden decision taken by the child. Direct teaching and intensive practice have relatively little effect. Acquisition follows a regular sequence of milestones which can be loosely correlated with other aspects of the child's development. In other words, there is an internal mechanism both to trigger it off and to regulate it. There is unlikely to be a strict 'critical period' for acquiring it, though early exposure is an advantage, since younger brains have more plasticity.

However, it would be wrong to think of language as something which is governed *only* by internal mechanisms. These mechanisms require external stimulation in order to work properly. The child needs a rich verbal environment during the acquisition period.

This suggests that the so-called nature–nurture controversy mentioned in Chapter 1 may be misconceived. Both sides are right: nature triggers off the behaviour, and lays down the framework, but careful nurture is needed for it to reach its full potential. The dividing line between 'natural' and 'nurtured' behaviour is by no means as clear cut as was once thought. In other words, language is 'natural' behaviour – but it still has to be carefully 'nurtured' in order to reach its full potential.

But, although we have now shed considerable light on the problem of innateness, we have not yet begun to answer the crucial question, exactly *what* is innate? We noted in Chapter 1 that Chomsky argued in favour of postulating a 'rich internal structure'. What in his opinion does this structure consist of? This is the topic considered in the next chapter.

5 The blueprint in the brain
What grammatical information might conceivably be innate?

There are very deep and restrictive principles that determine the nature of human language and are rooted in the specific character of the human mind.

CHOMSKY
Language and Mind

It is relatively easy to show that humans are innately predisposed to acquire language. The hard part is finding out exactly *what* is innate. People have indulged in speculation about this for centuries. Over two thousand years ago the Egyptian king Psammetichus had a theory that if a child was isolated from human speech, the first word he spontaneously uttered would come from the world's oldest inhabitants. Naturally he hoped this would be Egyptian. He gave instructions for two new-born children to be brought up in total isolation. When eventually the children uttered the work BEKOS, Psammetichus discovered to his dismay that this was the Phrygian word for 'bread'. He reluctantly concluded that the Phrygians were more ancient than the Egyptians.

Nobody takes Psammetichus's theory seriously today – especially as the few reliable accounts we have of children brought up without human contact indicate that they were totally without speech when they were found. The famous French boy, Victor of Aveyron, who was discovered naked rooting for acorns in the Caune woods in 1797, did not speak Phrygian or any other language. He merely grunted like an animal.

Although the speculations of Psammetichus can safely be ignored, the ideas of Noam Chomsky on the topic of innateness must be taken seriously. As we have already noted, he claims that for language acquisition to be possible, a child must be endowed with a 'rich internal structure', and the biological evidence examined in the last two chapters is consistent with his claim. The notion of a rich innate schema contrasts strongly with the point of view popularly held earlier in the century that children are born with 'blank sheets' as far as language is concerned. Consequently, some people consider

Chomsky to be new-fangled and daring, someone who has set out to shock the world with outrageous and novel proposals. But Chomsky denies this. He points out that he is following in the footsteps of eighteenth-century 'rationalist' philosophers, who believe in the existence of 'innate ideas'. Such philosophers held that 'beyond the peripheral processing mechanisms, there are innate ideas and principles of various kinds that determine the form of the acquired knowledge in what may be a rather restricted and highly organized way' (Chomsky 1965, p. 48). Descartes, for example, suggested that when a child sees a triangle, the imperfect triangle before his eyes immediately reminds him of a true triangle, since we already possess within us the idea of a true triangle.

But leaving philosophical predecessors aside, what does this 'rich internal structure' consist of? What exactly does Chomsky regard as innate? In his words: 'What are the initial assumptions concerning the nature of language that the child brings to language learning, and how detailed and specific is the innate scheme?' (Chomsky 1965, p. 27).

Chomsky gave an explicit account of his early views in his linguistic classic *Aspects of the Theory of Syntax* (1965), though he has repeated them in a number of other places with minor variations. But in recent years he has changed his mind on various points, sometimes quite fundamentally. His later views are set out most clearly in *Knowledge of Language: Its Nature, Origin and Use* (1986). The following account begins with his 1965 statements. It then explains why he regards these as unsatisfactory, and outlines his more recent ideas.

Chomsky's early ideas: LAD and LAS

Chomsky has never regarded his proposals on the matter of innateness as definitive, merely outline suggestions. 'For the present we cannot come at all close to making a hypothesis that is rich, detailed and specific enough to account for the fact of language acquisition' (1965, p. 27). Nevertheless, his ideas are specific enough to be interesting – even if they are, in his own judgement, incomplete.

Chomsky started out with the basic assumption that anybody who acquires a language is not just learning an accumulation of random utterances but a set of 'rules' or underlying principles for forming speech patterns: 'The person who has acquired knowledge of a language has internalized a system of rules that relate sound and meaning in a particular way' (Chomsky 1972a, p. 26). It is these 'rules' which enable a speaker to produce an indefinite number of novel utterances, rather than straight repetitions of old ones. As we saw in Chapter 1, an essential characteristic of language is its 'creativity' – people do not just run through a repertoire of stereotyped phrases when they speak. Instead, they are continually producing novel utterances such as 'My baby swallowed four ladybirds', or 'Serendipity upsets me'. But where do the rules come from? How do speakers discover them? Somehow, children have to construct their own set of rules from the jumble of speech they hear going on around them. This is a formidable task. Chomsky pointed out that children are to some extent in the same situation as a linguist faced with an unknown language. Both child and linguist are surrounded by a superficially unintelligible confusion of sound which they must somehow sort out.

So let us first consider how a *linguist* deals with this unknown language situation. She possibly starts by finding simple sound sequences which refer to single objects, such as TREE, NOSE, CONGER EEL. But this stage is not particularly interesting from a syntactic point of view. Learning off lists of vocabulary items is a relatively simple task, as is clear from the ease with which the chimps Sarah and Washoe managed to do this. In addition, Genie, the Californian teenager discussed in the last chapter, finds the acquisition of vocabulary easy – it is the grammatical rules which are slowing her down. For a linguist working on an exotic language, the interesting stage is likely to come when she starts to notice recurring syntactic patterns among the data. As soon as she has found some, she begins to make guesses or *hypotheses* concerning the principles which underlie the patterns. For example, suppose she repeatedly finds the utterances WOKKI SNIZZIT, WOKKI UGGIT and WOKKI SNIFFIT. She might hazard, as a first guess that the sequence WOKKI always has to be followed by a sequence which ends in -IT. But if, later, she finds utterances such as LIKKIT WOKKI and UKKING WOKKI, she would have to abandon her original, over-simple theory, and form a new, more complex hypothesis to account for the fresh data. She continues this process of forming hypotheses, testing them, then abandoning them when they prove inadequate until, ideally, she has compiled a set of rules which can account for all the possible sequences of the language she is studying.

A child, according to Chomsky (1965), is constructing an internalized grammar in the same way. He looks for regularities in the speech he hears going on around him, then makes guesses as to the rules which underlie the patterns. His first guess will be a simple one. His second amended hypothesis will be more complex, his third, more elaborate still. Gradually his mental grammar will become more sophisticated. Eventually his internalized rules will cover all the possible utterances of his language. Fodor (1966, p. 109) describes the situation clearly:

Like the scientist, the child finds himself with a finite body of observations, some of which are almost certain to be unsystematic. His problem is to discover regularities in these data that, at the very least, can be relied upon to hold however much additional data is added. Characteristically the extrapolation takes the form of the construction of a theory that simultaneously marks the systematic similarities among the data at various levels of abstraction, permits the rejection of some of the observational data as unsystematic, and automatically provides a general characterization of the possible future observations.

If this hypothesis-testing view of language acquisition is correct, a child must be endowed with an innate *hypothesis-making device* which enables him, like a miniature scientist, to construct increasingly complex hypotheses.

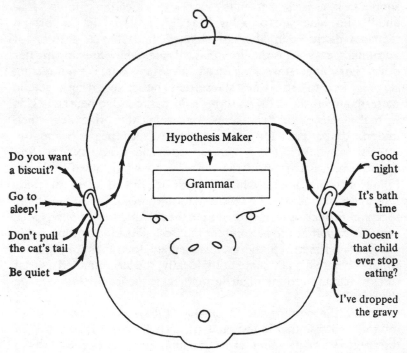

However, there are a number of differences between a linguist working on an unknown language, and a child acquiring language for the first time. The linguist has considerably more help at his disposal. He can say to a native speaker of the language he is working on, 'Does LEGLESS DADDY-LONG-LEGS make sense?' 'Is ATE UP IT grammatical?' 'Is PLAYING CARDS ambiguous?' and so on. The child cannot do this. Yet the amazing fact remains: it is the child who acquires the complete grammar. No linguist has ever written a perfect grammar of any language. This suggests that by itself, an internal hypothesis-making device is not sufficient to account for the acquisition of language. The child must have rather more information at his disposal. It cannot be information about any particular language because babies learn all languages with equal ease. A Chinese baby brought up in England will learn English as easily as an English baby in China will learn Chinese. The wired-in knowledge must, therefore, said Chomsky, consist of *language universals*. Children learn language so fast and so efficiently because they 'know' in outline what languages look like. They know what is, and what is not, a possible language. All they have to discover is *which* language they are being exposed to. In Chomsky's words, his theory

attributes tacit knowledge of linguistic universals to the child. It proposes that the child approaches the data with the presumption that they are drawn from a language of a certain antecedently well-defined type, his problem being to determine which of the (humanly) possible languages is that of the community in which he is placed. [Chomsky 1965, p. 27]

The child is perhaps like a pianist waiting to sight-read a piece of music. The pianist will know in advance that the piece will have a rhythmic beat, but he will not know whether it is in two, three or four time until he sees it. He will know that the notes are within a certain range – but he will not know in what order or combinations they come.

But it is not very satisfactory to speak airily of 'innate linguistic universals'. What *are* these shadowy phenomena?

Language universals, Chomsky suggested (1965), are of two basic types, *substantive* and *formal*. Substantive universals represent the fundamental 'building blocks' of language, the substance out of which it is made, while formal universals are concerned with the form or shape of a grammar. An analogy might make this distinction clearer. If, hypothetically, Eskimos were born with an innate knowledge of igloo-building they would have *two* kinds of knowledge.

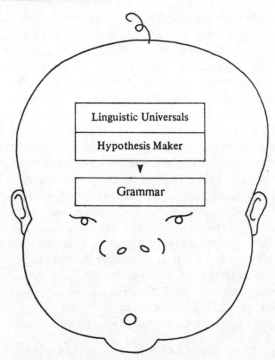

On the one hand they would know in advance that the *substance* out of which igloos are made is ice and snow, just as thrushes automatically know that their nests are made of twigs, not bricks or worms or glass. On the other hand, their innate knowledge of igloo-building would include the information that igloos are round in *shape*, not square or diamond-shaped or sausage-like, just as thrushes instinctively build round nests, not ones shaped like bathtubs.

To return to the substantive universals of human language, a child might know instinctively the possible set of sounds to be found in speech. She would automatically reject sneezes, belches, hand-clapping and foot-stamping as possible sounds, but accept B, O, G, L, and so on. She would dismiss PGPGPG as a possible word, but accept POG, PIG, PEG or PAG.

But the idea of *substantive* universals is not particularly new. For a long time linguists have assumed that all languages have nouns, verbs and sentences even though the exact definitions of these terms is in dispute. And for a long time linguists have been trying to identify a 'universal phonetic alphabet' which 'defines the set of possible signals from which signals of a particular language are drawn' (Chomsky 1972a, p. 121). Such a notion is not very surprising, since humans all possess similar vocal organs. More revolutionary, and therefore more interesting, are the *formal* universals proposed by Chomsky. These, we noted, are concerned with the form or shape of a grammar, including the way in which the different parts relate to one another.

According to Chomsky, children would 'know' in advance how their internalized grammar must be organized. It must have a set of *phonological* rules for characterizing sound patterns and a set of *semantic* rules for dealing with meaning, linked by a set of *syntactic rules* dealing with word arrangement.

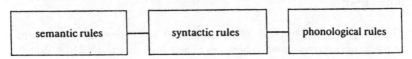

Furthermore, children would instinctively realize that in its rules language makes use of *structure-dependent* operations. This, as we noted earlier (Chapter 1), involves at least two types of knowledge: firstly, an understanding of hierarchical structure – the notion that several words can fill the same slot as one:

Cows	EAT	GRASS
LARGE BROWN COWS	HAVE EATEN UP	THE GRASS

secondly, a realization that each slot functions as a unit which can be moved around:

3	2	1
THE GRASS	HAS BEEN EATEN UP	BY LARGE BROWN COWS

However, this is an over-simplification. In this case, the original sentence has *not* just been rearranged (and *been* and *by* added) because mere rearrangement (and *been* and *by* addition) would result in *THE GRASS HAVE BEEN EATEN BY UP LARGE BROWN COWS. Observations of this type led Chomsky to an interesting and controversial conclusion. He maintained that what had been rearranged was *not* the surface sentence LARGE BROWN COWS HAVE

EATEN UP THE GRASS but a 'deeper', more abstract form of the sentence. The underlying form would show the basic similarity between actives and passives. It would be likely to look more like one than the other (probably the active), though it would not be identical to the surface form of either.

Chomsky assumed that every sentence had an 'inner' hidden *deep structure* and an outer manifest *surface structure*. This was a simple and elegant way of accounting for the relationship between sentence pairs such as active and passive. Other important reasons behind the assumption that every sentence has both an underlying and a manifest structure were mentioned in Chapter 1. The two levels of structure are linked by rules known as *transformations*. Chomsky noted that:

The grammar of English will generate, for each sentence, a deep structure, and will contain rules showing how this deep structure is related to a surface structure. The rules expressing the relation of deep and surface structure are called 'grammatical transformations'. (CHOMSKY 1972a, p. 166]

According to this view, several sentences which are quite different on the surface could be related to *one* deep structure. The four sentences:

CHARLES CAPTURED A HEFFALUMP
A HEFFALUMP WAS CAPTURED BY CHARLES
IT WAS A HEFFALUMP WHICH CHARLES CAPTURED
WHAT CHARLES CAPTURED WAS A HEFFALUMP

were all related to a similar underlying structure.

Alternatively, different deep structures could undergo transformations which made them similar on the surface:

Deep structure (simplified)

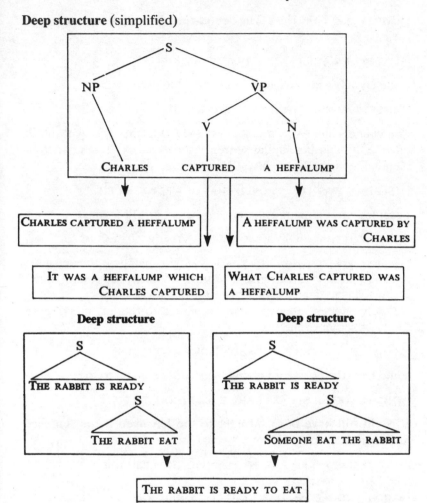

Chomsky assumed that children would somehow 'know' about deep structures, surface structures and transformations. They would realize that they had to reconstruct for themselves deep structures which were *never* visible on the surface.

In addition, children would know that there were constraints on the ways in which deep structures could be altered by the transformational rules. Clearly, underlying structures could not be randomly scrambled up. Children would be automatically aware of some quite complex constraints on rearrangement possibilities. For example, there seems to be some type of 'natural' constraint on moving items to the right. The deep structure underlying a sentence such as:

[THAT PAUL WAS ILL]   UPSET LAVINIA

could equally well have been rearranged to produce

IT UPSET LAVINIA   [THAT PAUL WAS ILL].

The clause THAT PAUL WAS ILL was moved to the right with no ill effects. But another similar sentence shows a surprising restriction on moving this clause rightwards:

[THAT PAUL WAS ILL]   PROVED THAT HE ATE TOO MUCH

becomes, after moving THAT PAUL WAS ILL, the ill-formed

*IT PROVED THAT HE ATE TOO MUCH   [THAT PAUL WAS ILL].

For no very clear reason, THATPAULWASILL resists being moved more than a small way to the right. Children, Chomsky suggested, might instinctively understand this type of prohibition.

   Oddly enough, elements can be moved to the left much more freely. A sentence such as:

CHARLIE HAS ASKED ZAK TO BUY [SOME AVOCADOS]

could have the phrase involving 'avocados' brought to the left:

[WHICH AVOCADOS] HAS CHARLIE ASKED ZAK TO BUY?

It could still have been brought to the left even if the sentence had been much longer:

CHARLIE HAS ASKED ZAK TO TELL VIC TO PERSUADE ALOYSIUS TO
   BUY [SOME AVOCADOS]
[WHICH AVOCADOS] HAS CHARLIE ASKED ZAK TO TELL VIC TO
   PERSUADE ALOYSIUS TO BUY?

However, if the original sentence had been:

CHARLIE HAS ASKED ZAK TO BUY [SOME AVOCADOS] AND [SOME
   AUBERGINES],

the 'avocado' phrase cannot be brought to the front:

*[WHICH AVOCADOS] HAS CHARLIE ASKED ZAK TO BUY AND [SOME
   AUBERGINES]?

Children may automatically know that if two things are joined together in this way, one alone cannot be separated out and brought to the front.

Or, to take another example, consider the sentence:

IGNATIUS HAS STOLEN A PIG.

If we wanted to ask which pig was involved, we would normally bring the phrase about the pig to the front:

WHICH PIG HAS IGNATIUS STOLEN?

But supposing the original sentence had been:

ANGELA KNOWS WHO HAS STOLEN A PIG.

It would then be impossible to bring the 'pig' phrase to the front. We could not say:

*WHICH PIG ANGELA KNOWS WHO HAS STOLEN?

According to Chomsky 'some general principle of language determines which phrases can be questioned' (1980, p. 44), and children would somehow 'know' this.

To summarize so far, we have been outlining Chomsky's 'classic' (1965) viewpoint. He assumed that children were endowed with an innate hypothesis-making device, which enabled them to make increasingly complex theories about the rules which would account for the language they heard going on around them. In making these hypotheses, children were guided by an inbuilt knowledge of language universals. These provided a 'blueprint' for language, so that the child would know in outline what a possible language looked like. This involved, firstly, information about the 'building blocks' of language, such as the set of possible sounds. Secondly, it entailed information about the way in which the components of a grammar were related to one another, and restrictions on the form of the rules. In particular, Chomsky assumed that children automatically knew that language involved two levels of syntax – a deep and a surface level, linked by 'transformations'. With this help a child could speedily sift through the babble of speech he heard around him, the so-called 'primary linguistic data' and hypothesize plausible rules which would account for it.

But another problem arises. There may be more than one possible set of rules which will fit the data. How does a child choose between them? At that time, Chomsky suggested that children must in addition be equipped with an *evaluation* procedure which would allow them to choose between a number of possible grammars, that is, some kind of measure which would enable them to weigh up one grammar against another, and discard the less efficient. This was perhaps the least satisfactory of Chomsky's proposals, and many psycholinguists regarded it as wishful thinking. There were no plausible suggestions as to how this evaluation procedure might work, beyond a vague notion that a child might prefer short grammars to long ones. But even this was disputed, since it is equally possible that children have very messy, complicated grammars, which only gradually become simple and streamlined (e.g. Schlesinger 1967). So the problem of narrowing down the range of possible grammars was left unsolved.

According to Chomsky (1965 version), then, a hypothesis-making device, linguistic universals, and (perhaps) an evaluation procedure constituted an innately endowed Language Acquisition Device (LAD) or Language Acquisition System (LAS), (LAD for boys and LAS for girls, as one linguist facetiously remarked). With the aid of LAD any child could learn any language with relative ease – and without such an endowment language acquisition would be impossible.

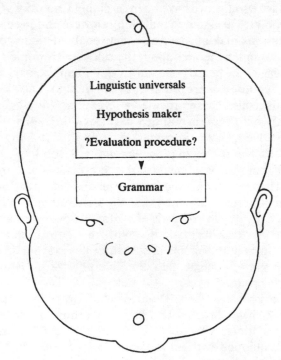

However, this simple threefold system has disappeared from Chomsky's recent writings. What made him change his mind, and what does he now propose?

Chomsky's later views: setting switches

Suppose children knew in advance that the world contained two hemispheres, a northern and a southern. In order to decide which, they simply needed to watch water swirling down the plug hole of a bath, since they were pre-wired with the information that it swirled one way in the north, and another way in the south. Once they had observed a bath plug hole, then they would automatically know a whole lot of further information: an English child who discovered bath-water swirling clockwise would know that it had been placed in the northern hemisphere. It could then predict that the sun would be in the south at the hottest part of the day, and that it would get hotter as one travelled southwards. An Australian child who noticed water rotating anticlockwise would immediately realize the opposite.

This scenario is clearly science fiction. But it is the sort of situation Chomsky now envisages for children acquiring language. They are pre-wired with a number of possible options which language might choose. They need to be exposed to relatively little language, merely some crucial trigger, in order to find out which route their own language has chosen. Once they have discovered this, they automatically know, through pre-programming, a considerable amount about how languages of this type work.

Let us consider how Chomsky hit on such an apparently bizarre idea. *Learnability* remained Chomsky's major concern. How is language learnable, when the crumbs and snippets of speech heard by children could not possibly (in Chomsky's view) provide sufficient clues to the final system which is acquired? The unworkability of the evaluation procedure in LAD made the problem acute. There seemed no way in which the child could narrow down its guesses sufficiently to arrive at the grammar of a human language. The learnability problem has also been called the 'logical problem of language acquisition': how, logically, do children acquire language when they do not have enough information at their disposal to do so?

The logical answer is that they have an enormous amount of information pre-wired into them: the innate component must be considerably more extensive than was previously envisaged. Children, therefore, are born equipped with *Universal Grammar*, or

UG for short: 'UG is a characterization of these innate, biologically determined principles, which constitute one component of the human mind – the language faculty' (Chomsky 1986, p. 24). This is 'a distinct system of the mind/brain' (1986, p. 25), separate from general intelligence.

UG is envisaged as considerably more rigid and structured than the old, and somewhat vaguer notion of innate universals. It is 'a computational system that is rich and narrowly constrained in structure and rigid in its essential operations' (1986, p. 43). Let us see how it differs.

Imagine an orchestra, playing a symphony. The overall effect is of a luscious tropical jungle, a forest of intertwined melodies. Yet, if one looks at the score, and contemplates the various musical instruments, one gets a surprise. Each instrument has its own limitations, such as being confined to a certain range of notes. Most of the instruments are playing a relatively simple tune. The overall, intricate Turkish carpet effect is due to the skilled interaction of numerous simple components.

Chomsky, then, views UG and language as something like an orchestra playing a symphony. It consists of a number of separate components or *modules*, a term borrowed from computers. Chomsky notes: 'UG . . . has the modular structure that we regularly discover in investigation of cognitive systems' (1986, p. 146). Within each module, there are sets of principles. Each principle is fairly straightforward when considered in isolation. The principles become complex when they interact with those from other modules.

The general framework is not entirely new. He still retains the notion of deep and surface structure (or D-structure and S-structure as he now calls them). But the number of transformations has been drastically reduced in number – there may be only one! But this one, which moves structures about, is subject to very severe constraints. Innate principles specify what can or cannot happen, and these are quite rigid. Chomsky's major concern, therefore, is in specifying the principles operating within each module, and showing how they interact.

At the moment it is still unclear how many modules are involved, and what they all do. But the general idea behind the grammar is reasonably clear. For example, one module might specify which items can be moved, and how far, as with the word WHO, which can be moved to the front of the sentence:

WHO DID SEBASTIAN SAY OSBERT BIT?

Another might contain information as to how to interpret a sentence such as:

SEBASTIAN SAID OSBERT BIT HIM INSTEAD OF HIMSELF.

This would contain principles showing why SEBASTIAN had to be linked to the word HIM, and OSBERT attached to the word HIMSELF. These two types of principles would interact in a sentence such as:

WHO DID SEBASTIAN SAY OSBERT BIT INSTEAD OF HIMSELF?

As we have noted, most of the principles, and the way they interleave with one another are innately specified and fairly rigid.

However, a narrowly constrained rigid UG presents another dilemma. Why are not all languages far more similar? Chomsky argues that UG is only partially 'wired-up'. There are option points within the modules, with switches that can be set to a fixed number of positions, most probably two. Children know in advance what the available options are. This is preprogrammed and part of a human's genetic endowment. A child will therefore scan the data available to him or her, and on the basis of a limited amount of evidence will know which way to throw the switch. In Chomsky's words: 'We may think of UG as an intricately structured system, but one that is only partially "wired-up". The system is associated with a finite set of switches, each of which has a finite number of positions (perhaps two). Experience is required to set the switches. When they are set, the system functions' (Chomsky 1986, p. 146).

Chomsky supposes that the switches must be set on the basis of quite simple evidence, and that a switch, once set in a particular direction, will have quite complex consequences throughout the language. These consequences will automatically be known by the child.

As an example, Chomsky suggests that children might know in advance that language structures have one key word, or *head*. They then have to find out the position of the subsidiary words (or *modifiers*). These could be placed either before or after the head. In English, heads are generally placed before modifiers:

Head	Modifier
DROP	THAT SLIPPER!
DOWN	THE DRAIN

So we get sentences such as:

THE DOG DROPPED THE SLIPPER DOWN THE DRAIN.

A language such as Turkish would reverse this order, and say the equivalent of THAT SLIPPER DROP, THE DRAIN DOWN. The end result is that Turkish looks quite different on the surface. It would say, as it were:

THE DOG THE DRAIN DOWN THE SLIPPER DROPPED.

However, this superficial strangeness is to a large extent the result of one simple option, choosing to place modifiers on a different side of the head.

UG, then, is envisaged as a two-tier system: a hard-wired basic layer of universal *principles*, applicable to all languages, and a second layer which is only partially wired in. This contains a finite set of options which have to be decided between on the basis of observation. These option possibilities are known as *parameters*, and Chomsky talks of the need 'to fix the parameters of UG' (Chomsky 1981, p. 4). The term *parameter* is a fairly old mathematical one, which is also used in the natural sciences. In general, it refers to a fixed property which can vary in certain ways. For example, one

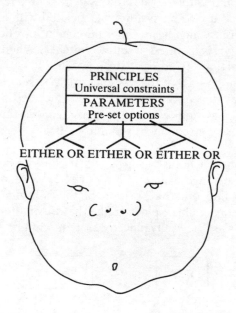

might talk of 'temperature' and 'air pressure' as being 'parameters' of the atmosphere. So in language, a parameter is a property of language (such as head position, discussed above) whose values could vary from language to language.

We are therefore dealing with 'a system of unifying principles that is fairly rich in deductive structure but with parameters to be fixed by experience' (Chomsky 1980, p. 66). The interlocking nature of the system will ensure that minor alterations will have multiple consequences: 'In a tightly integrated theory with a fairly rich internal structure, change in a single parameter may have complex effects, with proliferating consequences in various parts of the grammar' (Chomsky 1981, p. 6). In particular, 'a few changes in parameters yield typologically different languages' (Chomsky 1986, p. 152).

Once the values of the parameters are set, 'the whole system is operative' (Chomsky 1986, p. 146), and a child has acquired its *core language*. Only minor peripheral elements now remain to be learned: 'Suppose we distinguish *core language* from *periphery*, where a core language is a system determined by fixing values for the parameters of UG, and the periphery is whatever is added on in the system actually represented in the mind/brain of a speaker-hearer' (Chomsky 1986, p. 147). In this system 'what we "know innately" are the principles of the various subsystems . . . and the manner of their interaction, and the parameters associated with these principles. What we learn are the values of the parameters and the elements of the periphery' (Chomsky 1986, p. 150).

Children have relatively little to do in this new system: 'We view the problem of language acquisition as . . . one of fixing parameters in a largely determined system' (Chomsky 1986, p. 151). Indeed, many of the old rules which children had to learn just appear automatically, because the principles underlying them are there already. Take the 'rule' that objects follow verbs, as in THROW THE BALL, EAT YOUR CAKE. The child might 'know' that languages behave consistently as far as heads and modifiers are concerned (as discussed above). Once the 'head' parameter is set, then the rule appears without any tedious learning, as does the rule that prepositions precede nouns, as in IN THE BATH, ON THE TABLE. As Chomsky notes: 'There has been a gradual shift of focus from the study of rule systems . . . to the study of systems of principles, which appear to occupy a much more central position in determining the character and variety of possible human languages' (Chomsky 1982, pp. 7–8). If this minimal effort by the child is correct, then it makes sense to think of the language system as a 'mental organ', which grows mainly by itself, in the same way that the heart grows in the body.

Is Chomsky right? Or is he just an armchair theorist who tries to solve problems by waving a magic wand labelled 'innateness'? His proposals are not necessarily an 'all-or-nothing' package deal. He may be right in some respects, and wrong in others, so his suggestions can be looked at one by one.

But the obvious next step is to look at child language, and to consider two important preliminary issues. First of all, are children's utterances structured? Or are early attempts at talking merely clumsy efforts to copy adult speech, with words juxtaposed at random? Furthermore, are there any signs of a universal framework in the early beginnings of speech? These will be the topics discussed in the next chapter.

6   Chattering children
Are children following 'rules' when they learn to speak?

They can't talk straight
Any more than they can walk straight.
Their pronunciation is awful
And their grammar is flawful

OGDEN NASH
It must be the milk

According to Ogden Nash, the behaviour of children and drunks is equally confusing. Linguists would perhaps agree with him. Listening to infants speaking is like being in topsy-turvy land. The problems of children faced with adult language sometimes seem trivial to a linguist who is trying to decipher infant burbles. But far worse than the problem of decipherment is the difficulty of interpreting the utterances. One writer remarked that writing about the acquisition of language

is somewhat like the problem of reconstructing a dinosaur while the bones are still being excavated. It can happen that after you have connected what you earnestly believe are the hind legs you find that they are the jaw bones. [MCNEILL 1970, p. vii]

Consequently, before we consider the main topics of this chapter – whether children's utterances are structured, and whether there is a universal framework underlying early speech – we must outline some of the problems of interpretation which arise when linguists attempt to analyse child language. We shall do this by considering one-word utterances.

Ba, qua, ha and other one-word utterances

One-word utterances present a microcosm of the difficulties faced by linguists examining child language. Consider the following situation. Suppose a child says BA when she is in the bath, again says BA when given a mug of milk, and also says BA to the kitchen taps. How are we to interpret this? There are at least four possible explanations.

110   *The Articulate Mammal*

The first possibility is that the child is simply naming the objects to prove she knows them, but has over generalized the word BA. That is, she has learnt the name BA for 'bath' and has wrongly assumed that it can apply to anything which contains liquid. A typical example of this type of over generalization was noted by one harassed mother in a letter to the London *Evening Standard*:

My baby is Moon-struck. She saw the moon in the sky at six o'clock last week and ever since she's gaped at the sky shouting for the moon. Now she thinks anything that shines is the moon; street lamps, headlights, even the reflected light bulb in the window. All I hear is yells about the moon all day. I love my baby but I'm so ashamed. How does one get patience?

However, this plain over generalization interpretation may be too simple a view of what is happening when the child says BA. A second, and alternative, explanation has been proposed by the famous Russian psychologist Vygotsky (1893–1934). He suggests that when children over generalize they do so in a quite confusing way. They appear to focus attention on one aspect of an object at a time. One much quoted example concerns a child who used the word QUA to refer to a duck, milk, a coin, and a teddy bear's eye (Vygotsky 1962, p. 70). QUA 'quack' was, originally, a duck on a pond. Then the child incorporated the pond into the meaning, and by focusing attention on the liquid element, QUA was generalized to milk. But the duck was not forgotten, since QUA was used to refer to a coin with an eagle on it. Then, with the coin in mind, the child aplied QUA to any round

coin-like object, such as a teddy bear's eye. Vygotsky calls this phenomenon a 'chain complex' because a chain of items is formed, all linked by the same name. If he is correct, then in the case of BA, we can suggest that the child originally meant 'bath'. Then, by focusing her attention on the liquid element she generalized the word to 'milk'. Meanwhile, remembering the bath taps, she used BA to mean 'kitchen taps'.

Yet even Vygotsky's 'chain complex' interpretation seems over-simple in the view of some researchers. A third, and less obvious, point of view is that of David McNeill, a psychologist at the University of Chicago. He has argued that one-word utterances show a linguistic sophistication which goes far beyond the actual sound spoken. He claims that the child is not merely involved in naming exercises, but is uttering *holophrases*, single words which stand for whole sentences. For example, BA might mean 'I am in my bath' or 'Mummy's fallen in the bath'. He justifies his viewpoint by claiming that misuse of words shows evidence of grammatical relationships which the child understands, but cannot yet express. For example, a 1-year-old child said HA when something hot was in front of her. A month later she said HA to an empty coffee cup and a turned-off stove. Why did she do this? McNeill suggests that

by misusing the word the child showed that 'hot' was not merely the label of hot objects but was also something said of objects that could be hot. It asserted a property. [MCNEILL 1970, p. 24]

He also claims that the same child understood the notion of location because she pointed to the empty top of the refrigerator, where bananas were normally kept, and said NANA. He concludes that 'there is a constant emergence of new grammatical relations, even though no utterance is ever longer than one word' (McNeill 1970, p. 23). So, McNeill might perhaps suggest that BA, when applied to kitchen taps and milk, showed an understanding of location: 'There are taps like this on the bath tub', 'There is liquid like this in the bath'.

McNeill's claim that children understand a wide variety of grammatical relationships and that one-word utterances are sentences in embryo seems over-imaginative to many researchers. However, the idea that single-word utterances may be more than mere labels has also been examined by Lois Bloom, a researcher at Columbia University, who has put forward a fourth possibility (Bloom 1973).

After a careful analysis of the single words spoken by her daughter, Allison, she suggests that there is no simple answer to the problem of interpretation because the meaning of a one-word utterance varies according to the age of the child. For example, when Allison said MUMMY at the age of sixteen months, she seemed to mean, simply, 'That's Mummy'. But at the age of nineteen months she appeared to be trying to express some kind of interaction between Mummy and the surrounding environment, as when she pointed to her mother's cup and said, MUMMY.

However, Bloom was unable to tell exactly what kind of interaction was intended. Did Allison mean 'That's Mummy's cup', or was she saying 'Mummy's drinking from a cup too'? Because of this intrinsic ambiguity, Bloom is cautious about assigning specific meanings to BA-type words which relate either to objects, or to interaction between objects. She is more optimistic about the interpretation of words such as NO, MORE and A'GONE in which 'conceptual notions are so conveniently tied to the actual words in the child's speech' (Bloom 1973, p. 140). For example, Allison showed by her use of the words NO and A'GONE that she could cope with the notion of non-existence. Bloom, therefore, concludes (perhaps not surprisingly) that single words are grammatically fairly uninteresting. Their importance lies in the light they throw on a child's conceptual representation of experience.

Other researchers have tried to analyse what the child is trying to *do* with one-word utterances (e.g. Halliday 1975; Wells 1974; Griffiths 1986). If a child says GA, is she simply naming an object such as a cat? Is she asking for the cat? Or is she trying to control the actions of her parents by telling them to let the cat in? All of these are possible. The probable 'translation' may even depend on the temperament of the child. Some children simply enjoy naming things, others prefer to use words to get the attention of the adults around them.

An extra reason for caution is that some youngsters may not even realize that they are 'naming' things when they first utter words (McShane 1979, 1980). They may simply be taking part in a ritual game. Many middle-class parents sit down with their children and leaf through picture books, naming the objects which appear on each page, such as 'apple', 'ball', 'cat', 'duck', and so on. The child may shriek BA delightedly when she reaches the page with the round blue blob in the middle, but may not for some weeks realize that this sequence of sounds is actually the 'name' of a certain type of round object, a ball. As McShane puts it: 'The child first learns the words and later learns that these words are names' (1979, p. 890). The sudden realization that things have names appears to lead to a surge of 'labelling' everyday objects such as CAR, MILK, BALL, APPLE, followed by a surge of 'describing', with the use of words such as BLUE, GONE, BROKE, HIT. This in turn, he suggests, leads to the beginning of structured speech.

But the situation is by no means clear cut. Some children go through this sudden 'naming insight' stage, others seem to know that thing have names before they start to utter any words (Harris *et al.* 1988). And occasionally, the 'single word' stage may even be missed out. There are reports of a working-class black community in Pennsylvania where it is considered odd to talk to babies, and parents make no attempt to interpret children's early babbles as labels. These children often begin to communicate by picking up whole phrases, which they use with a wide range of intonations and meanings. One toddler, Teegie, used 'You shut up' to mean 'No', 'Leave me alone', 'Give me that', and 'Take it, I don't want it' (Heath 1983). But these children learned language perfectly well via this route. A young child is 'faced with having to discover what talking is all about' (Griffiths 1986, p. 281), and there seems to be no one way in which this realization comes about.

This brief excursus has by no means exhausted the views on one-word utterances found in the literature. It does, however, illustrate one important point: when the data are so confusing, it is no wonder that differences of opinion abound in child language studies. All researchers, to some extent, see what they want to see. This accounts for the extraordinarily diverse viewpoints which arise over apparently simple issues.

Having pointed out the type of problem that is likely to arise, we must now return to the main topics of this chapter, which are the following: first, are children's utterances structured? Do children have their own 'rules' which differ from those of adult speakers? Second, is there any sign of a universal framework in the early stages of acquisition? We shall consider these questions by looking first at children's two-word utterances. We shall then go on to examine how children acquire more complicated aspects of language such as word endings and negation.

Two-by-two

There are basically two ways of analysing two-word utterances. We may choose either the 'Let's pretend he's talking Martian' technique or the 'Let's guess what she's trying to say' method. In the first, linguists approach the child's speech as if it were an unknown exotic language. Having freed their minds of preconceived notions connected with their knowledge of English, they write a grammar based entirely on the word patterns they discern in the child's speech. In the second method, linguists try to provide an interpretation of what the child is saying by using their knowledge of the language and by observing the situation in which the words were uttered.

In their earliest attempts at analysing two-word utterances, linguists followed the 'Let's pretend he's talking Martian' technique. Martin Braine (1963), of the University of California at Santa Barbara, listed all the two-word utterances produced by three 2-year-olds, Steven, Gregory and Andrew. The results were superficially puzzling. There were a number of inexplicable sequences such as MORE TAXI, ALLGONE, ALLGONE STICKY, NO BED, BUNNY DO, IT DOGGIE. Such utterances could not be straight imitations, as it is unlikely that any adult ever said MORE TAXI, ALLGONE SHOE, or BUNNY DO. Anyway, straight imitation would put too great a strain on the child's memory. Braine counted over 2500 different combinations uttered by one child. Are these then just accidental juxtapositions? Apparently not.

To his surprise, Braine noted that the combinations did *not* seem to be random. Certain words always occurred in a fixed place, and other words never occurred alone. Andrew, Steven and Gregory all seemed to be following definite, though primitive rules when they put two words together. They had two distinct classes of word in their speech. One class contained a small number of words such as ALLGONE, MORE, THIS, NO. These words occurred frequently, never alone, and in a fixed position. They are sometimes labelled *pivots*, because the utterance appears to pivot round them. The other class contained many more words which occurred less frequently, but in any position and sometimes alone. These words often coincided with adult nouns such as MILK, SHOE, BUNNY and so on. They are sometimes called *open* class words, since an 'open' class is a set of words which can be added to indefinitely.

For example, Steven always used WANT, GET, THERE, IT as pivots in first position, and DO as a pivot in second position. His open class words included a wide variety of names such as BABY, CAR, MAMA, DADA, BALL, DOLL, BUNNY, HORSIE. Steven seemed to have internalized a rule which said, 'A sentence consists of *either* a type 1 pivot

followed by an open class word (P^1 + O), *or* an open class word
followed by a type 2 pivot (O + P^2)':

Pivot 1	Open
WANT	BABY
GET	BALL
THERE	BOOK
IT	DADDY

Open	Pivot 2
BUNNY	DO
DADDY	

Several other researchers who independently tried the exotic
language technique confirmed this phenomenon by finding other
children who formed word combinations in the same way as Andrew,
Steven and Gregory (Brown and Fraser 1964; Miller and Ervin
1964). For a time, linguists were quite excited. They thought they
might have discovered a universal first grammar, a so-called *pivot
grammar*. But, alas, disillusion gradually crept in. One by one,
researchers noted that a number of children did not fit into this simple
pattern. Although all children showed strong preferences for placing
certain words in a particular position in an utterance, these
preferences were not always strong enough to be regarded as 'rules'.
In addition, some children used so-called pivots such as MORE, NO,
by themselves, which disagreed with Braine's finding that pivot
words do not occur alone. And other children confused the picture
by having pivot constructions as only a small portion of their total
utterances.

Perhaps the biggest difficulty for pivot grammar is the appearance
of utterances such as MUMMY SOCK, DADDY CAR, KITTY BALL, which
occur in the speech of many children. Here two *open* class words
seem to be juxtaposed, with no pivot in sight! Braine dismissed this
problem by saying that O + O constructions were a second stage,
which occurred only *after* the P + O and O + P phase. But this does
not seem to be true of all children. Of course, there is nothing wrong
with stating that some youngsters make sentences which can be
P + O, O + P or O + O. It just does not tell us very much to say that, 'As
well as pivot constructions, almost any other two words can occur
together.' But even if such empty statements were acceptable, it is
not necessarily correct to assume that O + O utterances are random
juxtapositions. There may be more reason behind them than appears
at first sight, and the words may be related to one another in a highly

structured way. It is quite inadequate to characterize a sentence such as DADDY CAR as O + O, since such a description cannot distinguish between several possible interpretations:

1   'Daddy is washing the car.'
2   'That's Daddy's car.'
3   'Daddy is under the car.'

To summarize the achievements of pivot grammars, it seems that they are not as much use as was once hoped. They only describe the rules used by a small number of children – or perhaps, more accurately, they characterize only a small portion of the output of most children. If one used pivot grammars in order to answer the question 'Are two-word utterances structured?', the answer is 'Partially – children use pivot constructions but supplement them by apparently combining open class words at random'.

Disillusioned by the pivot grammars which resulted from the 'Let's pretend he's talking Martian' technique, linguists in recent years have tended to favour the second, 'Let's guess what she's trying to say' approach. This is more time-consuming, since researchers must note not just the utterances themselves, but also the accompanying actions. Luckily, what young children say usually relates directly to what they do and see:

If an adult or an older child mounts a bicycle, there is no need for him to inform anyone who has seen him do it that he has done it. But a young child who mounts a tricycle will often 'announce' the fact: *I ride trike!* [BLOOM 1970, p. 9]

One of the first linguists to make a careful study of two-word utterances following this method is again Lois Bloom (1970). She kept a careful account of the actions accompanying the utterances of three children, Kathryn, Eric and Gia, and has provided convincing interpretations of what they were trying to say. For example, it is quite clear what twenty-one-month-old Kathryn meant on the two occasions when she uttered the words MOMMY SOCK. The first time, she said it as she picked up her mother's sock, indicating that she meant 'This is Mummy's sock'. The second time was when her mother was putting Kathryn's sock on Kathryn, so Kathryn was saying 'Mummy is putting on my sock for me'. 2-year-old Gia said LAMB EAR apparently meaning 'That's the lamb's ear' when her mother pointed to the ear on a toy lamb, and said, 'What's this?' She said GIRL BALL when looking at a picture of a girl bouncing a ball, and presumably meant 'The girl is bouncing a ball'. She said FLY BLANKET when a fly settled on her blanket, probably meaning 'There is a fly on my blanket'.

There is a possible objection to these interpretations. Is Bloom not reading too much into these utterances? Perhaps Gia was just saying 'That is a lamb and an ear', 'That is a girl and a ball'. 'That is a fly and a blanket'. Or perhaps she was just bringing up a 'topic' of conversation, and then making a 'comment' about it: 'I'm talking about a *fly*, and it has involved itself with my *blanket*', I'm referring to a *girl* who is connected with a *ball*'. This type of suggestion was first put forward in the mid 1960s to explain two-word utterances (Gruber 1967).

How can one eliminate these possibilities? The answer is, the highly consistent word order makes it unlikely that the sequences are random juxtapositions. Whenever Gia seemed to be expressing location she put the object she was locating first, and the location second: FLY BLANKET 'The fly is on the blanket', FLY BLOCK 'The fly is on the block', BLOCK BAG 'The block is in the bag'. When she referred to subjects and objects, she put the subject first, and the object second: GIRL BALL 'The girl is bouncing the ball', GIRL FISH 'The girl is playing with a fish'. And she expressed possession by putting the possessor first, the possession second: LAMB EAR 'That's the lamb's ear', GIA BLUEYES 'That's Gia's doll, Blueyes'. If Gia was accidentally juxtaposing the words we would expect BLANKET FLY or EAR LAMB as often as FLY BLANKET or LAMB EAR. And the possessive sentences makes it highly unlikely that Gia was using a 'topic' and 'comment' construction. It would be most odd in the case of GIA BLUEYES to interpret it as 'I am talking about myself, Gia, and what I want to comment on is that I have a doll Blueyes'.

Of course, Gia is expressing these relationships of location, possession, and subject – object in the same order as they are found in adult speech. But the important point is that she seems to realize automatically that it is necessary to express relationships consistently in a way Washoe the chimp perhaps did not. She seems to *expect* language to consist of recurring patterns, and seems naturally disposed to look for regularities or rules. But before stating conclusively that Gia's utterances are rule-governed we must consider one puzzling exception. Why did Gia say BALLOON THROW as well as THROW BALLOON when she dropped a balloon as if throwing it? Why did she say BOOK READ as well as READ BOOK when she was looking at a book? Surely this is random juxtaposition of the type we have just claimed to be non-existent? A closer look at Gia's early utterances solves the mystery.

In her earliest two-word sequences, Gia *always* said BALLOON THROW and BOOK READ. She had deduced wrongly that the names of people and objects precede action words. This accounts for 'correct' utterances such as GIRL WRITE and MUMMY BACK as well as 'mistakes' such as BALLOON THROW and SLIDE GO, when she placed some keys on a slide. Soon she began to have doubts about her original rule, and experimented, using first one form, then the other. Utterances produced at a time when the child is trying to make up her mind have aptly been labelled 'groping patterns' by one linguist (Braine 1976). Eventually, after a period of fluctuation, Gia acquired the verb–object relationship permanently with the correct order THROW BALLOON, READ BOOK.

The consistency which Bloom found in the speech of Kathryn, Eric and Gia, has been confirmed by numerous researchers who have worked independently on other children. In conclusion, then, our answer to the question 'Are two-word utterances structured?' must be 'Yes'. From the moment they place two words together (and possibly even before) children seem to realize that language is *rule-governed*, not just a random conglomeration of words. They express each relationship consistently, so that, for example, in the actor-action relationship, the actor comes first, the action second as in MAMA COME, KITTY PLAY, KATHY GO. Exceptions occur when a wrong rule has been deduced, or when a child is groping towards a rule. And even at the two-word stage, children are creative in their speech. They use combinations of words they have not heard before.

However, we have talked so far only about children who are learning English, which has a fixed word order. But some languages have a variable order, and mark grammatical relationships with other devices, such as word endings. How do children cope in these circumstances? Recent research suggests that the answer varies from language to language (Slobin 1985). Turkish is a language in which the endings are particularly clear and easy to identify, and Turkish children are reported to adopt consistent endings with variable word order. But in Serbo-Croatian, where word endings are confusing and inconsistent, children prefer to disregard the endings and use a fixed word order to begin with, even though there is variation in the word order used by the adults around them.

In brief, the evidence suggests that children express relationships between words in a consistent way, whether they use word order or devices such as word endings. This raises a further question: do children from different parts of the world express the *same* relationships? Apparently, children everywhere say much the same things at the two-word stage. Roger Brown notes that 'a rather small set of operations and relations describe all the meanings expressed . . . whatever the language they are learning' (Brown 1973, p. 198). Because of this similarity, psycholinguists at one time hoped that they might be able to make a definitive list of the concepts expressed at this stage, and predict their order of emergence. But it soon became apparent that there was considerable variation between different children, even when they spoke the same language. Every researcher produced a slightly different list, organized in a slightly different order.

Perhaps the best known list is that of Brown (1973, p. 173). He suggests a set of eight 'minimal two-term relations', supplemented by three 'basic operations of reference', set out in the chart below.

Relations	1 Agent action	MUMMY PUSH
	2 Action and object	EAT DINNER
	3 Agent and object	MUMMY PIGTAIL
	4 Action and location	PLAY GARDEN
	5 Entity and location	COOKIE PLATE
	6 Possessor and possession	MUMMY SCARF
	7 Attributive and entity	GREEN CAR
	8 Demonstrative and entity	THAT BUTTERFLY
Operations	9 Nomination	THIS (IS A) TRUCK
	10 Recurrence	MORE MILK
	11 Non-existence	ALLGONE EGG

The examples here show clearly that young children can cope with different types of meaning relationships. But to what extent do these two-word utterances embody specifically *grammatical* knowledge? At one time, certain psycholinguists thought that children were born with an inbuilt understanding of some basic grammatical relations. For example, it was claimed that a child who said DRINK MILK showed an innate knowledge of the verb–object relationship (McNeill 1966; 1970). However, most people have now shifted away from this viewpoint. As one researcher notes, the assumption that children understand grammatical relationships in a way comparable to adults is 'an act of faith based only on our knowledge of the adult language' (Bowerman 1973, p. 187). We must admit that these early utterances do not show any firm evidence of specific grammatical knowledge. They merely reveal an awareness that meaning relationships need to be expressed consistently.

This leaves us with a considerable problem. If we assume that two-word utterances show grammatical knowledge (which would be fanciful) then we have to specify exactly what kind of grammar we are dealing with. If, on the other hand, we do not regard them as showing evidence of grammar, then we have to find out when children start having a primitive syntax. In this case, we have to assume that language learning is a discontinuous process. Children start with one kind of system, and then shift over to another, syntactic one. We may be dealing with a tadpole-to-frog phenomenon (Gleitman and Wanner 1982), in which the immature tadpole behaves rather differently from the mature frog.

A number of researchers support the notion of discontinuity. Perhaps children initially use their general cognitive ability to express meaning relationships in a consistent way. When they have acquired a certain number, they start to sort them out in their mind. This possibly triggers an innate syntactic capacity (e.g. Pinker 1984). We shall discuss this possible switch-over to syntax in Chapter 7.

Getting started

We need to ask a further question. How do children set about acquiring these early utterances? Do they discover how to express one concept at a time? Or do they deal with several simultaneously? A psycholinguist who has examined this question is Martin Braine, of pivot grammar fame. Braine found that children coped with several concepts at the same time, but used each one in a very restricted set of circumstances (Braine 1976). For example, just prior to his second birthday, his own son, Jonathan, could express possession, (MUMMY SHOE), recurrence (MORE JUICE) and attribution (BIG DOG), but only with a narrow range of words. In the case of possession, the only possessors were MOMMY and DADDY. Jonathan had apparently acquired a formula for dealing with possession, but a formula of very limited scope, MOMMY or DADDY + object, as in MOMMY SHOE 'Mummy's shoe', DADDY PIPE 'Daddy's pipe'. Jonathan's formula for dealing with recurrence was even more limited, consisting of the word MORE + object. He used this whenever he wanted more food, as in MORE JUICE, or when he noticed more than one of something, as in MORE BEE. His attribution formula consisted of the words BIG or LITTLE + object, as in BIG PLANE, BIG DOG, LITTLE LAMB, LITTLE DUCK.

Gradually, Jonathan expanded the range of words he used in each formula. Approximately one month later, he had added extra names to his possession formula, as in ELLIOT COOKIE 'Elliot's cookie', ANDREW BOOK 'Andrew's book'. He extended his recurrence formula with the words TWO and OTHER, as in TWO SPOON, OTHER BALL, 'There's another ball'. He also attributed the colours RED, GREEN, BLUE to objects as in RED BALLOON, as well as the properties OLD and HOT, as in OLD COOKIE, HOT TEA. Somewhat unexpectedly, he also included the word HURT in his attribution formula, producing phrases such as HURT KNEE, HURT HAND, HURT FLY. At around this time he started to express a new concept, that of location, though he restricted the object located mainly to the word SAND, as in SAND EYE 'sand in my eye,' SAND TOE 'sand on my toe'. He also began to produce actor–action phrases, in which he usually chose the word DADDY as actor, as in DADDY WORK, DADDY SLEEP. The emergence of Jonathan's limited scope formulae is set out in the diagram on p. 122.

Do all children acquiring language behave like Jonathan? Braine examined the early utterances of a number of other children, and concluded that each one had adopted a 'limited scope formulae' approach at the two-word stage, though the actual formulae varied from child to child. Numerous children seem to go about learning language in a roughly similar fashion, even though there is considerable individual variation in the precise track they follow.

However, there may be more variation than Braine realized at the time. It is possible that most of the children studied in the 1960s were subconsciously picked out because they were easy to understand (Peters 1983). And they were easy to understand because they fitted in with our preconceptions about what happens as children learn to talk – that they learn single words, then put these words together. But reports are coming in of children who do not behave like this. Some learn whole sequences of sounds, then only gradually break them down into words, as with a child called Minh (Peters 1977, 1983). Minh's words were often fuzzy and indistinct, but he paid considerable attention to intonation patterns. Over time, his words became separate and distinct, but he did not go through the gradual building-up process found in the speech of many children. As one researcher notes: 'There is no one way to learn language. Language learning poses a problem for the child, and, as with other complex problems, there is no single path to a solution' (Nelson 1973, p. 114).

	Possession		Recurrence		Attribution		Location		Actor–Action	
Stage 1	MUMMY	SHOE	MORE	JUICE	BIG	PLANE				
	DADDY	PIPE		BEE	LITTLE	LAMB				
		etc.								
Stage 2	MUMMY	SHOE	MORE	TOY	BIG	LION	SAND	EYE	DADDY	WORK
	DADDY	BREAD	OTHER	BALL	LITTLE	BOY		TOE		SLEEP
	ELLIOT	JUICE	TWO	SPOON	RED	BALLOON		etc.		WALK
	ANDREW	BOAT		etc.	OLD	COOKIE				etc.
		etc.			HOT	TEA				
					HURT	KNEE etc.				

Simplified, from Braine 1976.

Where does all this leave us? We have noted that there is no rigid universal mould into which all early utterances will fit, even though children express the same kind of things at the two-word stage. Moreover, these two-word utterances are structured in the sense that children express relationships such as actor–action, location and possession consistently. But we have not been able to show that these are essentially and primarily grammatical relationships that are being expressed. Consequently, in order to assess the claim that children's language is rule-governed in a strictly linguistic sense, we must look at later aspects of language acquisition – at the development of word endings and more complex constructions such as the rules for negation in English.

The case of the wug

This is a Wug

Now there is another one. There are two of them. There are two . . . ??

'Wugs' you should say, if you understand the rules which underlie English plurals. And that is the reply given almost unanimously by a group of children who were given this test. The researcher wanted to prove that they hadn't just memorized each plural as they heard it, but had an internalized rule which could apply even to words they had never heard (Berko 1958).

And it wasn't just wugs the children coped with correctly, so no one could argue that they misunderstood the word as 'bugs'. Another picture showed a man standing on the ceiling, with the words: 'This is a man who knows how to bing. He is binging. He did the same thing yesterday. Yesterday he − '? 'Binged' said nearly all the children tested. Admittedly, they had higher results for words they already knew. More children got the plural of GLASS right than the plural of a nonsense word TASS (TASS and GLASS rhyme in American English, having the same vowel as the word MASS). But no one can doubt that they were applying rules which they had worked out for themselves.

An even more striking example of the child's internalized rules is the development of irregular verbs such as COME and CAME, GO and WENT, BREAK and BROKE. As noted in Chapter 4, children start by acquiring the correct *irregular* forms for the past tense, CAME, WENT, BROKE. Some of these are acquired fairly early, since they are very common words (Ervin 1964; Slobin 1971a). One might suppose that practice makes perfect and these words would remain correctly formed. But not at all. As soon as children learn the *regular* past tense for words such as HELPED, PLAYED, WALKED and WASHED, they give up using the correct irregular form, and start using the over-generalized forms COMED, GOED, BREAKED. And when they re-acquire the irregular verbs, they first produce semi-regular forms which have a normal ending, as in LOST, LEFT (Slobin 1971a). All this indicates that children have a strong tendency to look for and apply rules, at least as far as English noun and verb endings are concerned.

But it is perhaps not surprising that children are able to generalize plurals and past tenses. After all, word endings tend to rhyme. Children are known to have a fascination for rhymes, and they frequently make up little poems such as 'I am a bug, sitting on a rug, warm and snug, with my mug'. So the extension of an -s from BUGS, MUGS and RUGS to WUGS is not particularly startling.

What further evidence of 'rules' can we find? We can note that from the moment children place three or more words together, they seem to show an instinctive awareness of *hierarchical structure*, the realization that several words can fill the same structural 'slot' as one:

THAT	FLOWER
THAT	A BLUE FLOWER

PUT	HAT	ON
PUT	THE RED HAT	ON

However, the sentences just quoted look like ordinary adult ones with a few words left out. This means that we need more evidence to test Chomsky's assertion that children are operating with an internalized set of 'rules' which do not correspond to the adult ones. Several researchers have hunted for this evidence, and seem to have found it. Ursula Bellugi of Harvard University notes: 'We have found several periods where the child's sentences show systematic deviations from adult language, as if they were constructed according to a different set of rules' (Bellugi 1971, p. 95). She and Edward Klima analysed the development of negatives and interrogatives by studying the utterances produced by the now famous Harvard trio Adam, Eve and Sarah (Klima and Bellugi 1966). As already noted in Chapter 4, the families of these children were totally unacquainted and independent of one another, and each child heard a different set of sentences as 'input'. Nevertheless, the children passed through surprisingly similar stages in their progress towards adult constructions. Each phase was characterized by regular 'rules' and the utterances could not be regarded merely as bad imitations of adult speech. The children seemed to be devising hypotheses to account for the regularities in the speech they heard around them. The development of negative sentences, outlined below, shows this clearly.

At first, Adam, Eve and Sarah seemed to be using a primitive rule, 'Put NO or NOT in front of the whole sentence.'

Neg	Sentence
No	WANT STAND HEAD
No	FRASER DRINK ALL TEA
No	PLAY THAT

But this rule did not last long. Next came the realization that the negative goes *inside* rather than in front of the sentence. The children devised a new rule which said, 'Put the negative *after* the first noun phrase and before the rest of the sentence.'

NP	Neg	Rest of sentence
HE	NO	BITE YOU
THAT	NO	MUMMY
I	CAN'T	CATCH YOU
I	DON'T	SIT ON CROMER COFFEE

At this stage, CAN'T and DON'T seemed to be treated as alternatives to NO. The children had not yet realized that they consist of *two* elements. To them, CAN'T and DON'T were single negative units which could be substituted for NO or NOT. However, this substitution was not completely free. Just as in correct adult speech you never find CAN –ING (e.g. *I CAN SINGING) or DON'T –ING (e.g. *I DON'T SMOKING) – so the children never said *I CAN'T CATCHING YOU or *I DON'T CRYING. They had grasped the fact that CAN'T and DON'T do not occur before verbs ending in -ING.

The next stage came when the children realized that CAN'T and DON'T contained two separate elements, CAN + NOT, DO + NOT. This was guaranteed by the fact that CAN and DO began to occur in the children's speech in non-negative sentences. This led to a more sophisticated negative rule in which the negative was placed in the *third* slot in a sentence, after the noun and auxiliary or copula and before the rest of the sentence.

The difference between this and the standard adult rule is that the children had not yet realized that the tense need only be included once.

NP	Aux (or Cop)	Neg	Rest of the sentence
PAUL	CAN	N'T	HAVE ONE
YOU	DO	N'T	WANT SOME SUPPER
I	DID	N'T	SPILLED IT
YOU	DID	N'T	CAUGHT ME
I	AM	NOT	A DOCTOR
THAT	WAS	NOT	ME

A final stage occurred when the children amended sentences such as YOU DIDN'T CAUGHT ME to YOU DIDN'T CATCH ME.

So, independently, Adam, Eve and Sarah each went through similar intermediate stages in their acquisition of the negative:

1 Neg + Sentence NO WANT STAND HEAD
2 NP + Neg + VP HE NO BITE YOU
3 NP + Aux + Neg + Rest of Sentence I DID N'T CAUGHT IT

Each of these can be regarded as a hypothesis to account for the rules of negation in English. The first is a simple hypothesis. The second is slightly less simple, and the third is almost the same rule as that used by adults. Klima and Bellugi are justified in their remark that 'It has seemed to us that the language of children has its own systemacity, and that the sentences are not just an imperfect copy of those of an adult' (Klima and Bellugi 1966, p. 191).

So Chomsky (1965) was probably right to regard the child as a miniature scientist who makes successive hypotheses to account for the data. But there is one major difference. When a scientist discards a hypothesis, he abandons it totally, and works only with the new one he is testing. Children do not behave like this. The stages do not follow one another cleanly and suddenly – they overlap quite considerably. As Klima and Bellugi note: 'A characteristic of child language is the residue of elements of previous systems' (Klima and Bellugi 1966, p. 194). For example, beside I AM NOT A DOCTOR, IT'S NOT COLD, and THAT WAS NOT ME, the children still produced sentences such as THIS NOT ICE CREAM, I NOT CRYING, PAUL NOT TIRED.

This type of fluctuation is noticeable in all aspects of child language. For example, Roger Brown notes, in the case of word endings, that children do not 'abruptly pass from total absence to reliable presence. There is always a considerable period, varying in length, in which production-where-required is probabilistic' (Brown 1973, p. 257). When he analysed the speech of the child Sarah, he found extraordinary swings in her use of the suffix -ING. At the age of 2 years she used it correctly 50 per cent of the time in sentences such as I (AM) PLAYING. But six months later this had dropped to 20 per cent. One month after this it shot up to 80 per cent, then went down again to around 45 per cent. She was over 3 years old before -ING occurred steadily and correctly in all her utterances.

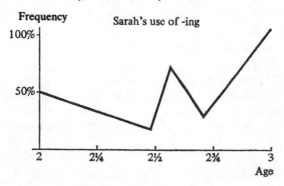

Frequency — Sarah's use of -ing

And it is not only production of speech which fluctuates, but comprehension also. Richard Cromer tested children's understanding of constructions such as THE WOLF IS TASTY TO BITE, THE WOLF IS HAPPY TO BITE, THE DUCK IS HORRIBLE TO BITE. Using glove puppets of a wolf and a duck, he asked the subjects to show him who was biting whom. To his surprise he concluded that 'children may be very inconsistent in their answers from one day to the next' (Cromer 1970, p. 405).

What causes this baffling inconsistency? There may be more than one reason. Firstly, children make mistakes. Just as adults make grammatical errors such as DIDN'T YOU SAW BILL? instead of 'Didn't you see Bill'? or 'Didn't you say you saw Bill?', so do children. But this does not mean the utterances are random jumbles of words. The rules are there, despite lapses. A second reason for inconsistency may be selective attention. Children may choose to concentrate on one aspect of speech at a time. If Sarah is working out rules for plurals one month, she may ignore the -ING ending temporarily. As a schoolboy learning Latin said, 'If I get the verb endings right, you can't expect me to get the nouns right as well!'

However, mistakes and selective attention cannot account completely for the extreme fluctuations in Sarah's use of -ING. Linguists have realized that inconsistency is a normal transitional stage as children move from one hypothesis to the next. It seems to occur when a child has realized that her 'old' rule is wrong or partially wrong, and has formulated a new one, but remains confused as to the precise instances in which she should abandon her older primitive rule (Cromer 1970). For example, Cromer suggests that when they hear sentences such as THE DUCK IS READY TO BITE, children start out with a rule which says 'The first noun in the sentence is doing the biting'. As they get older, they become aware that this simple assumption does not always work. But they are not quite sure why or when their rule fails. So they experiment with a second rule, 'Sometimes it is the first noun in the sentence which is doing the biting, but not always'.

When a child has made an inference that is only partially right, he can get very bewildered. Partially correct rules often produce right results for the wrong reasons, as in sentences such as I DON'T WANT IT, where DON'T is treated as a single negative element. A further example of the confusion caused by a partially effective rule is seen in the Harvard child Adam's use of the pronoun IT. He produced 'odd' sentences such as MUMMY GET IT LADDER, SAW IT BALL, alongside correct ones such as GET IT, PUT IT THERE. He appeared to be treating IT as parallel in behaviour to THAT which can occur either by itself, or attached to a noun: BRING ME THAT, BRING ME THAT BALL.

BRING ME	IT (BALL)
BRING ME	THAT (BALL)

( ) Parentheses denote optional items.

But this was not the only wrong conclusion Adam reached. He also wrongly assumed that IT had an obligatory -S when it occurred at the beginning of a sentence, so he produced IT'S FELL, IT'S HAS WHEELS, as well as superficially correct utterances such as IT'S BIG. Presumably this error arose because Adam's mother used a large number of sentences starting with IT'S . . ., IT'S RAINING, IT'S COLD, and so on. When Adam's 'funny' rules produced correct results half the time, it is not surprising that he took time to abandon them.

Perhaps the situation will become clearer if we look in detail at the emergence of one particular wrong word ending in the speech of one child.

Consider the following utterances produced by a child named Sally when she was nearly 3:

ME MADEN THAT
ME TIPPEN THAT OVER
ME HADEN STAWBERRIES AT LUNCHTIME
ME JUST BUYEN IT
SOMETHING MAKEN A FUNNY NOISE.

Sally seems to have decided that one way to deal with the past is to add -EN on to the ends of verbs. How did this strange personal 'rule' emerge? Did Sally just wake up one morning and start saying TIPPEN OVER, BUYEN, MADEN, or what happened? Fletcher (1983) has examined Sally's verbs in -EN in some detail. He started recording her speech one November when she was almost 2½ years old. She began producing verbs ending in -EN in December. That month, there were three of them: BROKEN (which occurred 13 times), then FALLEN (once), and TAKEN (once). Note that these three are all forms which actually occur in adult speech, even though Sally used them in her own idiosyncratic way, to denote a simple past tense. In the middle of January a new form, PUTTEN, emerged, alongside the existing three. This was the first non-existent form which she

produced. In February, Sally used two more existing forms, GIVEN
and EATEN, and eight more invented forms: BOUGHTEN, BUILDEN,
RIDEN, GETTEN, CUTTEN, MADEN, WANTEN, TOUCHEN. The peak
of Sally's inventiveness came in March when she added on one actual
word, WAKEN, and eighteen made-up ones: HADEN, STEPPEN,
HURTEN, LEAVEN, BRINGEN, COMEN, DRAWNEN, HITTEN, LETTEN,
RUNNEN, WASEN, SEE-EN, ROCKEN, HELPEN, SPOILEN, MAKEN, TIPPEN,
HAVEN. In April, there were no new forms noted, but in May nine
new invented ones appeared: LETTEN, WRAPPEN, SHOULDEN, HIDEN,
WALKEN, BUYEN, CLOSEN, PLAYEN and a strange verb CAVEN, whatever Sally meant by that. In June the real form BITTEN was added.
In July, a mere three invented forms emerged, WEAREN, LEAVEN,
LIKEN, then in August just one, STAYEN. This was the last of the invented
forms. Finally, an actual one, FORGOTTEN, appeared in December. The
rise and fall of forms in -EN took just nine months. This is represented
on the graph.

Sally's over-generalizations in -EN

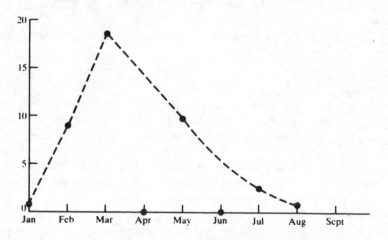

What can we learn from this? Of course, Sally's speech was not
recorded every moment of the day, so there may be some element
of chance in the data. But she was probably recorded often enough
(two or three times a week) for the sequence of events presented here
to be reasonably accurate.

First, Sally seems to have picked out from adult speech several
words ending in -EN which actually occur. She may well have heard
them in sentences such as YOU'VE BROKEN IT, I'VE TAKEN YOUR DOLL

upstairs, and failing to take notice of the shortened form 'VE (HAVE) she perhaps believed that she was dealing with a simple past tense – though this is speculation. What we *do* know is that she spent over a month using a small number of actual forms, and one in particular, BROKEN, which kept recurring. She then perhaps experimentally brought in a new one, PUTTEN. Her hypothesis that -EN was a correct ending was probably confirmed by hearing more actual -EN forms, since her next new form was GIVEN. She then became confident in her -EN endings, and had a surge of them in February and March. Soon after, she began to have doubts, and forms in -EN started to tail off, while Fletcher notes that her verbs in -ED were gradually increasing at this time, occurring in sentences such as:

ME CALLED IT PEANUT BUTTER
SOME MILK DRIPPED, DROPPED ON THE FLOOR.

Eventually, the over generalized forms in -EN faded away completely.

This scenario suggests that a new construction works its way into a child's speech in a manner similar to that found in language change. In language change, first of all a few words get the new pronunciation, though not every time they occur. Then, when these few have acquired a firm hold, the change spreads rapidly to a large number of other words. Then finally, the change slowly rounds up the stragglers (Aitchison 1981). The word by word progress of a change through the vocabulary is known as *lexical diffusion*. In the case of Sally, the situation started off normally. The new ending got a firm footing in a few words, then spread rapidly to a large number. But as Sally had made a false hypothesis, the overgeneralized forms gradually decreased in number, then disappeared.

But how did Sally ever discover that her MAKEN, PUTTEN, BUILDEN forms were wrong? Children are impervious to correction, as we saw earlier (Chapter 4). So how do they discover their errors? This is a complex problem, which we shall return to in the next chapter. In this case, however, there may be a simple answer. Children seem to expect different words to mean different things, an expectation which has been called 'the principle of contrast' (Clark 1987). When she heard someone say, perhaps, DADDY BUILT THAT SNOWMAN, Sally may have realized that this was equivalent to her own DADDY BUILDEN THAT SNOWMAN. This may have led her to reassess her own 'rule', and eventually emend it.

We must conclude, then, that children are not just copying adult utterances when they speak. They seem to be following grammatical rules they devise themselves, and which produce systematic divergences from the adult output. Chomsky (1965) appears to have been substantially correct in attributing to children an innate hypothesis-forming device which enables them to form increasingly complex theories about the rules which underlie the language they are exposed to. Like scientists, children are constantly testing new hypotheses. But, as we have seen, the scientist metaphor falls down in one vital respect. Scientists, once they have discarded a hypothesis, forget about it and concentrate on a new one. Children, on the other hand, appear to go through periods of experimentation and indecision in which two or more hypotheses overlap and fluctuate: each rule wavers for a long time, perhaps months, before it is finally adopted or finally abandoned.

Also, children's hypotheses often apply only to rather small corners of language at a time. Occasionally one finds a broad, sweeping 'rule' such as 'Put NO in front of the sentence to negate it'. But this type of across-the-board generalization is quite rare, and mostly children concentrate on much smaller pieces of structure. Language acquisition is turning out to be a much messier process than was once assumed.

We can now summarize the main conclusions of this chapter. In spite of difficulties connected with interpreting the data, we have come to some firm conclusions. Children automatically 'know' that language is rule-governed, and they seem to make a succession of hypotheses about the rules underlying the speech they hear around them. However, these hypotheses overlap and fluctuate in a way that the hypotheses of scientists do not.

We also considered whether there is a universal framework underlying early speech. We noted that children everywhere seem to produce roughly comparable utterances at the two-word stage. However, it would be an exaggeration to claim that this represents a 'universal framework'. All we can say is that children at this stage tend to express similar meaning relationships in a consistent way.

Therefore, in order to assess whether Chomsky is right in his assumption that children learning language make use of fairly specific outline facts which are somehow innate, we must look in more detail at the way children cope with acquiring speech beyond the two-word stage. We also need to consider whether there are other ways of explaining language development.

7   Puzzling it out
Exactly how do children learn language

Teach your child to hold his tongue; he'll learn fast enough to speak.

BENJAMIN FRANKLIN

According to Chomsky, children learn language so efficiently and so fast because they know in advance what languages look like. They are wired, he argues, with a substantial amount of innate knowledge.

So far, it has not been very difficult to show that children have some inkling of what languages are like. As we noted in the last chapter, children seem to 'know' that language is rule-governed – that a finite number of principles govern the enormous number of utterances they hear going on around them. They also have an instinctive awareness that languages are hierarchically structured – the knowledge that several words can go in the same structural slot as one. A child might say:

	I LOVE	TEDDY
or	I LOVE	MY TEDDY
or	I LOVE	MY OLD BLUE TEDDY

Furthermore, children realize that language makes use of operations which are structure-dependent, so that each 'slot' in a sentence functions as a unit which can be moved around, as in

WHERE	MY TEDDY?	
DON'T TAKE	MY TEDDY	AWAY
	MY TEDDY	HERE

However, an innate knowledge that language is rule-governed, that it has a hierarchical structure, and that it makes use of structure-dependent operations by no means explains the whole of language acquisition. We still need to know exactly *how* children develop language ability so efficiently. We would also like to find out *why* it is that English children follow such remarkably similar paths in the development of their language. These are mysteries which cannot just be swept aside with the vague explanation of 'innate programming'. We must investigate the matter more fully.

Content Cuthbert or Process Peggy?

Two types of explanation have been put forward to account for the mysterious nature of language acquisition. First of all, there is Chomsky's *content* approach. Secondly, an alternative *process* approach has been proposed. What is the difference between these two? Briefly, a content approach postulates that a child's brain naturally *contains* a considerable amount of specific information about language. A process approach, on the other hand, suggests that children have inbuilt puzzle-solving equipment which enables them to *process* the linguistic data they come across.

A content approach, such as Chomsky's, claims that children come to language learning with certain expectations. They are pre-wired with some quite specific information about language, and so approach the data they hear with advance knowledge. Of course Chomsky does not assume that this knowledge is ready waiting, the moment the child is born. It takes time to mature. But when the time is right it requires relatively little exposure to language for the knowledge to emerge. It may be like the growth of teeth or breasts. Given normal surroundings, these appear without any great effort on the part of the acquirer.

However, Chomsky's theory that children innately contain large chunks of specific information about language is disputed by a number of people. These researchers claim that, instead of possessing advance information, children are born with some sort of process mechanism which enables them to analyse linguistic data (Derwing 1973; Slobin 1971b). They suggest that

the child's mind is somehow 'set' in a predetermined way to process the sorts of structures which characterize human language . . . . That is not to say that the grammatical system itself is given as innate knowledge, but that the child has innate means of processing information and forming internal structures, and that when these capacities are applied to the speech he hears, he succeeds in constructing a grammar of his native language. [SLOBIN 1971b, p. 56]

The crucial point is this: are children wired with knowledge of Universal Grammar, as Chomsky suggests? Or do they come equipped with special techniques for performing linguistic analysis? Are children's heads loaded with information? Or with puzzle-solving equipment? Are we dealing with a 'Content Cuthbert' or a 'Process Peggy'?

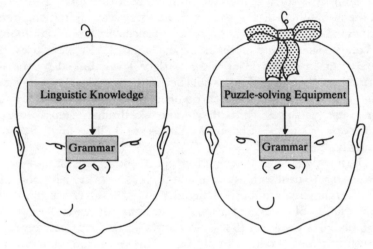

Content Cuthbert or Process Peggy?

In both the content and process approaches the child may end up with the same set of linguistic universals. But in the second case they are the *result* of inbuilt analytic procedures. They are not there at the beginning.

Because the end result may be the same in both cases, it is sometimes claimed that the two points of view are virtually indistinguishable, and should be regarded as two sides of one coin. But there is a crucial difference. Chomsky's content approach presupposes that the pre-wired knowledge is specific to language, and is independent of general intelligence. But the process approach comes in two versions, an intelligent Peggy and a linguistic Peggy. In the intelligent version, Peggy makes use of the same general cognitive abilities as she would to cope with everything else she comes across in the world. In the linguistic version, her processing mechanisms are geared specifically to language.

So are we dealing with a Content Cuthbert? an intelligent Process

Peggy? or a linguistic Process Peggy? We shall consider each of these possibilities in turn.

Does Content Cuthbert exist?

If Chomsky is correct, then we would expect to find evidence for Content Cuthbert displayed in at least three ways. First, children would indicate that they know in advance certain basic facts about language. They would, perhaps, expect language to have two levels of structure, a deep level and a surface level, linked by transformations. Second, children would be aware of universal constraints. They could never utter a sentence which would be an impossible one for human languages. Third, they would take dramatic steps forward as they 'set switches' (Chapter 5). Let us see if all, or any, of these things happen.

The first possibility, that children 'know' about transformations is not as easy to deal with as one might think, since Chomsky and his followers have continuously changed their proposals concerning the appearance of transformational grammar since it was first formulated (Newmeyer 1986). Nowadays, it contains relatively few transformations – perhaps only one. This one transformation is found in WH-questions (questions beginning with WHAT, WHO, WHY, etc.). These have involved a transformation at all stages of the theory, though the exact formulation of it has varied. Let us therefore examine how children acquire them.

All adults can relate a sentence such as

JEMIMA HAS BOUGHT A YAK

to the corresponding question

WHAT HAS JEMIMA BOUGHT?

According to Chomsky, these sentences are likely to be related to similar underlying structures:

Deep structure (simplified) of

JEMIMA HAS BOUGHT A YAK
WHAT HAS JEMIMA BOUGHT?

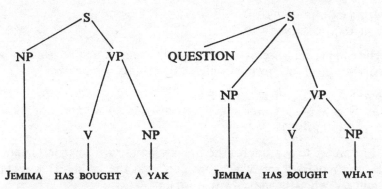

If children had to infer deep structures, we would expect them to go through a stage in the acquisition of WH-questions in which they say: JEMIMA HAS BOUGHT WHAT?

which is nearer to the deep structure. Alternatively, recent models of transformational grammar have suggested that when a WH-word is moved out of its original deep structure place, there is a faint 'trace' left to remind one where it was. Therefore, we might expect the child to get confused between the moved form and the trace, and to say something like

WHAT HAS JEMIMA BOUGHT WHAT?

But when we looked at the development of WH-questions in Chapter 4, we found no sign of these hypothetical intermediate stages. From the very beginning, children put the WH-word at the front, as:

WHAT COWBOY DOING?
WHERE MILK GO?

As far as WH-questions are concerned, therefore, it looks as if children start off by learning the surface location of the WH-word, and have no idea that it might have been moved from a slot at the end of the sentence. This is clearly embarrassing for Chomsky's viewpoint.

However, the situation is slightly more complicated later, when children add in auxiliaries such as CAN, SHALL, DID. At first, they fail to switch around the subject and the auxiliary, and produce sentences such as:

WHAT HE CAN RIDE ON?
WHY KITTY CAN'T STAND UP?

instead of the correct, inverted version

WHAT CAN HE RIDE ON?
WHY CAN'T KITTY STAND UP?

The child version seems to be nearer the deep structure. And a few children produce a form in which the auxiliary is repeated:

WHY DID PETER DID SLEEP HERE?
WHAT SHALL WE SHALL HAVE? [HURFORD 1975; BELLUGI 1971; FLETCHER 1979].

How are we to account for this? Has a faint 'trace' been left behind by the moved form, which has confused the child? This seems unlikely, when the moved WH-word left no trace.

There is probably a much simpler explanation. Perhaps the child simply hears the standard order of noun followed by auxiliary more often than the shifted around form. This would be reinforced by the fact that questions which occur as the second of two clauses, retain the unaltered order, as in

I KNOW WHAT WE ARE HAVING FOR LUNCH
(not *I KNOW WHAT ARE WE HAVING FOR LUNCH).

The doubled up forms such as

WHAT SHALL WE SHALL HAVE?

perhaps occur when the child has realized that a verbal auxiliary follows the WH-word, and so inserts an extra auxiliary into the original sentence. In brief, the child seems to be paying attention to aspects of the surface structure, not looking for deep structures.

Perhaps here we need a word of warning about the ambiguity and looseness with which some authors speak of children 'acquiring transformations'. As soon as children can relate the following two sentences:

MY DINOSAUR ATE A JAM TART
WHAT DID MY DINOSAUR EAT?

some authors say they have 'acquired the question transformation'. What they actually mean is that children can form questions. But it is only strictly correct to speak of 'acquiring transformations' if we can show that children have inferred a deep structure to which the transformations can apply. As we have tried to demonstrate, this is not the case. We have concluded that it is not necessary to infer deep structures in order to be able to speak. Children grasp constructions such as WH-questions by learning surface patterns, and how to manipulate them. It is still an open question whether at a later stage adults and older children have Chomsky-like deep structures. The acquisition of such underlying structures could occur months or even years later. They might do this 'by way of "inductive" inferences from an already acquired stock of surface structures . . . . The child learns at first only the surface structures which it can observe, and only subsequently he extrapolates from these to a more parsimonious and effective set of rules' (Schlesinger 1967, p. 398).

In summary, then, Chomsky's assumption that a child looks at language expecting to find two levels of structure seems to be wrong. Instead, 'The resulting picture of linguistic acquisition will imply a child who stays close to the surface in constructing his grammar and who often only slowly comes to appreciate transformational relations among syntactic structures' (Maratsos 1978, p. 249).

We can now turn to the topic of universal constraints. If children are aware of these, they should never utter a sentence which would be an impossible one for human languages. Supposedly, anything quite weird will be ruled out by 'a biological mandate against wild grammars' (Goodluck 1986, p. 55). This ensures that 'each developing grammar will fall within the bounds of adult language systems as characterized by linguistic theory' (Goodluck 1988, p. 64).

So do children always obey universal constraints? This might seem a strange question to ask. After all, adults don't produce strange sentences such as:

*WHICH AVOCADOS HAS CHARLIE ASKED ZAK TO BUY AND SOME
   AUBERGINES?
*WHICH PIG ANGELA KNOWS WHO HAS STOLEN?

Surely, therefore, we are quite unlikely to find similar sentences in child language?

Surprisingly, perhaps, a three-year old boy called Seth has produced a series of 'forbidden' utterances (Wilson and Peters 1988). Consider the following:

Seth: WE'RE GONNA LOOK AT SOME HOUSES WITH JOHNNIE.
    WHAT ARE WE GONNA LOOK FOR SOME?
    WHAT ARE WE GONNA LOOK FOR SOME WITH JOHNNIE?

Seth appears to have picked on the phrase SOME HOUSES. He has then replaced HOUSES with the word WHAT, and brought this WH-word to the front, but left the word SOME behind. Supposedly, children should know automatically that it is impossible to split up a phrase such as SOME HOUSES, and move half of it away. And this was not an isolated example, so cannot be attributed to a chance mistake. This 'prohibited' construction occurred several times, as when Seth was sorting through magnetic letters:

Seth: IS THIS A FUNNY T?
Father: NO, THAT'S A FUNNY I.
Seth (holding up another): WHAT IS THIS A FUNNY, DAD?

A possible reason for Seth's extraordinary behaviour is that he is partially blind. Because of this, his father often asked him to finish off sentences, as when playing with the magnetic letters:

Father: THAT'S A . . .   Seth: ALEPH
Father: THAT'S A NICE . . .   Seth: OTHER KAF.

So Seth may have assumed that it was necessary to have a word following the verb at the end of a sentence. At the same time, he knew that WH-words had to go to the front. When he combined these two 'rules of thumb', he produced the 'impossible' sentences.

Seth ended up chopping the strange sentences out of his speech, so they were only a small detour on the way to fluent English. But Seth's case suggests that children are not pre-wired with absolute information about language universals from the beginning. They may need to get there gradually, especially if they are in any way disadvantaged, as Seth was.

The gradual acquisition of universal constraints is supported by another study, which looked at them from the point of view of comprehension.

One American linguist set out to discover how children understand sentences involving the phrase EACH OTHER (Matthei 1981). Now if you have a sentence such as

THE BOYS WANTED THE GIRLS TO LIKE EACH OTHER

the only possible interpretation is that each girl should like all the other girls. Any other interpretation, according to Chomsky, would go against universal constraints. So a number of children between the ages of 4 and 6 were presented with sentences such as

THE CHICKENS SAID THAT THE PIGS TICKLED EACH OTHER.

They were asked to perform the actions described with farmyard animals. Unfortunately for Chomsky, most of them seemed quite unaware of the proposed constraints. The majority interpreted the sentence as if the chickens and pigs were tickling one another, though a few made the chickens tickle one another. In fact, it has been repeatedly shown that young children often do not pay attention to the syntax, and either answer at random, or utilize a 'probable world strategy', that is, interpret sentences by arranging the words to give the most plausible meaning (Cromer 1976, 1981).

Of course, one can always argue that the child really 'knew' about the constraint, but failed to reveal this knowledge. Perhaps the experiment was badly designed, or the youngsters did not fully understand what they had been asked to do. Or perhaps the children were simply 'overloaded', in that they had been asked to cope with too many things at once. A child forced to deal simultaneously with language and non-verbal responses might appear less competent than it really is 'Hamburger and Crain 1984).

But the most plausible conclusion is that children do not have any firm, fixed beliefs about language as they acquire it. So far, they do not seem to know what to look for, or what to avoid – though some of this knowledge clearly develops over the course of time. Let us now consider Chomsky's latest 'switch-setting' views.

Do children 'set switches'?

Universal Grammar (UG) is partly like a switchboard with its switches in neutral position, according to Chomsky (Chapter 5). Children know in advance about the possible routes which languages can take. But they have to find out which particular option has been selected by the language they are learning. Once they discover this, they flick each switch, and 'the system functions'. Is this true?

Children's omissions have loomed largest in discussions of Chomsky's 'switch-setting' theory. Why do English children say things such as:

HUG KITTY
MEND CAR

instead of

I'M HUGGING THE KITTEN
HE'S MENDING THE CAR?

Most children could have strung more words together if they'd wanted to, because the brief HUG KITTY type of utterance often alternates with longer ones such as:

MUMMY HUG KITTY
DADDY MEND CAR.

According to one viewpoint, children behave like this because they have temporarily set a switch wrong (Hyams 1986, 1987). They leave out the subject pronouns (I, HE, etc.) as well as the auxiliary verbs (AM, IS, etc.) because they have wrongly assumed that English is a 'pro-drop' language like Italian – one which optionally drops pronouns at the beginning of sentences. In Italian, one can say 'I am here' in two ways, either:

SONO QUI ('am here') or IO SONO QUI ('I am here').

Children have set a switch which wrongly assumes that English is a language of this type. So they omit both the subject pronouns and the auxiliaries which are attached to them.

How, then, do children ever start to speak proper English, if they have made a fundamental switching error? Supposedly, they reach a point in maturation when they notice the presence of items such as THERE, IT as in:

THERE'S A HOLE IN YOUR BUCKET.
IT'S RAINING.

They therefore realize that English cannot drop its pronouns at the beginning of a sentence, and re-set the switch in the right direction.

This ingenious proposal raises several problems. First, children leave out numerous other things, not just pronouns and auxiliaries, as in:

PIG WATER 'The pig's in the water.'
MUMMY BATHROOM 'Mummy's in the bathroom.'

A really good theory would link *all* the omissions together. Second, setting or re-setting a switch should have 'proliferating consequences', according to Chomsky. In this case, setting the switch the wrong way caused the omission of both subject pronouns and auxiliaries. So re-setting should have done the reverse, and caused the instantaneous appearance of both. In fact, the auxiliaries creep in one by one, over several months (O'Grady 1989).

Moreover, there are several possible alternative explanations for children's early omissions. Perhaps they simply leave out unstressed items (e.g. Aitchison 1988). Or perhaps they can cope at this stage with only 'full' lexical items, and not with the grammatical 'little words' such as *is*, *'s*, which do not always have a clear meaning (Radford 1988). Or they may not yet understand why some verbs have subjects (e.g. PENELOPE SLEPT), and others do not, as when they come after TO (e.g. PENELOPE WANTED TO SLEEP) (O'Grady 1989). In short, the notion of 'throwing a switch' is only one, not entirely plausible explanation, for children's omissions. We must therefore conclude either that Chomsky is wrong, or that this particular switch has been wrongly identified.

Chomsky himself mentioned another possible switch, that of 'head position' (Chapter 5). Children might know in advance that language structures have a head (key word), and that languages tend to put the modifiers (words relating to the head) consistently either before or after it. Does this suggestion work?

Children are on the whole consistent in their treatment of heads and modifiers. But this may be because they are sensitive to the order of the words they hear. There is no need to assume an English child has 'set a parameter' when it says WANT MILK, rather than *MILK WANT. Furthermore, if a switch had been set, we would expect children to iron out various inconsistencies. They should say *AGO TWO WEEKS instead of TWO WEEKS AGO, where the modifier occurs (exceptionally) after the words it modifies. But they show no real signs of behaving like this.

Perhaps the biggest weakness of the switch-setting theory is that no-one can agree how many switches there are, nor how exactly they are set (Roeper and Williams 1987). This may be because language acquisition is just too messy a process to be explained by the flick of a switch.

Let us now summarize our conclusions about Content Cuthbert. This approach does not seem to be borne out by the evidence. Children do not appear to have firm advance expectations about language. They are not aware that language may be organized on two levels. They do not necessarily steer clear of sentences which are prohibited by language universals. They do not acquire chunks of language by flicking a switch.

Of course, Chomskyan language universals may still exist. But they are not there 'ready to go' at a relatively early stage, triggered by simple data, and requiring very little effort on the child's part, as Chomsky suggests. If they do exist, they develop gradually, perhaps with some false starts, as some Chomskyan supporters now suggest (e.g. Borer and Wexler 1987).

Let us now consider whether Process Peggy provides a better explanation for language acquisition.

Is Process Peggy a general problem solver?

In its strongest form, the process approach proposes that Process Peggy is simply making use of a wider set of puzzle-solving abilities which she brings to bear on the world in general. Proponents of this viewpoint put forward various non-linguistic factors which they consider to be critical for guiding the child forward through the thickets of language. We shall consider three of these: children's needs, their general mental development, and parental speech.

Obviously, all of these must be taken into consideration. But can any of these factors, or all of them together, account for why children acquire language so efficiently? We need to ask not only *what* propels children onwards, but also *why* there are certain broad outline similarities in the way children acquire language.

According to the 'everyday needs' approach, children are by nature sociable little animals who need to interact with other humans. They also have certain material needs, such as MILK or JUICE. They are therefore concerned primarily with interacting with other people, and with getting what they want. They acquire speech in order to help them in this quest (e.g. Donaldson 1978). Within a particular culture, there is relatively little variation in the interests and requirements of different children. Therefore, it is not surprising that children develop language in a parallel fashion, even though they have never met one another.

This viewpoint is certainly borne out by children in the very early stages of development. As we noted in Chapter 6, children all over the world seem to talk about very similar things at the two-word stage. We find requests such as WANT MILK, rejections such as NO WASH, questions such as WHERE DADDY?, and so on, in widely separated children. Some people have suggested that this state of affairs lasts throughout the language learning period. That is, they suggest that children are concerned primarily with the external world, both with finding out about it, and with getting what they want. As they attempt to learn about and manipulate some aspect of their environment, they look for ways to talk about it. Language, therefore, mirrors the preoccupations of the child at each stage.

In a trivial way, this is undoubtedly true, in that children talk about the things which concern them. But it cannot account for similarities in the development of language *structure*. Nor can it explain why children proceed to further stages of language development when their own primitive structures have the desired effect. For example, if a child says WHERE KITTY? She is likely to be told what she wants to know – where the cat is. Why, therefore, should she, and most other children, proceed to (probably) WHERE KITTY GO?, then some weeks or months later to WHERE KITTY HAS GONE?, and finally to WHERE HAS KITTY GONE? In brief, the argument that the child learns language in order to help her to manipulate the world does not explain why she does not stop learning as soon as she starts obtaining what she wants, nor why we find parallel structural developments in different children.

A child called John provides further problems for the notion that children develop language in order to cope with everyday needs (Blank, Gessner and Esposito 1979). John used language creatively, and had a firm grasp of linguistic structures – but he did not use language to communicate. He disliked interacting with others so much that he never spoke directly to anyone, even his parents. He simply talked to himself as he played with his toys: 'Let's go shopping. Where's the money? OK here's the change. Open the door. Pretend its a shopping centre. OK get elevator. Push button.' John provides evidence against the view that children are sociable beings who cater for their needs by communicating with others.

Let us, therefore, look at another factor, which is considered by many to be important in understanding the stages by which children acquire language. This is general mental development, or rather, general cognitive development as it is more usually expressed. Some people have suggested that language acquisition is both dependent on it, and caused by it. Like the 'everyday needs' view, such a belief is obviously justified to a limited extent, since 'It is tautological that linguistic development presupposes cognitive development in the uninteresting sense that one cannot express a concept that one doesn't have' (Fodor, Bever and Garrett 1974, p. 463). Certain concepts seem to be easier for children to grasp than others. For example, English, Italian, Turkish and Serbo-Croatian children were asked to describe where an object such as a nut was placed in relation to one or more other items, such as plates or glasses (Johnston and Slobin 1979; Slobin 1982). They could all cope with the nut being IN, ON, BESIDE, or UNDER a plate before they could describe it as being BETWEEN two plates.

It is also true that certain cognitive abilities and language structures tend to emerge simultaneously. For example, one researcher has claimed that the development of comparative constructions (I AM BIGGER THAN YOU) occurs at a time when the child can recognize that a pint of milk remains the same whether it is poured into a long thin container or a short fat one (Sinclair-de-Zwart 1969). However, the simultaneous development of different abilities does not prove that one is dependent on the other, since in the normal child, many aspects of growth take place at around the same time. As one researcher notes 'Hair growth and language development might be positively correlated, but few psycholinguists would wish to posit interesting links between the two' (Curtiss 1981).

Perhaps the best way to test whether language acquisition and cognitive development are inextricably linked is to search for children who show some discrepancy between cognitive and linguistic abilities. If such a discrepancy can be found, then clearly the link is not an inevitable one. And there are reports of several children whose general cognitive development is unrelated to their grasp of language structure.

Consider Marta (Yamada 1988). Marta had been a limp, floppy infant. In spite of coming from a loving, supportive home, her general development was delayed. She could not sit alone until she was fifteen-months old. She was also severely mentally retarded, and as a teenager was unable to perform tasks which even normal 2-year-olds can carry out successfully. When she was given a stack of pictures to sort, she did not separate humans from objects, as normal children tend to do. She did not understand numbers, and did not know her age. Her short-term memory was limited, and she could not repeat back sequences of more than three unrelated items.

In contrast, her speech was fluent and richly structured, and had apparently been so since around the age of 9. When her speech was studied in her teens, she produced sentences such as:

SHE DOES PAINTINGS, THIS REALLY GOOD FRIEND OF THE KIDS WHO I
WENT TO SCHOOL WITH LAST YEAR, AND REALLY LOVED.

She used syntactic structures which are acquired relatively late in normal development, such as 'full' passives, as in:

I GOT IT CUT ALREADY BY A MAID (when talking about her hair)
I DON'T WANT TO GET EATEN BY ONE (about crocodiles at the zoo).

Marta was not just repeating back sentences she'd heard, as shown by occasional errors, as in:

WHEN I FIRST WENT THERE THREE TICKETS WERE GAVE OUT BY A
POLICE LAST YEAR.

She could also repeat back correctly a sentence such as:

AN APPLE WAS EATEN BY JENI,

something which is difficult for children who have not acquired the
passive.

But the passive was not the only advanced construction she had
acquired. Consider:

I SHOULD'VE BROUGHT IT BACK
I DON'T LIKE HIM PUTTIN' PAPER TOWELS IN MY MOUTH
DID YOU HEAR ABOUT ME NOT GOING TO THIS SCHOOL?
HE WAS SAYING THAT I LOST MY BATTERY-POWERED WATCH
THAT I LOVED.

These all show a considerable degree of linguistic sophistication as
far as syntax is concerned.

But Marta's speech was by no means 'normal'. Her utterances
were often semantically odd, or inappropriate, as in:

I WAS 16 LAST YEAR AND NOW I'M 19 THIS YEAR
I WAS LIKE 15 OR 19 WHEN I STARTED MOVING OUT O' HOME
SHE WAS THINKING THAT IT'S NO REGULAR SCHOOL, IT'S JUST PLAIN
OLD NO BUSES
WELL, WE WERE TAKING A WALK, MY MOM, AND THERE WAS THIS
GIANT, LIKE MY MOTHER THREW A STICK.

In brief, she finds it easy to deal with the structure of language,
but difficult to cope with the type of concepts which language
normally expresses.

Genie, the Californian girl whose development was outlined in
Chapter 4, illustrates the reverse situation (Curtiss 1977). Genie is
able to cope with complex feelings and concepts, but her ability to
deal with language structure is minimal. She expresses herself mainly
by means of content words strung together with little syntactic
structure as in, THINK ABOUT MAMA LOVE GENIE, or DENTIST SAY
DRINK WATER. Her utterances are appropriate, and often con-
ceptually sophisticated, even though telegraphic, as in:

Adult: HOW MANY SIDES DOES A TRIANGLE HAVE?
Genie: THREE
Adult: HOW MANY SIDES DOES A CIRCLE HAVE?
Genie: ROUND

As Curtiss notes: 'Genie's semantic sophistication suggests a conceptual level far surpassing what one would imagine from her otherwise rather primitive utterances' (1981, p. 21) – an impression borne out by her relatively good performance in a wide range of intelligence tests.

Marta, therefore, shows that severe conceptual deficits can exist alongside a highly developed language ability, while Genie illustrates the opposite – that conceptual ability can outstrip language structure to a considerable extent. These case studies suggest that cognitive development cannot provide the definitive key to acquisition of language structure – even though it is clearly important for meaningful communication.

Caregiver language

NO, YOU SHOULDN'T MAKE A HOLE IN THE BOTTOM
NO, LET DADDY DO IT FIRST
NO, I DON'T THINK YOU'LL BE ABLE TO CUT STRAIGHT
NO, DON'T CUT TOO MUCH ON THE FRONT
NO, I DON'T THINK YOU SHOULD PUT MORE HOLES IN IT
NO, DON'T CUT TWO HOLES.

These six examples of NO placed in front of the sentence occurred in a fifteen minute recording session in which 2-year-old Nicholas was 'helping' his father to carve a pumpkin (De Villiers and De Villiers 1979). This construction seemed to be a favourite one for Nicholas's father. Not surprisingly, the majority of Nicholas's early negatives (76 per cent) involved opposition to some suggestion proposed by his parents, and his means of expressing this was by placing NO in front of the sentence, as in NO DADDY DRESS ME.

Faced with such examples, a number of people have suggested that *motherese, caretaker language,* or *caregiver language* (speech addressed to children) can solve the mystery of why so many children go through similar stages in the acquisition of language. Children, according to this view, just absorb and copy the speech they hear around them. They learn so fast, it is claimed, because speech addressed to children is rather different from that to adults (Chapter 4), and so grabs their attention. In many communities, this special way of talking to children begins as soon as the baby is born:

'Wha's a matter, Bobby, yo' widdle tum-tum all empty? Here you are, a growin' boy, and dese folks won't feed you. You tell 'em, they can't just let you cry, not while Aunt Sue is 'round . . . You're a-gonna be a big boy, just like your daddy. Mamma gonna hafta get some new rompers soon . . . Okay, okay, look, look, there's mamma, she's comin', she gonna get dat bottle right now and get it ready for you. It's a hungry boy, it is'. [HEATH 1983, p. 118]

This stream of speech was addressed to Bobby by a helpful neighbour when he was only a month or so old. It contains many of the characteristics found repeatedly in child-directed speech (Ferguson 1978). It tends to be slower, spoken with higher pitch, and with exaggerated intonation contours. The utterances are shorter, with the average length being approximately one-third of that found in speech addressed to adults (Newport, Gleitman and Gleitman 1977). The sentences are well-formed, simple in structure, and repetitious, in that the same lexical items recur, though in slightly different combinations. Special 'baby' words are sometimes used, such as DOGGIE, BIRDIE, GEE-GEE, CHUFF-CHUFF, TUM-TUM. The topic is usually related to the 'here and now' – things that are present both in place and time.

The link between caregiver speech and child language is not straightforward. Neither correction by the parents, nor immediate repetition by the child has any significant effect (Chapter 4). And 'repairs' – cases in which caregivers try to 'mend' a communication which has been ignored or misinterpreted – turn out to be too infrequent to be of consistent use. Reformulations such as:

OPEN YOUR MOUTH. OPEN IT
SPIT OUT THE SNAIL, SPIT THE SNAIL OUT. SPIT IT OUT
GIVE MUMMY THE SNAIL. GIVE THE SNAIL TO MUMMY

account for only around 4 per cent of maternal speech (Shatz 1982).

However, it seems reasonable to expect that words and constructions which occur frequently in adult speech will be produced early by children. And this certainly seems to be borne out in some studies. For example, in the development of verbal auxiliaries (words such as *can, will, might, have*, etc.) the order of acquisition roughly follows the frequency of these words in adult speech (Wells 1979).

Statistically, therefore, there is a link between items produced frequently by parents, and those acquired early by the child. But the problem with statistical correlations is that they do not hold for every construction, nor for every child. The development of some aspects of language may be related to their frequency of use by parents, but by no means all. Roger Brown found numerous exceptions. He comments that although it is a truism that children do not develop constructions they do not normally hear, he is even 'prepared to conclude that frequency is not a significant variable' (Brown 1973, p. 368). Furthermore, correlations which are valid for groups of people can sometimes disappear when each individual child and its parents are examined separately (Wells 1979). We must conclude, therefore, that overall frequency of use is only a rough guide to the order of acquisition, and is by no means a definitive map.

Since simple frequency counts have not proved entirely helpful, some researchers have suggested that motherese directs child language in a more subtle way. They have proposed that parents have an inbuilt sensitivity to their children. According to this view, parents gradually increase the complexity of their speech as the child becomes ready for each new stage. This has sometimes been called the 'fine-tuning' hypothesis (Cross 1977), in the sense that parents subconsciously attune their output to their child's needs. And a few people have claimed that, far from children possessing an innate language learning device, mothers possess an innate language teaching device! Those who support this viewpoint assume that there will be a close correlation between the structure of the mother's speech and that of the child at every stage of development. Is this true?

Recent research confirms that parents attune their speech to their children's needs, but suggests they attune them to a child's interests, rather than his or her language structure. That is, parents talk about topics which are relevant to the child such as picking up blocks, or drinking juice, but show no evidence that they are grading their syntax, or introducing constructions one at a time, as one might expect if they were subconsciously guiding their children from one stage of language to another. There is no sign of a step-by-step programme, except in the broad general sense that as the child gets older, the parents' speech tends to become less repetitious, with longer sentences and more complex subject matter. Moreover, researchers who examined the speech of fifteen mothers interacting with their young daughters, concluded that if one was designing a curriculum for language teaching, motherese was highly unsuitable! (Newport, Gleitman and Gleitman 1977). In a good language teaching programme, you would expect teachers to introduce constructions one at a time and to concentrate first on simple active declarative sentences (TOBY WANTS A BATH, or MARION IS EATING A

BUN), then move on to constructions in which words are omitted or the order shifted round as in imperatives (TURN OFF THE TAP! COME HOME!) or questions (WHAT IS TONY EATING? WHY ARE YOU CRYING?). Instead, they found mothers did the reverse. That is, they used all these constructions jumbled together with more questions and imperatives (62 per cent) than declaratives (30 per cent)! Oddly enough, there were more declaratives in the *second* session, six months later, than in the first, and even more in the speech addressed to other adults! These researchers, therefore, assert that 'Motherese is not a syntax-teaching language'.

Children, therefore, have an inbuilt filter which allows them to choose what they pay attention to: 'The child is selective in WHAT he uses from the environment provided; he is selective about WHEN in the course of acquisition he chooses to use it' (Gleitman, Newport and Gleitman 1984). Child 'uptake' is not matched in any straight-forward way with adult input.

There is one final piece of 'proof' that uptake matters more than input. Reports are coming in of societies where parents do not modify their speech when talking to infants. In 'Tracton', a working-class black community in the southeast of the USA, adults do not regard babies as suitable partners for regular conversation (Heath 1983). They rarely address speech specifically to very young children. Moreover, Tracton inhabitants find it odd when they hear white people gurgling over infants: 'White folks uh hear dey kids say sump'n, dey say it back to 'em' (Heath 1983, p. 84). Tracton children are an integral part of family life, so they hear plenty of speech around them. Somehow, they acquire language as efficiently as anyone else.

Adults can, however, help their children by talking about things that interest them, and engaging in joint enterprises (Wells 1979): 'Now, then, Shirley, are you going to help mummy peel the potatoes? Can you get me six out of that basket?' The tendency of girls to be mildly ahead of boys in their language may be due to the different treatment meted out by parents. Girls are often kept in to help with the chores in many families, but boys are sent out to play games. Mothers, rather than footballs, aid progress in language.

We must conclude, then, that motherese cannot explain the various stages through which children pass as they acquire language. We must admit that it is an important factor which must be taken into consideration, and that parental speech is considerably more coherent than Chomsky suggests. Yet as Cromer (1981, p. 65) notes:

To show that the input signal to many children is far clearer than had been assumed in no way explains how the grammatical structures that the child uses are developed.

Or, in the words of the nineteenth-century German philosopher-linguist Wilhelm von Humboldt: 'Language cannot really be taught . . . One can only offer the thread along which language develops on its own' (quoted in Slobin 1975, p. 283).

A linguistic Process Peggy

Process Peggy, then, is not a general problem-solver. Neither everyday needs nor general intelligence nor caregiver speech can account for her special language abilities – though all these factors are important if she is to develop normally. She must be innately programmed to tackle language. In this section, we shall discuss how she might set about her linguistic puzzle-solving.

In the beginning, she possibly uses her general intelligence to get going (Chapter 6). She may behave like a computer, which often needs a fairly general programme to start up before it can use a more specific one. Computer operators talk about 'booting up' or 'bootstrapping' a computer – giving it some preliminary commands, which will then allow it to cope with more detailed programmes. So some linguists talk about a 'bootstrapping' approach to language (Pinker 1984, 1987).

Linguistic bootstrapping might work as follows. Children learn words such as DOGGY, KITTY, BITE, DRINK, BALL, MILK, which correlate well with actors, actions and objects. They therefore build these up in various semantic relationships (Chapter 6):

KITTY DRINK (ACTOR + ACTION)
DRINK MILK (ACTION + OBJECT).

And they may combine these into longer sequences:

KITTY DRINK MILK (ACTOR + ACTION + OBJECT).

Up to this point, general intelligence may be at work, rather than syntactic ability. The basic scaffolding relies on meaning.

Then they switch over to syntax. Exactly how they do this is disputed. According to one suggestion, syntax begins when children discover some discrepancy in their semantic scaffolding. They may discover that ACTION words such as BITE, DRINK can sometimes be replaced by words such as WANT, GOT, LIKE, which do not involve any kind of action:

KITTY WANT MILK
KITTY LIKE MILK.

The child may therefore realize that the 'slot' a word occupies in the sentence matters more than its strict correlation with an action in the external world. At this point, the child has acquired a linguistic category, that of verb.

To take a slightly different example, children may notice that different semantic relationships have some underlying structural similarity:

BLUE SOCK 'It's a blue sock' (ATTRIBUTE + OBJECT)
MUMMY SOCK 'It's mummy's sock' (POSSESSOR + OBJECT).

They may notice that both BLUE and MUMMY fall into the same slot, the one in front of SOCK, and combine them in their minds. Once two different types of word have been combined under one heading, this is syntax, not meaning.

To summarize, a possible way of moving from a semantic grammar to a syntactic one is to discover that there is not necessarily a direct correlation between types of word and the world. The child therefore discovers abstract relationships underlying the semantic ones. This is the beginning of syntax. Just as some children have a 'naming-insight' which triggers a surge forward in vocabulary (Chapter 6), so some children may acquire a syntactic insight, which triggers an innate processing device.

Children cannot persist in using meaning to guide them, because language just does not correlate sufficiently with the world around. If children carried on classifying verbs as actions, they would probably make strange over-generalizations such as:

SHE IS NOISYING
SHE IS BUSYING.

They would wrongly assume that NOISY, BUSY were verbs, because they describe actions. Similarly, they would fail to recognize words such as LIKE, HATE, GOT as verbs, because they do not involve an action. But children do not seem to have this type of problem (Maratsos 1982).

Somehow, children are specially pre-programmed to notice linguistic regularities, and to give them priority over semantic ones, as shown by children learning French or German (Maratsos 1982). A language such as French has a somewhat odd gender system (by English standards), since every word has to be labelled as masculine or feminine. Sometimes this correlates with natural gender: UN GARCON 'a boy' (m.), UNE DAME 'a lady' (f.), but at other times it does not, as in UN CANIF 'a knife' (m.), UNE FOURCHETTE 'a fork' (f.). Certain word endings (such as -IEN) are typically masculine, while others (such as -IENNE) are typically feminine. Children pay more attention to this type of information than to matching up gender with the external world. This was demonstrated by an ingenious experiment (Karmiloff-Smith 1979).

The researcher showed children a picture of two little boys, and told them: 'Here are two FORSIENNES'. She then showed them another picture, which had just one of the little boys in it, and asked: 'What's this?' The children replied: 'It's UNE FORSIENNE.' They automatically used the feminine UNE 'a' because this goes with the ending -IENNE. They did not seem bothered that a boy seemed to be assigned to the feminine gender. If they had required language to correlate closely with the world, they should have been puzzled. But they were not. We conclude that linguistic consistency matters more than language–world matching.

Children therefore switch over to a syntactic processing system fairly early on in life. But how does this work? Dan Slobin of the University of California at Berkeley has been working on this problem for a number of years. He claims to have isolated a number of 'operating principles' used by children as they process language. Let us consider these.

Operating principles

Children find certain types of constructions easier to cope with than others. They begin by acquiring 'easy' constructions, and will then move on to more difficult ones. This commonsense assumption underlies Slobin's pioneering work. We need therefore to find out what constitutes 'difficulty' for a child in linguistic terms. We can learn a certain amount by simply looking at constructions which are acquired early, and seeing what they have in common (after, of course, checking that the frequency of use by adults is not a major factor for the construction in question). For example, children acquire relative clauses (clauses introduced by relative pronouns such as WHO, WHICH, THAT) in a certain order. They produce relative clauses which follow the main clause such as

MUNGO SAW AN OCTOPUS [WHICH HAD 20 LEGS]

before ones which are placed inside the main clause:

THE OCTOPUS [WHICH HAD 20 LEGS] ESCAPED

even though there seems to be little difference in the frequency with which adults produce these two types. We can also draw certain conclusions from looking at children's errors: why, for example, do children so often leave out the auxiliary verb, as in DADDY (IS) SWIMMING, MUMMY (IS) COOKING? However, the best way of discovering which constructions children find easy, and which difficult, may be the study of children speaking different languages, and in particular, bilingual children (Slobin 1973, 1977, 1982, 1985a).

Slobin points out that children who grow up learning two languages together do not normally acquire a particular construction simultaneously in both languages. For example, children who are acquiring Hungarian and Serbo-Croatian as twin native languages use Hungarian locatives (INTO THE BOX, ON THE TABLE) long before they produce the equivalent Serbo-Croatian ones. Clearly, there cannot be any conceptual difficulty connected with the notion of locative, because the Hungarian ones are used in the correct circumstances. We conclude that there must be something intrinsically difficult about Serbo-Croatian locatives from the linguistic point of view.

Let us examine the locatives in these two languages, and then go on to consider Slobin's conclusions (which were based on far more evidence than we can consider here).

The Hungarian locative, on the one hand, is formed by means of a suffix attached to a noun. Each locative expression, INTO, ON, and so on, is a single unambiguous syllable, placed after a noun:

HAJÓBAN 'Boat-in, in the boat'
HAJÓBÓL 'Boat-out-of, (getting) out of the boat'.

The Serbo-Croatian locatives, on the other hand, are not nearly as clear cut. The Serbo-Croatian word U can mean either 'into' or 'in'. You can tell the difference between the two uses of Serbo-Croatian U by looking at the end of the following noun:

U KUĆU 'into the house'
U KUĆI 'in the house'.

But the situation is further complicated because the noun endings are not used only in conjunction with this preposition, but have other uses as well. Worse still, another preposition, к 'towards', which you might expect to be followed by the same suffix as υ 'into', in fact takes a quite different noun ending. So in Serbo-Croatian we find the same prepositional form with more than one meaning, and followed by more than one noun ending. And we find prepositions with similar meanings followed by different noun endings, as well as the same noun endings used for a variety of purposes. No wonder the children get confused!

Slobin concludes that children find some constructions easy to learn and others difficult because they have certain expectations about language (Slobin 1973, 1977, 1985b). They expect language to be consistent, and assume that there will be one unit of form to match each unit of meaning. They expect words to be systematically modified, especially by means of endings. They assume that word-order is important. They are puzzled by interruptions and re-arrangements of linguistic units.

Slobin expresses these expectations as a set of 'operating principles' – self instructions which the child might subconsciously give himself as he attempts to analyse linguistic data. For example:

1 Allot one form only to each unit of meaning.
2 Pay attention to the ends of words.
3 Pay attention to the order of words.
4 Avoid interruptions.

Of course, Slobin's list contains many more principles than the four listed above (which appear in a slightly different form in his recent work, Slobin 1985b). But there is considerable evidence to support his point of view, particularly in respect of the four principles mentioned here. Let us briefly comment on each, giving some examples.

The principle of one form per unit of meaning seems to persist right through the acquisition period. It lies behind children's over-generalizations. Once a child has correctly identified the plural ending on words such as DUCKS, COWS, HORSES, he naturally assumes that this ending can be extended to other words, as in SHEEPS, MOUSES, GOOSES. Children confidently expect the same plural ending to be applicable everywhere (with minor phonetic variations). Several researchers have noted that children show an inbuilt resistance to using two different forms to mean the same thing (e.g. MacWhinney 1978; Bloom *et al.* 1980; Clark 1987). Conversely, children do not like to allot more than one meaning to any word or word-ending.

Karmiloff-Smith (1979) has shown that this principle is still at work in children between the ages of 5 and 8. In a study of the acquisition of the articles LE/LA 'the' and UN/UNE 'a' in French, she notes that until around the age of 8 'the child does not place on one word the burden of conveying more than one meaning' (Karmiloff-Smith 1979, p. 224). For example, French UN/UNE can either mean 'a' or 'one'. When children first became aware of the double meaning, several of them in her experiments tried to invent ways of distinguishing between the two meanings, by altering the syntax. In the following conversation, an 8-year-old correctly says UNE BROSSE for 'a brush', but incorrectly uses the phrase UNE DE BROSSE for 'one brush'. The experimenter had shown the child a picture of a boy in a room with three brushes, and a girl in a room with one brush, and had asked: 'Two whom would I say, lend me a brush?' The child replied:

. . . 'it's the boy because he's got a brush (une brosse), no it's the girl because she has one brush (une de brosse), . . . no, the boy because he could give you any of his brushes.' [KARMILOFF-SMITH 1979, p. 1981]

The second operating principle mentioned above, 'Pay attention to the ends of words' seems to be subconsciously followed even when children are not dealing with specific inflectional endings. When English children confuse two different words, they often get the last part right: THE LION AND THE LEPRECHAUN instead of 'the lion and the unicorn', ICE CREAM TOILET, for 'ice cream cornet' (Aitchison and Straf 1981). And it is well known that children tend to omit or confuse the first syllable of a word, particularly if it is unstressed, as in RITTACK, RIDUCTOR, RIFECTION for 'attack', 'conductor', 'infection' (Smith 1973, p. 12). But this is not only because the syllable is unstressed. It is also because the syllable occurs at the beginning of the word. In Czech, where initial syllables are stressed, it is the unstressed final syllables which are better remembered by children, according to one researcher (Pacesova 1968, reported in Slobin 1973). And further evidence that suffixes are more salient than prefixes or items placed in front of a word comes from the fact that English children omit prepositions that are essential to the sentence (e.g. MUMMY GARDEN) at a time when they have already started using the correct endings on words (e.g. DADDY SINGING).

The third operating principle 'Pay attention to the order of words' is illustrated by the consistency with which children preserve the adult word order in English (see Chapter 6), while their resistance to alterations in the 'normal' order is shown by their tendency to acquire the process of noun-auxiliary inversion relatively late. As we noted, children produce sentences such as WHERE DADDY HAS GONE? before the correct, inverted form WHERE HAS DADDY GONE?

Finally, the principle 'Avoid interruptions' is shown by the development of the verbal construction known as the progressive. This describes an on-going action:

POLLY IS SNORING
ARTHUR IS WHISTLING.

It is a discontinuous sandwich-like construction because the progressive sequence IS . . . ING is interrupted by the verb:

| POLLY | IS | SNOR | ING |
| ARTHUR | IS | WHISTL | ING |

It is clear that IS . . . ING functions as a single unit, because when an on-going action is described we do not find one without the other. English does not have sentences such as

*POLLY IS SNORE
*ARTHUR WHISTLING.

The Harvard children, Adam, Eve and Sarah all used the -ING part of the progressive early (Brown 1973). Both Adam and Eve acquired it earlier than any other ending. But they all omitted the IS (AM, ARE, etc.) part;

WHAT COWBOY DOING?
WHY YOU SMILING?

The full IS . . . ING construction appeared only after a long delay. In both Adam's and Sarah's speech, the gap was longer than twelve months. For a year, it seems, they just did not fully recognize the connection between the IS and the -ING. And there appears to be nothing inherently difficult about the phonetic forms AM, IS, ARE. This is shown by the fact that for all three children AM, IS, ARE occurred with nouns, as in

HE IS A COWBOY

some time before AM, IS, ARE, in progressive constructions.

It seems that all three children were puzzled by the discontinuity involved. They assigned -ING to the progressive early, but were baffled by the preceding IS. In other words, discontinuities seem to go against children's natural intuitions about what language is like. This point is again illustrated by the development of relative clauses. As we noted earlier, those which do not interrupt the main clause such as:

THE FARMER WAS ANGRY WITH THE PIG [WHICH ATE THE TURNIPS]

develop before those which do:

THE PIG [WHICH ATE THE TURNIPS] ESCAPED.

Moreover, if children are asked to repeat a sentence in which a main clause is interrupted by a relative clause, they tend to alter the sentence in order to avoid this happening. A child asked to repeat the sentence

THE OWL [WHO EATS CANDY] RUNS FAST

repeated it as:

THE OWL EAT A CANDY AND HE RUN FAST (Slobin and Welsh 1967).

Operating principles are not the whole answer, however. The four described above cannot account for the whole of acquisition. But as soon as we start adding to them – Slobin (1985b) lists forty – then they start to clash with one another. Every time we find one which doesn't work, we can claim it is because another one is in operation, cancelling out the first. This leads to the whole idea being vacuous (Bowerman 1985). Unless we can find out which have precedence, and how children cope in cases of conflict, then we are back at square one – looking for some basic principles which guide children through the morass of possibilities.

Some people have suggested that the principles interact with particular languages. If one operating principle works well, due to the structure of the language concerned, then it gets given priority over others (Bates and MacWhinney 1987a; MacWhinney 1987). For example, English has a fairly rigid word order. Children will repeatedly come across the same order for (say) verb + adverb (WALK SLOWLY, HOLD IT CAREFULLY, SHUT IT QUIETLY). Counter-evidence such as SOFTLY FALLS THE LIGHT OF DAY is rare. So evidence of word order is both easily available and reliable. So English children will pay particular attention to the order of words. In another language, such as Turkish, the ends of words may get extra scrutiny. According to this view, then, all the various operating principles are competing with one another, and the structure of the language determines which ones will win out over the others. But more work is needed to discover if this plausible idea works. There is still a considerable amount of work to be done before we fully understand the operation of the operating principles, and how they are guided.

Advancing and retreating

But how do children advance? And how do they retreat? Being endowed with a processing mechanism which involves certain outline expectations about language does not tell us exactly *how* a child acquires any particular construction. Nor does it tell us how children manage to abandon their mistakes. Let us consider these matters.

A construction does not pop up suddenly, like a chicken out of an egg. There may be quite a gap between its *emergence* (first appearance) and its *acquisition* (reliable use). A typical profile of a developing structure was outlined earlier, when we discussed Sally's past tenses (Chapter 6). Judging from Sally's behaviour, children learn the first examples of a construction by rote, without fully analysing them. In this way, a structure gets a firm hold in a few places. The child then tentatively experiments by extending it to new examples. If she gets reinforcement for these experiments, the construction is likely to proliferate, affecting more and more vocabulary items. As an end result, a rule is acquired.

This general pattern of 'lexical diffusion' (Chapter 6) occurs in more complex constructions also, such as sentences which contain the sequence TO + verb (Bloom, Tackeff and Lahey 1984):

FELIX TRIED TO REACH THE APPLE
I WANT THAT DOG TO STAY OUTSIDE

The earliest examples of this construction occur without any overt appearance of TO, as in:

I WANNA PEE-PEE
I WANNA TAKE KITTY

where the child had no realization that TO is a separate item. When a distinct TO did appear, children behaved as if it was fastened to the end of the previous verb, each of which was one of a small group of newly acquired verbs, such as TRY TO, LIKE TO, SUPPOSED TO, as in:

I LIKE TO   SEE GRANDMA
I TRY TO   STAY CLEAN.

Gradually, they added in more and more verbs. They also re-analysed their old WANNA sequences, and produced utterances such as:

I WANT TO   HOLD THE KITTY.

Finally, they began to acquire sentences in which a noun occurred between the first verb and TO:

I'LL HELP YOU   TO FIND THE BUTTONS
I WANT THIS DOLL   TO STAY HERE.

They therefore realized that TO was more closely associated with the second verb.

We have some notion, therefore, about how children typically advance as they acquire language. But the problem of retreat is trickier – how they backtrack in cases where they have gone wrong.

Retreating is hard to understand primarily because children are impervious to correction (Chapter 4). Negative evidence ('No, that's wrong') is ignored. So some internal correction mechanism must be at work. Nobody agrees on what this is (Bowerman 1987, 1988; Randall 1987). Let us consider three proposals concerning it, which we may label the 'contrast', 'explain variation', and 'flow with the tide' views.

The Principle of Contrast (Clark 1987) suggests that children are innately pre-programmed with the expectation that different forms will have different meanings (Chapter 6 and earlier this chapter). Various linguists have noticed this tendency, and given it slightly different labels. Sally (Chapter 6) provided a possible example. She may have realized that her private forms such as BUILDEN, HELPEN were no different from adult BUILT, HELPED. This may have led her to reconsider her own forms, and revise her rule.

The 'explain variation' viewpoint complements the 'contrast' principle and may work in cases where contrast fails. Supposedly, if children hear adults using two different forms which superficially mean the same thing, they look for a reason. This may lead them to alter their own grammar. For example, children might hear adults say:

MARION BAKED A CAKE FOR PETER
MARION BAKED PETER A CAKE.

If the Principle of Contrast worked, then the child should be resistant to acquiring both of these constructions with a word such as BAKE. Yet both are eventually acquired. But the problem is considerably worse than this, because some other verbs can only take one of the constructions:

DONALD OPENED THE DOOR FOR PAMELA
*DONALD OPENED PAMELA THE DOOR

The second of these is impossible, yet children say things such as:

MOMMY, OPEN HADWEN THE DOOR [MAZURKEWICH AND WHITE 1984].

How does this child discover that OPEN does not behave like BAKE?

A partial explanation is that children somehow notice that not all verbs can behave like BAKE. They then look around for a reason to predict which ones do, and which ones don't. In this case, they may discover that the person who is the recipient usually has to be able to possess the object in order to come in front of it. That is, you can say:

MARION BAKED PETER A CAKE
PETER'S CAKE WAS BAKED BY MARION

but not:

*DONALD OPENED PAMELA THE DOOR
*PAMELA'S DOOR WAS OPENED BY DONALD

(The second sentence is of course possible in itself, but it does not have the same meaning as DONALD OPENED THE DOOR FOR PAMELA). This discovery may lead them to reorganize their ideas as to which verbs take which structures.

'Flowing with the tide' is a fairly recent and highly controversial suggestion. This proposes that the child is highly responsive to the input she receives. Take the case of Sally. As she hears numerous new words, she notices that most of these have endings of the BUILT, HELPED type. As the numbers of words with the new (correct) ending increase, the child readjusts the old (incorrect) forms to fit in with the pattern of endings she now perceives to be the dominant one (Rumelhart and McClelland 1987). But although this type of ebbing and flowing may occasionally work with simple aspects of grammar, such as word endings, the 'flowing with the tide' approach involves a number of problems (Pinker and Prince 1988). For example, it assumes that the child is constantly readjusting everything all the time. Yet there is plenty of evidence that children's grammar reorganization happens in fits and starts, and does not always tie in neatly with the input she receives.

In conclusion, we do not fully understand the mechanisms behind children's retreats. The puzzle of why children do not simply rush ahead and produce enormously over generalized grammars 'constitutes one of the most intriguing and difficult challenges for all students of language acquisition' (Bowerman 1988, p. 73).

The state of the art

In this chapter we have tried to see exactly how children extract grammar from the data they hear around them. Chomsky appears to be wrong when he suggests that children are born with detailed linguistic knowledge which is triggered by only minimal exposure to language. In place of a Content Cuthbert, a child whose mind contains chunks of information about language, we should substitute a Process Peggy, a child whose mind is set up with puzzle-solving equipment.

Process Peggy seems to be geared specifically to language. Her achievements cannot be explained by her daily needs, her general cognitive ability, or her parents' speech, though these undoubtedly help her as she struggles to solve linguistic puzzles.

We now have some general idea of the kinds of linguistic expectations which Process Peggy brings to language, and how she advances as she acquires each new construction. But we are much less clear about how she backtracks, that is, how she discovers she has made a mistake, and reorganizes her grammar.

The exact proportion of specific language mechanisms to other aspects of intelligence is also unclear. It may be that the two are so inextricably mixed, we never shall succeed in fully untangling them. This is another question for the future.

Although we have now completed our discussion of language acquisition, there is one point which remains quite open. What kind of internal grammar does someone who has completed the acquisition of language have? In other words what does the internalized grammar of an adult look like? Is it a transformational grammar? This is the next question to be considered. But before that, we have a brief excursus in which we discuss the following topic: how did Chomsky conceive the idea of a transformational grammar in the first place?

8 Celestial unintelligibility
Why propose a transformational grammar?

'If any one of them can explain it,' said Alice, 'I'll give him sixpence. *I* don't believe there's an atom of meaning in it.'

'If there's no meaning in it,' said the King, 'that saves a world of trouble, you know, as we needn't try to find any. And yet I don't know,' he went on, 'I seem to see some meaning after all.'

LEWIS CARROLL
Alice in Wonderland

Linguists, particularly transformational linguists, are sometimes accused of being 'too abstract' and 'removed from reality'. For example, one reviewer has condemned 'that celestial unintelligibility which is the element where the true student of linguistics normally floats and dances' (Philip Toynbee, *Observer*). Yet almost all linguists, not just psycholinguists, are trying to find out about a speaker's mental 'grammar' – the internalized set of rules which enables someone to speak and understand their language. As Chomsky notes:

The linguist constructing a grammar of his language is in effect proposing a hypothesis concerning this internalized system. [CHOMSKY 1972a, p. 26]

So the question which naturally arises is this: if linguists are really trying to form theories about an internalized system, why did they hit on something as complex and abstract as transformational grammar? Surely there are other types of grammar which do not seem as odd? Some of the reasons for setting up a transformational grammar were mentioned in Chapter 1. But the question will be considered again from a different angle here.

Jupiter's stick insects

Suppose . . . a space ship full of English speakers had landed on Jupiter. They found the planet inhabited by a race of green stick insects who communicated by sitting down and wiggling their stick-like toes. The English speakers learned the Jupiter toe-wiggle language easily. It was a sign language like Washoe's in which signs stood for words, with no obvious structure. So communication was not a serious problem. But the Emperor of Jupiter became highly envious of these foreigners who were able to walk about *and* communicate at the same time. They did not have to stop, sit down, and wiggle their toes. He decided to learn English.

At first, he assumed the task was easy. He ordered his servants to record all the sentences uttered by the English speakers, together with their meanings. Each morning he locked himself into his study and memorized the sentences recorded on the previous day. He carried out this routine unswervingly for about a year, dutifully learning every single sentence spoken by the foreigners. As he was an inhabitant of Jupiter, he had no natural ability for understanding the way a language worked. So he did not detect any patterns in the words, he simply memorized them. Eventually, he decided he knew enough to start testing his knowledge in conversation with the Englishmen.

But the result was a disaster. He didn't seem to have learnt the sentences he needed to use. When he wanted to ask the Englishmen if they liked sea-urchin soup, the nearest sentence he could remember having learnt was 'This is funny-tasting soup. What kind is it?' When it rained, and he wanted to know if rain was likely to harm the foreigners, the most relevant sentence was 'It's raining, can we buy gumboots and umbrellas here?'

He began to have doubts about the task he had set himself of memorizing all English sentences. Would it ever come to an end? He understood that each sentence was composed of units called words, such as JAM, SIX, HELP, BUBBLE which kept recurring. But although he now recognized most of the words which cropped up, they kept appearing in new combinations, so the number of new sentences did not seem to be decreasing. Worse still, some of the sentences were extremely long. He recalled one in which an English speaker had been discussing a greedy boy: 'Alexander ate ten sausages, four jam tarts, two bananas, a Swiss roll, seven meringues, fourteen oranges, eight pieces of toast, fourteen apples, two ice-creams, three trifles and then he was sick.' The Emperor wondered despairingly what would have happened to the sentence if Alexander hadn't been sick. Would it have gone on for ever? Another sentence worried him, which an English speaker had read out of a magazine. It was a summary of previous episodes in a serial story: 'Virginia, who is employed as a governess at an old castle in Cornwall, falls in love with her employer's son Charles who is himself in love with a local beauty queen called Linda who has eyes only for the fisherman's nephew Philip who is obsessed with his half-sister Phyllis who loves the handsome young farmer Tom who cares only for his pigs.' Presumably the writer ran out of characters to describe, the Emperor reasoned. Otherwise, the sentence could have gone on even further.

The Emperor had therefore deduced for himself two fundamental facts about language. There are a finite number of elements which can be combined in a mathematically enormous number of ways. And it is *in principle* impossible to memorize every sentence because there is no linguistic bound on the length of a sentence. Innumerable 'sub'-sentences can be joined on to the original one, a process known as *conjoining*:

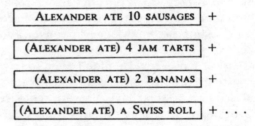

Alternatively, sub-sentences can be inserted or *embedded* inside the original one:

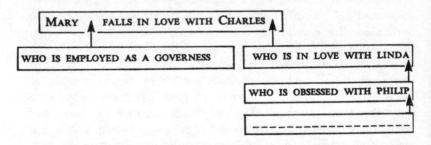

This property of language is known as RECURSIVENESS from the Latin to 'run through again' – you can repeatedly apply the same rule to one sentence, a process which could (in theory) go on for ever. Of course, in practice you would fall asleep, or get bored or get a sore throat. But these are not *linguistic* reasons for stopping. This means that no definite set of utterances can ever be assembled for any language.

The Emperor of Jupiter eventually concluded that memorization of all English sentences was impossible. He realized it was the *patterns* behind the utterances which mattered.

How should he discover what these were? One way would be to make a list of all the English words he had collected, and to note whereabouts in the sentence each one occurred. He started to do this. But he hit on problems almost immediately. He had a feeling that some of his sentences had mistakes in them, but he was not sure which ones. Was 'I hic have hic o dear hic hiccups' a well-formed English sentence or not? And what about 'I mean that what I wanted I think to say was this'?

His other problem was that he found gaps in the patterns, and he didn't know which ones were accidental, and which not. For example, he found four sentences containing the word ELEPHANT:

THE ELEPHANT CARRIED TEN PEOPLE
THE ELEPHANT SWALLOWED TEN BUNS
THE ELEPHANT WEIGHED TEN TONS
TEN PEOPLE WERE CARRIED BY THE ELEPHANT.

But he did not find:

TEN BUNS WERE SWALLOWED BY THE ELEPHANT
TEN TONS WERE WEIGHED BY THE ELEPHANT.

Why not? Were these gaps accidental? Or were the sentences ungrammatical? The Emperor did not know, and grew very depressed. He had discovered another important fact about language: collections of utterances must be treated with caution. They are full of false starts and slips of the tongue. And they constitute only a small subset of all possible utterances. In linguistic terms, a speaker's *performance* is likely to be a random sample bespattered with errors, and does not necessarily provide a very good guide to his *competence*, the internalized set of rules which underlie them.

The Emperor of Jupiter realized that he needed the help of the foreigners themselves. He arrested the spaceship captain, a man called Noam, and told him that he would free him as soon as he had written down the rules of English. Noam plainly knew them, since he could talk.

Noam was astounded. He pleaded with the Emperor, pointing out that speaking a language was an ability like walking which involved knowing *how* to do something. Such knowledge was not necessarily conscious. He tried to explain that philosophers on earth made a distinction between two kinds of knowing: knowing *that* and knowing *how*. Noam knew *that* Jupiter was a planet, and factual knowledge of this type was conscious knowledge. On the other hand, he knew *how* to talk and *how* to walk, though he had no idea how to convey this knowledge to others, since he carried out the actions required without being aware of how he actually managed to do them.

But the Emperor was adamant. Noam would not be freed until he had written down an explicit set of rules, parallel to the system internalized in his head.

Noam pondered. Where could he begin? After much thought he made a list of all the English words he could think of, then fed them into a computer with the instructions that it could combine them in any way whatsoever. First it was to print out all the words one by one, then all possible combinations of two words, then three words, then four words, and so on. The computer began churning out the words as programmed, and spewed out (in the four-word cycle) sequences such as:

DOG INTO INTO OF
UP UP UP UP
GOLDFISH MAY EAT CATS
THE ELEPHANT LOVED BUNS
DOWN OVER FROM THE
SKYLARKS KISS SNAILS BADLY.

Sooner or later, Noam reasoned, the computer would produce every English sentence.

Noam announced to the Emperor that the computer was programmed with rules which made it potentially capable of producing all possible sentences of English. The Emperor was suspicious that the task had been completed so quickly. And when he checked with the other foreigners, his fears were confirmed. The others pointed out that although Noam's computer programme could in theory generate *all* English sentences, it certainly did not generate *only* the sentences of English. Since the Emperor was looking for a device which paralleled a human's internalized grammar, Noam's programme must be rejected, because humans did not accept sentences such as:

DOG INTO INTO OF.

It was also unlikely that they would accept

GOLDFISH MAY EAT CATS
or SKYLARKS KISS SNAILS BADLY.

But there was nothing really wrong with these grammatically: these were accidental facts about the diet of goldfish and the amatory preferences of skylarks which need not be included in the grammar.

So Noam went away again and thought hard. It dawned on him that all sentences were straightforward word 'strings': they were composed of words strung together, one after the other. And the order in which they occurred was partially predictable. For example, THE had to be followed either by an adjective such as GOOD, LITTLE or by a noun such as FLOWER, CHEESE, or occasionally an adverb such as CAREFULLY as in

THE CAREFULLY NURTURED CHILD SCRIBBLED OBSCENE GRAFFITI ON THE WALLS.

Perhaps, he pondered, one's head contained a network of associations such that each word was in some way attached to the words which could follow it in a sentence. He started to devise a grammar which started with one word, which triggered off a choice between several others, which in turn moved to another choice, until the sentence was complete:

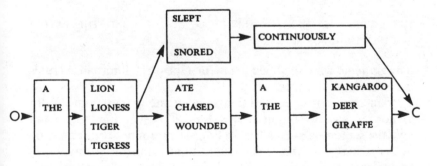

This simple device could account for quite a number of different sentences:

A LION ATE A KANGAROO
THE TIGRESS CHASED THE GIRAFFE,

and so on. If he continued to elaborate it, perhaps it could eventually include all possible sentences of English.

He presented it to the Emperor, who in turn showed it to the other

Englishmen. They pointed out a fatal flaw. Such a device could not possibly account for a speaker's internalized rules for English, because English (and all other languages) has sentences in which non-adjacent words are dependent on one another. For example, you can have a sentence:

THE LIONESS HURT HERSELF.

If each word triggered off the next only, then you would not be able to link the word following HURT with LIONESS, you would be just as likely to have

*THE LIONESS HURT HIMSELF.

Similarly, a sentence starting with EITHER, as in

EITHER BILL STOPS SINGING OR YOU FIND ME EAR PLUGS

would not fit into this system, since there would be no means of triggering the OR. Furthermore, in this left-to-right model, all the words had equal status, and were linked to one another like beads on a necklace. But in language, speakers treat 'chunks' of words as belonging together:

THE LITTLE RED HEN / WALKED SLOWLY / ALONG THE PATH / SCRATCHING FOR WORMS.

Any grammar which claimed to mirror a speaker's internalized rules must recognize this fact.

Noam, therefore, realized that an adequate grammar must fulfil at the very least two requirements. First, it must account for *all* and *only* the sentences of English. In linguistic terminology, it must be *observationally adequate*. Secondly, it must do so in a way which coincides with the intuitions of a native speaker. Such a grammar is spoken of as being *descriptively adequate*.

Noam decided, as a third attempt, to concentrate on a system which would capture the fact that sentences are split up into chunks of words which go together. He decided that a multi-layered, 'downward branching' system was the answer. At the top of the page he wrote the letter S to represent 'sentence'. Then he drew two branches forking from it, representing the shortest possible English sentence (not counting commands).

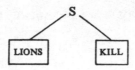

Then each branch was expanded into a longer phrase which could optionally replace it:

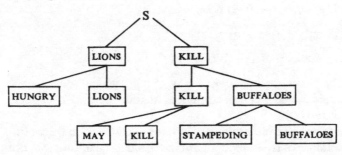

This tree diagram clearly captured the *hierarchical* structure of language, the fact that whole phrases can be the structural equivalent of one word. It diagrammed the fact that HUNGRY LIONS functions as a single unit in a way that KILL STAMPEDING does not.

The Emperor of Jupiter was delighted. For the first time he began to have an inkling of the way language worked. 'I want some soup . . . some seaweed soup . . . some hot seaweed soup . . . some steaming hot seaweed soup,' he murmured to himself, realizing the importance of Noam's new system.

The other Englishmen praised the system, but grudgingly. They admitted that the tree diagram worked very well for sentences such as

HUNGRY LIONS MAY KILL STAMPEDING BUFFALOES.

But they had one major objection. Did Noam realize just how many trees might be required for the whole language? And did he realize that sentences which speakers felt to be closely related would have quite different trees? For example:

HUNGRY LIONS MAY KILL STAMPEDING BUFFALOES

would have a tree quite different from

STAMPEDING BUFFALOES MAY BE KILLED BY HUNGRY LIONS.

And a sentence such as

TO CHOP DOWN LAMP-POSTS IS A DREADFUL CRIME

would have a different tree from

IT IS A DREADFUL CRIME TO CHOP DOWN LAMP-POSTS.

Worse still, had Noam noticed that sentences which were felt to be quite different by the speakers of the language had exactly the *same* trees?

THE BOY WAS LOATH TO WASH

had exactly the same tree as

THE BOY WAS DIFFICULT TO WASH.

Surely Noam could devise a system in which sentences felt by speakers to be similar could be linked up, and dissimilar ones separated?

After much contemplation, Noam realized he could economize on the number of trees needed, and he could also capture the intuitions of speakers that certain sentences were similar if he regarded similar sentences as belonging to the same basic tree! Actives and passives, for example, could be related to an underlying tree:

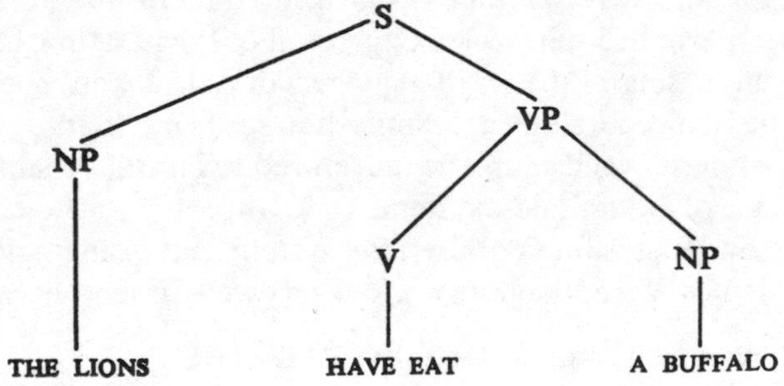

Then this 'deep structure' tree could be 'transformed' by operations known as transformations into different surface structure. It provided the basis for both the lions have eaten a buffalo and a buffalo has been eaten by lions.

Using the same principle, Noam realized that he could explain the similarity of

TO CHOP DOWN LAMP-POSTS IS A DREADFUL CRIME

IT IS A DREADFUL CRIME TO CHOP DOWN LAMP-POSTS.

Conversely, the difference between

THE BOY WAS LOATH TO WASH

THE BOY WAS DIFFICULT TO WASH

could be explained by suggesting that the sentences are connected to different deep structure strings.

The Emperor of Jupiter was delighted with Noam's latest attempt, and the other Englishmen agreed that Noam seemed to have hit on a very good solution. He appeared to have devised a clear, economical system which was able to account for *all* and *only* the sentences of English, and which also captured the intuitions of the speakers about the way their language worked. A further important bonus was that the system could possibly be used for French, Chinese, Turkish, Arawak, or any other language in the strange human world.

However, the Emperor was still somewhat puzzled. Had Noam explained to him how to actually *produce* English sentences? Or had he merely drawn him a map of the way in which related sentences were stored in an Englishman's head? Noam was rather vague when asked about this. He said that although the map idea seemed nearer the truth, the map nevertheless had important implications for the way in which sentences were produced and recognized. The Emperor was extremely puzzled by this statement. However, he decided that Noam had done some splendid work, and so should be set free, and rewarded handsomely. Meanwhile, the Emperor made a mental note that when he had some more spare time, he would have to contemplate more thoroughly the question of how Noam's proposals related to the way humans produced and recognized sentences.

Let us summarize what the Emperor of Jupiter had discovered about the nature of human language and the type of 'grammar' which can account for it. Firstly, he discovered that it is in principle impossible to memorize every sentence of a language, because there is no linguistic limit on the length of a sentence.

Secondly, he found that any collection of utterances must be treated with the utmost care. It contains slips of the tongue, and represents only a random sample of all possible utterances. For this reason it is important to focus attention on a speaker's underlying system of rules, his 'competence' rather than on an arbitrary collection of his utterances, or his 'performance'. Thirdly, the

Emperor realized that a good grammar of a language will not only be observationally adequate – one which can account for all the possible sentences of a language. It will also be descriptively adequate – that is, it will reflect the intuitions of the native speaker about his language. This meant that a simple, left-to-right model of language, in which each word was triggered by the one before it, was unworkable. It was observationally inadequate because it did not allow for non-adjacent words to be dependent on one another. And it was descriptively inadequate because it wrongly treated all words as being of equal value and linked together like beads on a string, when in practice language is hierarchically structured with 'chunks' of words going together.

Fourthly, the Emperor of Jupiter noted that a hierarchically structured top-to-bottom model of language was a reasonable proposal – but it did not link up sentences which were felt by the speakers to be closely related, such as

TO CHOP DOWN LAMP-POSTS IS A DREADFUL CRIME

and

IT IS A DREADFUL CRIME TO CHOP DOWN LAMP-POSTS.

On the other hand it wrongly linked up sentences such as

THE BOY WAS LOATH TO WASH

and

THE BOY WAS DIFFICULT TO WASH,

which seemed to be quite different. So finally, he became convinced that the most satisfactory system was a transformational model of language, in which sentences felt to be similar share the same deep structure. He came to believe that all sentences had both a hidden, deep structure and an obvious surface structure which might look quite different, and he accepted that these two levels were linked by processes known as transformations.

However, the Emperor remained puzzled about how this model of an internalized grammar might tie in with the way humans produce and comprehend sentences. He felt that Noam had been quite unclear on the topic.

Several of the things discovered by the mythical Emperor of Jupiter are points made by Noam Chomsky in his early, slim, but extremely influential work, *Syntactic Structures* (1957). In this, he explains why a left-to-right or 'finite-state' model of language is deficient, and also why a top-to-bottom or 'phrase structure' model is inadequate. He then justifies the need for a transformational grammar. He elaborated this basic model in his 'classic' work *Aspects of the Theory of Syntax* (1965). Within twenty years, however, his views had radically changed. Let us see how this alteration might be justified to the Emperor of Jupiter.

Return to Jupiter

Many years later, after he had orbited the universe several times, and been acclaimed as one of the pioneers of his century, Noam decided to return to Jupiter. He wanted to see how the Emperor was coping with his old transformational system. More importantly, he wanted to explain his new ideas on language.

Noam found the Emperor full of complaints. After Noam's departure from Jupiter, the Emperor had continued to work on Noam's system. He had been helped by some of Noam's spaceship colleagues who had stayed behind on Jupiter to do some research on the climate. But things just hadn't worked out as he had hoped.

The Emperor had two types of grumble. There were general grumbles about the whole system, and specific grumbles about particular transformations.

His main complaint was that the system just didn't work properly. He had hoped that by now he would have found a set of rules which could account for all the possible sentences of English, and no others. But in spite of working long hours, there were dozens of sentences which he'd heard Noam's colleagues speak, for which he hadn't been able to specify the full set of rules. And the very best set of rules he'd come up with still included numerous sentences which apparently weren't English.

Furthermore, he had considerable doubts about his trans-formational rules. As long as he got the right outcome, it didn't seem to matter very much how he got there. Almost anything could be transformed into anything! There seemed to be too much latitude. Surely the whole thing ought to be tightened up a bit?

Noam agreed with these general points. The Emperor had discovered for himself the same problems as Noam had noticed. It seemed almost impossible to find a definitive set of rules which could specify what was, and what was not, a permissible sentence of

English. The second, and more serious problem, was the enormous 'power' of the system: transformations appeared to be able to do almost anything. There were not enough constraints keeping them in check. A system which can do anything, as if with the wave of a magic wand, is not very informative.

Noam explained that he had been working very hard on the question of constraints. It was far more important, he had decided, to specify the general bounds within which human language worked, than to spend hours and hours fiddling with the exact rules which would account for any one particular language.

Encouraged by this, the Emperor started on his detailed complaints, which were mostly about transformations. First, he grumbled, some transformations were quite arbitrary, because they were linked to particular lexical items. You simply had to know which words were involved. For example, you could say:

FRED GAVE A GIRAFFE TO THE ZOO
FRED DONATED A GIRAFFE TO THE ZOO.

Then, a transformation supposedly specified that with GIVE, you could also say:

FRED GAVE THE ZOO A GIRAFFE.

But this transformation did not work with DONATE. You could not say:

*FRED DONATED THE ZOO A GIRAFFE.

Wasn't this odd? he asked.

Noam agreed that any transformation which was restricted to particular lexical items was not a proper transformation. Instead, it was part of the dictionary or 'lexicon' which existed in any speaker's mind. In his more recent system, he had moved information about the structures which could follow GIVE and DONATE into this dictionary.

The Emperor continued grumbling. Some transformations seemed to him pointless. Why did a sentence such as:

FENELLA THOUGHT THAT SHE WAS ILL

have a deep structure which included the word FENELLA twice, saying in effect:

FENELLA THOUGHT THAT FENELLA WAS ILL?

Wasn't this rather pointless? Couldn't one leave SHE in the deep structure, and add a note saying SHE referred to FENELLA?

Noam agreed that a transformation which changed FENELLA into SHE was quite unnecessary, and that the matter could be dealt with in the way the Emperor suggested. In any case, the linking up of a pronoun SHE to other words should be dealt with by the semantic component, not by a transformation.

The Emperor continued moaning. Why were there so many different transformations which all had more or less the same effect? Consider:

IT SEEMED THAT THE DUCHESS WAS DRUNK
IT WAS DIFFICULT TO PLEASE THE DUCHESS.

These two sentences were fairly like their deep structures, compared to two others, which involved bringing THE DUCHESS to the front:

THE DUCHESS SEEMED TO BE DRUNK
THE DUCHESS WAS DIFFICULT TO PLEASE.

Yet each sentence involved a different transformation! Supposedly, they had to be different, because the deep structures were different. Wasn't this unnecessary proliferation of transformations?

Noam agreed with this criticism. It was foolish to have different transformations which performed the same manoeuvre. In his recent system, they had been combined.

The Emperor in his moans and groans had outlined many of the problems which eventually surrounded old-style transformations. They were too powerful, there were too many of them, they were too disparate. Gradually, they were reduced in number. Some were handed over to other components of the grammar, others were combined. In the end, only one transformation survived. This moved items about, though within strict limits.

The Emperor was amazed! Fancy having a transformational grammar with hardly any transformations! How on Jupiter did such a system work?

Noam started waving his arms about in excitement as he propounded his new system. He was on the verge of specifying a genetic blueprint for language, he announced. There were a number of fixed principles, which worked for all languages. There were also others which allowed a limited amount of variation. If you specified these properly, you hardly needed any rules at all!

The Emperor looked doubtful. Perhaps Noam had contracted

space-sickness, which had sent him mad. How could one do without rules?

Noam tried to explain. Suppose you were designing a human being, he suggested. You had to give him or her a head. That would be a fixed principle. But the colour of the skin could vary in certain specified ways. As for doing away with rules, one might have a general principle saying: 'Limbs come in pairs'. Then one need not have separate rules which said: 'Humans have two arms' and 'Humans have two legs'. This sort of a system was applicable to language, he was convinced.

The Emperor was suspicious. Surely language was much too complicated to be dealt with in this simple way?

Not at all, argued Noam. On the contrary, language possibly consisted of a number of rather simple components. Each of the components worked in accordance with some quite straightforward principles, and they only appeared complex because of the way they interacted with principles from other components.

The Emperor seemed puzzled. So Noam used another analogy. 'Think of a human mouth,' he suggested. 'There's a mobile tongue which pushes food about. There are salivary glands which moisten it. And there are fixed teeth which grind it down. Each of these components is quite simple. Yet when they are working together, the interaction is quite complex, and the effect powerful!' (Matthei and Roeper 1983).

The Emperor was partially persuaded. He begged Noam to hand over his genetic blueprint for language. But Noam stalled. He hadn't yet worked out how many components were involved, he admitted, nor what the basic principles were. Matters would be clearer in a hundred or so years time, he predicted.

The Emperor felt quite frustrated. And he was even more puzzled as to how Noam's new system might link up with how humans understand and produce speech.

In this fictitious account, we have outlined several of the problems which caused disillusionment with transformations as they were formulated in the 'classic' (1965) version of transformational grammar. And we have put forward the general aims expressed by Chomsky first of all in *Lectures on Government and Binding* (1981), but expressed most clearly in *Knowledge of Language: Its Nature, Origin and Use* (1986). Chomsky is more concerned with specifying the nature of the human language system than with formulating a complete picture of any one language. He believes that a 'principles and parameters' approach (with parameter referring to a factor which can be set variably) will largely do away with rules. And he is convinced that the overall system is modular, in that it is composed of a set of modules (components) which are simple in themselves, but become complex when they interact with other modules.

But neither the new system nor the old system deals explicitly with how speakers and hearers actually *use* language. Let us now consider Chomsky's views on this topic.

Linguistic knowledge

Chomsky (1965) claimed that the grammar he proposed 'expresses the speaker-hearer's knowledge of the language'. This knowledge was latent or 'tacit', and 'may well not be immediately available to the user of the language' (Chomsky 1965, p. 21).

The notion of tacit or latent knowledge is a rather vague one, and may cover more than Chomsky intended. It seems to cover two types of knowledge. On the one hand, it consists of knowing *how* to produce and comprehend utterances. This involves using a rule system, but it does not necessarily involve any awareness of the rules – just as a spider can spin a web successfully without any awareness of the principles it is following. On the other hand, knowledge of a language also covers the ability to make various kinds of judgements about the language. The speaker does not only know the rules, but in addition, he knows something about that knowledge. For example, speakers can quickly distinguish between well-formed and deviant sentences. An English-speaker would unhesitatingly accept

HANK MUCH PREFERS CAVIARE TO SARDINES

but would quickly reject

*HANK CAVIARE TO SARDINES MUCH PREFERS.

In addition, mature speakers of a language can recognize sentence relatedness. They 'know' that

FADING FLOWERS LOOK SAD

is closely related to

FLOWERS WHICH ARE FADING LOOK SAD

and that

IT ASTONISHED US THAT BUZZ SWALLOWED THE OCTOPUS WHOLE

is related to

THAT BUZZ SWALLOWED THE OCTOPUS WHOLE ASTONISHED US.

Moreover, they can distinguish between sentences which look superficially alike but in fact are quite different, as in

EATING APPLES CAN BE GOOD FOR YOU.

(Is it good to eat a type of apple called an eating apple, or is any type of apple good to eat?), or

SHOOTING STARS CAN BE FRIGHTENING
SHOOTING BUFFALOES CAN BE FRIGHTENING.

(How do you know who is doing the shooting?)

There seems to be no doubt whatsoever that a 'classic' (1965) transformational grammar encapsulated this second type of knowledge, the speaker's awareness of language structure. People *do* have intuitions or knowledge of the type specified above, and a transformational grammar *does* seem to describe this. However, it is by no means clear how a transformational grammar relates to the first type of knowledge – the knowledge of how to actually *use* language. Although Chomsky claims that a speaker's internal grammar has an important bearing on the production and comprehension of utterances, he made it quite clear that this grammar 'does not, in itself, prescribe the character or functioning of a perceptual model or a model of speech production' (Chomsky 1965, p. 9). And he even labels as 'absurd' any attempt to link the grammar directly to processes of production and comprehension (Chomsky 1967, p. 399).

This viewpoint has persisted in his recent work, where he denies that knowledge has anything to do with ability to use a language: 'Ability is one thing, knowledge something quite different' (Chomsky 1986, p. 12), commenting that 'we should follow normal usage in distinguishing clearly between knowledge and ability to use that knowledge' (Chomsky 1986, p. 12). And as we have seen, the type of knowledge outlined in his more recent theories is considerably more abstract and deep-seated than that involved in a 'classic' transformational grammar.

In short, Chomsky is interested primarily in 'the system of knowledge that underlies the use and understanding of language' rather than in 'actual or potential behaviour' (Chomsky 1986, p. 24).

Let us put the matter in another way. Anyone who knows a language can do three things:

1	Produce sentences or 'encode'	LANGUAGE
2	Comprehend sentences or 'decode'	USAGE
3	Store linguistic knowledge	LANGUAGE KNOWLEDGE

We are saying that a transformational grammar seems undoubtedly to cover (3), but appears to be separate from, or only indirectly related to (1) and (2).

LANGUAGE USAGE		LANGUAGE KNOWLEDGE

This is a rather puzzling state of affairs. Is it possible for linguistic knowledge to be completely separate from language usage? If not, what could possibly be meant by saying that the two are 'indirectly related'? This is the topic of the next chapter.

9 The white elephant problem
Do we need a transformational grammar in order to speak?

'I have answered three questions, and that is enough,'
Said his father; 'don't give yourself airs!
Do you think I can listen all day to such stuff?
Be off, or I'll kick you downstairs!'

LEWIS CARROLL
Old Father William

In the last chapter we noted that a transformational grammar attempts to 'capture' a speaker's abstract knowledge of language. But it is not yet clear how knowledge relates to usage. According to Chomsky, the two are rather distant, since he denies that linguistic knowledge is directly related to the way we understand and produce utterances. This leads to a crucial and rather startling question: is a transformational grammar actually *irrelevant* to the problem of understanding and producing speech?

If we put this question to a hard-core linguist, he would probably answer: 'Of course language knowledge and language usage are not totally separate, they just have to be studied separately, because the relationship between them is indirect.'

If we persisted, and said, 'What exactly do you mean by an indirect relationship?' he would probably say: 'Look, please stop bothering me with silly questions. The relationship between language usage and language knowledge is not my concern. Let me put you straight. All normal people seem to have a tacit knowledge of their language. If that knowledge is there, it is my duty as a linguist to describe it. But it is not my job to tell you how that knowledge is used. I leave that to the psychologists.'

This, to a psycholinguist, seems an extremely unhappy state of affairs. She is just as much interested in language usage as language knowledge. In fact, she finds it quite odd that anybody is able to concentrate on one rather than the other of these factors, since they seem to her to go together rather closely. Consequently, in this chapter, we shall be briefly examining attempts made by psycholinguists over the last twenty or so years to assess the relationship between a transformational grammar and the way someone produces and comprehends sentences. We shall start by looking at the earliest psycholinguistic experiments on the topic, which were carried out in the early 1960s.

The years of illusion

When Chomsky's ideas spread across into the field of psychology in the early 1960s they made an immediate impact. Psychologists at once started to test the relevance of a transformational grammar to the way we process sentences. Predictably, their first instinct was to test whether there was a direct relationship between the two.

At this time, two different but similar viewpoints were put forward. The first is sometimes known as the 'correspondence hypothesis', and the second as the 'derivational theory of complexity' or DTC for short.

Supporters of the correspondence hypothesis postulated a close correspondence between the form of a transformational grammar, and the operations employed by someone when they produce or comprehend speech. Supposedly 'the sequence of rules used in the grammatical derivation of a sentence . . . corresponds step by step to the sequence of psychological processes that are executed when a person processes the sentence' (Hayes 1970, p. 5). The assumption was that when someone produces a sentence they first of all assemble the deep structure:

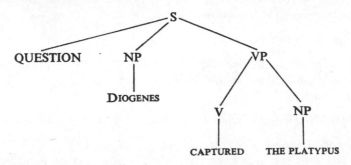

They then 'wind on' the transformations one by one, so that as an intermediate stage they might get:

QUESTION – THE PLATYPUS WAS CAPTURED BY DIOGENES

and finally

184   *The Articulate Mammal*

WAS THE PLATYPUS CAPTURED BY DIOGENES?

Decoding was thought to be the reverse of this procedure – a hearer was assumed to 'unwind' the transformations one by one. And finally, deep structure and transformations were presumed to be stored separately in the brain.

Supporters of DTC put forward a slightly weaker hypothesis. They suggested that the more complex the transformational derivation of a sentence – that is, the more transformations were involved – the more difficult it would be to produce or comprehend. They did not, however, assume a one-to-one correspondence between the speaker's mental processes and grammatical operations.

A number of experiments were devised to test these claims. Perhaps the two best-known are a sentence-matching experiment by George Miller of Harvard University (Miller 1962; Miller and McKean 1964), and a memorization experiment by Harris Savin and Ellen Perchonock, two psychologists from the University of Pennsylvania (Savin and Perchonock 1965).

George Miller reasoned that if the number of transformations significantly affected processing difficulty, then this difficulty should be measurable in terms of time. In other words, the more transformations a sentence had, the longer it should take to cope with. For example, a passive sentence such as

THE OLD WOMAN WAS WARNED BY JOE

should be harder to handle than a simple active affirmative declarative (or SAAD for short) such as

JOE WARNED THE OLD WOMAN,

since the passive sentence required an additional transformation. However, this passive should be easier to handle than a passive negative such as

THE OLD WOMAN WASN'T WARNED BY JOE

which required one more transformation still.

In order to test this hypothesis, Miller gave his subjects two columns of jumbled sentences, and asked them to find pairs which went together. The sentences to be paired differed from one another in a specified way. For example, in one section of the experiment actives and passives were jumbled, so that a passive such as

THE SMALL BOY WAS LIKED BY JANE

had to be matched with its 'partner'

JANE LIKED THE SMALL BOY.

And

JOE WARNED THE OLD WOMAN

had to be paired with

THE OLD WOMAN WAS WARNED BY JOE.

Miller assumed that the subjects had to strip the sentences of their transformations in order to match them up. The more they differed from each other, the longer the matching would take, he predicted.

Miller carried out this experiment twice, the second time with strict electronic time-controls (a so-called 'tachistoscopic' method). His results delighted him. Just as he had hoped, it took nearly twice as long to match sentences which differed by *two* transformations as it took to match sentences which differed by only one transformation. When he added the time needed to match actives with passives (approximately 1.65 seconds) to the time taken to pair affirmatives with negatives (approximately 1.40 seconds), the total added up to almost the same as that required for matching active with passive negative sentences (approximately 3.12 seconds).

Active ◄1·65►	*Passive*
JOE WARNED THE OLD WOMAN	THE OLD WOMAN WAS WARNED BY JOE
Affirmative ◄1·40►	*Negative*
JOE WARNED THE OLD WOMAN	JOE DIDN'T WARN THE OLD WOMAN
Active ◄3·12►	*Passive Negative*
JOE WARNED THE OLD WOMAN	THE OLD WOMAN WASN'T WARNED BY JOE

Miller seemed to have proved that transformations were 'psychologically real', since each transformation took up a measurable processing time – and his claim appeared to be strengthened by Savin and Perchonock's memorization experiment.

Savin and Perchonock asked their subjects to memorize short sentences followed by strings of unrelated words:

THE BOY HIT THE BALL – BUSH – COW – BUS – HOUR – CHAIR – RAIN –
  HAT – RED.
THE BOY DIDN'T HIT THE BALL – TREE – HORSE – SHIP – DAY – DESK –
  SNOW – COAT – GREEN.

The reason behind the experiment was as follows: a person's
immediate memory has a small constant capacity. It seems likely that
sentences which involve several transformations will take up more
memory space than those which involve only one or two. So they
predicted that the more transformations were added, the fewer
random words would be remembered. This prediction turned out to
be correct. With a straightforward SAAD sentence such as

THE BOY HIT THE BALL

subjects remembered on average five unrelated words. When one
extra transformation (such as passive or negative) was involved, they
remembered on average four words. When two extra transformations were added, subjects remembered only three words. The
conclusion drawn by Savin and Perchonock was that subjects
remembered sentences in their underlying form, with transformations tacked on separately as 'footnotes' which took up
measurable memory space.

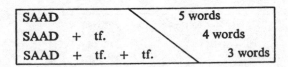

SAAD			5 words
SAAD	+ tf.		4 words
SAAD	+ tf.	+ tf.	3 words

Many psychologists were overjoyed at the results of these
experiments. Miller, it seemed, had shown that transformations took
up time in sentence matching experiments, and Savin and Perchonock
had demonstrated that they occupied memory space, and similar
experiments by other psychologists all pointed in the same direction
(e.g. Mehler 1963). Several people optimistically assumed that the
correspondence hypothesis was correct, and claimed that a new era
had dawned for psycholinguistics.

  But this period of illusion was shortlived. A time of disappointment and disillusion followed. Fodor and Garrett (1966) gave a
crushing paper at the Edinburgh University conference on psycholinguistics in March 1966, in which they clearly showed the emptiness
of the 'correspondence hypothesis' and DTC. They gave detailed
theoretical reasons why hearers do not 'unwind' transformations

when they decode speech. For example, the correspondence hypothesis entails the consequence that people do not begin to decode what they are hearing until a sentence is complete. It assumes that, after waiting until they have heard all of it, hearers then undress the sentence transformation by transformation. But this is clearly wrong, it would take much too long. In fact, it can be shown that hearers start to decode as soon as a speaker begins talking.

In addition, Fodor and Garrett pointed out flaws in the experiments carried out by Miller and Savin and Perchonock. The transformations, such as passive and negative, on which their results crucially depended, are atypical. Negatives change the meaning, and passives move the actor away from its normal place at the beginning of an English sentence. Passives and negatives are also longer than SAADs, so it is not surprising that they took longer to match and were more difficult to memorize. The difficulty of these sentences need not have anything to do with transformational complexity. Fodor and Garrett pointed out that there were other transformations which made no difference to processing difficulty. There was no detectable difference in the time taken to comprehend.

JOHN PHONES UP THE GIRL

and

JOHN PHONES THE GIRL UP.

If the correspondence hypothesis or DTC was correct, the second should be more difficult, because a 'particle separation' transformation has been applied, separating PHONES and UP. Worse still for the theory were sentences such as

BILL RUNS FASTER THAN JOHN RUNS
BILL RUNS FASTER THAN JOHN.

The second sentence had one more transformation than the first, because the word RUNS had been deleted. In theory it should be more difficult to comprehend, but in practice it was easier.

Fodor and Garrett followed their 1966 conference paper with another article in 1967 where they pointed out more problem constructions (Fodor and Garrett 1967). For example, DTC wrongly predicted that

THE TIRED SOLDIER FIRED THE SHOT

should be more complex to process than

THE SOLDIER WHO WAS TIRED FIRED THE SHOT

which (according to the 1965 version of transformational grammar) was closer to the deep structure. It also counter-intuitively treated 'truncated' passives such as

THE BOY WAS HIT

as more complex than full passives such as

THE BOY WAS HIT BY SOMEONE.

After this, researcher after researcher came up with similar difficulties. According to DTC,

THERE'S A DRAGON IN THE STREET

should have been more difficult to process than

A DRAGON IS IN THE STREET.

Yet the opposite is true. Similarly,

DEE IS HARD TO PLEASE

should be more complex than

FOR ANYONE TO PLEASE DEE IS HARD.

Yet in practice the first sentence is much simpler (Watt 1970).

Both the correspondence hypothesis and DTC had to be abandoned. Transformational grammar in its 'classic' form was not a model of the production and comprehension of speech, and derivational complexity as measured in terms of transformations did not correlate with processing complexity. Sentences that were transformationally complex were often simpler to produce and comprehend than those that were transformationally simple, and complexity itself was a far more complicated notion than was originally supposed. Clearly, Chomsky was right when he denied that there was a direct relationship between language knowledge, as encapsulated in a 1965 version of transformational grammar, and language usage.

The deep structure hypothesis

By the mid 1960s, the majority of psycholinguists had realized quite clearly that transformations as then formulated had no direct relevance to the way a person produces and understands a sentence.

However, the irrelevance of transformations did not mean that other aspects of transformational grammar were also irrelevant. So in the late 1960s another hypothesis was put forward – the suggestion that when people process sentences, they mentally set up a Chomsky-like deep structure. In other words, when someone produces, comprehends or recalls a sentence, 'the speaker-hearer's internal representation of grammatical relations is mediated by structures that are isomorphic to those that the grammatical formalism employs' (Fodor, Bever and Garrett 1974, p. 262). The experiments that were most relevant to this hypothesis were of two types: recall experiments and click experiments.

A number of recall experiments produced interesting results. Two of these will be described here. One was carried out by Blumenthal (1967) and the other by Wanner (1974).

Blumenthal asked his subjects to memorize pairs of sentences such as

GLOVES WERE MADE BY TAILORS
GLOVES WERE MADE BY HAND.

He then asked them to recall each sentence by prompting them with either the word TAILORS or the word HAND. When prompted by the word TAILORS, the subjects recalled the first sentence fairly well. But they were not nearly so successful with the second when prompted by the word HAND. What should we conclude from this? Blumenthal himself was fairly cautious in his assessment. He merely claimed that the experiment proved that simple slot-filling operations did not explain language, and that speakers are able to recognize the fundamentally different functions of TAILORS and HAND, although the sentences are superficially similar:

Apparently the implicit semantic and grammatical abilities of the Ss enabled them to infer different relational characteristics for sentences that were otherwise the same in observed phrase structure. [BLUMENTHAL 1967, p. 206]

But this is not particularly surprising, and tells us nothing new. More interesting were subsequent speculations as to why TAILORS was a better prompt than HAND. One suggestion was that subjects were remembering the deep structure configuration of the sentences.

In the deep structure, TAILORS was considerably more prominent. It was directly underneath, or 'dominated' by the S-node. In other words, it was one of the basic components of the sentence, and was essential to its intrinsic structure. But HAND was far less important.

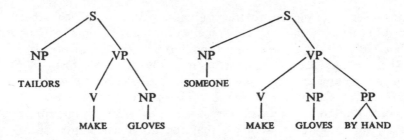

It appeared relatively low down on the deep structure tree. If subjects remembered sentences in terms of their deep structures, then it made sense that they should reconstruct them from the top of the tree downwards. But this was not the only possible explanation. TAILORS occurs frequently in speech without an accompanying BY, while HAND is often part of a set phrase BY HAND, so splitting up BY and HAND may have caused confusion, and hindered rather than aided recall.

The results of the recall experiment carried out by Wanner were less easy to explain away. He showed his subjects pairs of sentences such as

THE GOVERNOR ASKED THE DETECTIVES TO CEASE DRINKING
THE GOVERNOR ASKED THE DETECTIVES TO PREVENT DRINKING.

When prompted with the word DETECTIVES, the subjects tended to recall the first sentence more readily than the second. Why? It cannot be because the first sentence is more inherently memorable, since there was no difference in the level of recall of the two sentences when the word GOVERNOR was used as a prompt. One possible explanation put forward was that the word DETECTIVE occurred three times in the proposed deep structure of the first sentence, but only twice in that of the second sentence (once again, following a 1965 model).

This was an intriguing result. At first sight it seemed strongly to support the notion of a Chomskyan deep structure. But on closer inspection, the nature of the experiments might have falsified the results. The subjects were told in advance that the experiments involved memorization, and this might have affected their attitude. Two psychologists found that they got quite different results in a memorization experiment when they did not tell their subjects that they would be expected to recall the sentences (Johnson-Laird and Stevenson 1970). Furthermore, a number of psychologists have found that all memory of syntax and vocabulary normally fades very

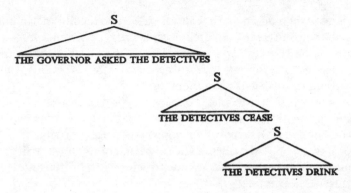

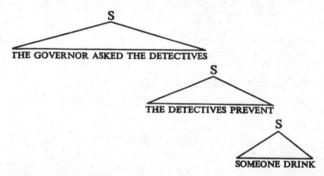

fast indeed, unless subjects are specifically told that they will be asked to recall the sentence. Memory for syntax of any kind is near to chance approximately half a minute after a sentence has been spoken (Sachs 1967). In normal circumstances, it seems, people remember only the gist of what has been said, and they often confuse this with a number of extra beliefs and expectations about the topic under discussion (Fillenbaum 1973). So it may be unrealistic to expect to find any syntax retained in normal recall. Johnson-Laird notes, 'No one knows how meaning is represented within memory, but there is no evidence to show that any form of syntactic structure is directly involved' (Johnson-Laird 1970, p. 269).

In brief, many psychologists now consider that recall experiments are irrelevant to the study of deep structure because of the natural tendency of humans to 'wipe away' the syntax and exact words of a sentence, unless they are carefully instructed to the contrary – in which case the experiment will reflect conscious memorization techniques which may be quite irrelevant to spontaneous language processing.

We must conclude, then, that although the two recall experiments we have discussed were *consistent* with the suggestion that humans utilize a Chomsky-like deep structure (1965 version) when they recall sentences, the experiments themselves are of dubious validity – and so we would be unwise to take them too seriously.

Let us now turn to the 'click' experiments carried out by Bever, Lackner and Kirk (1969). The object of these experiments was to test whether a person recovers a Chomsky-like deep structure (1965 version) when she decodes. The experimenters took pairs of sentences which had similar surface structures, but different deep structures. For example:

THE CORRUPT POLICE CAN'T BEAR CRIMINALS TO CONFESS QUICKLY
THE CORRUPT POLICE CAN'T FORCE CRIMINALS TO CONFESS QUICKLY.

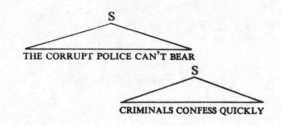

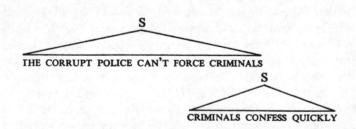

In the first sentence, the word *criminals* occurred once only in the deep structure, but in the second sentence it occurred twice, according to a 'classic' transformational model. If anyone doubts that these sentences have a different deep structure, try turning them round into the passive, and the difference becomes clear: the first sentence immediately becomes quite ungrammatical, though there is nothing wrong with the second:

*CRIMINALS CANNOT BE BORNE BY THE POLICE TO CONFESS QUICKLY

CRIMINALS CANNOT BE FORCED BY THE POLICE TO CONFESS QUICKLY.

In the experiment, the subjects were asked to wear headphones. Then the sentences were played into one ear, and a 'click' which occurred during the word CRIMINALS was played into the other. Subjects were asked to report whereabouts in the sentence they heard the click. In the first sentence, subjects tended to hear the click *before* the word CRIMINALS, where a Chomskyan deep-structure suggests a structural break:

THE CORRUPT POLICE CAN'T BEAR / CRIMINALS TO CONFESS QUICKLY.

But in the second sentence, the click stayed still, as if the hearers could not decide where the structural break occurred. They behaved as if CRIMINALS straddled the gap between the two sections of the sentence. Since CRIMINALS occurred twice in the deep structure, with the structural break between the two occurrences, this was a very encouraging result:

THE CORRUPT POLICE CAN'T FORCE CRIMINALS /
                              CRIMINALS TO CONFESS QUICKLY.

This suggested quite strongly that people recover a 'classic' deep structure when they decode a sentence.

But one swallow does not make a summer, and one experiment could not prove the validity of deep structure. In any case, as will be discussed below, any science proceeds by *disproving* hypotheses, not be proving them. Moreover, the significance of this particular experiment was disputed. Both its design and interpretation have been challenged. The results might have been due to the unusual experimental situation, or they could have been connected with meaning rather than with an underlying deep structure syntax (Fillenbaum 1971; Johnson-Laird 1974). The 'muddled history of clickology' (Johnson-Laird 1974, p. 138) is still a source of considerable controversy.

To summarize, the few experiments described in this section were *consistent* with the suggestion that people recover a Chomsky-like deep structure when they recall or understand sentences. But they were consistent with other hypotheses also. All that we could be sure about was that underlying every sentence was a set of internal relations which may well not be obvious on the surface. As Bever notes (1970, p. 286):

The fact that every sentence has an internal and external structure is maintained by all linguistic theories – although the theories may differ as to the role the internal structure plays within the linguistic description. Thus talking involves actively mapping internal structures on to external sequences, and understanding others involves mapping external sequences on to internal structures.

In other words, although it might seem rather *unlikely* that we recover a Chomskyan (1965) deep structure when we understand sentences, no one has actually disproved this possibility. No one has yet shown that the suggestion was totally false.

The point is, science proceeds by *disproving* hypotheses. Suppose you were interested in flowers. You might formulate a hypothesis, 'All roses are white, red, pink, orange or yellow.' There would be absolutely no point at all in collecting hundreds, thousands, or even millions of white, red, pink, orange and yellow roses. You would merely be collecting additional evidence consistent with your hypothesis. If you were genuinely interested in making a botanical advance, you would send people in all directions hunting for black, blue, mauve or green roses. Your hypothesis would stand until somebody found a blue rose. Then, in theory, you should be delighted that botany had made progress, and found out about blue roses. Naturally, when you formulate a hypothesis it has to be one which is capable of disproof. A hypothesis such as 'Henry VIII would have disliked spaceships' cannot be disproved, and consequently is useless. A hypothesis such as 'The planet Mars is made of chalk' would have been useless in the year AD 100, when there was no hope of getting to Mars – but it is a perfectly legitimate, if implausible, one in the twentieth century when planet probes and space travel are feasible.

This leads us back to Chomsky. Some people have claimed that deep structures cannot be disproved, and so are useless as a scientific hypothesis. It is true that, at the moment, it is difficult to see how to test them. But psycholinguistic experimentation is, in some ways, still in its infancy. Every year new techniques are introduced. In the last ten years or so an enormous amount of progress has been made. Perhaps with the development of further new techniques, ways will be found of definitively disproving theories about the 'inner structure' of a language. At the moment, as one psycholinguist notes, 'Presently available evidence on almost any psycholinguistic point is so scanty as to blunt any claim that this or that hypothesis has truly been disconfirmed' (Watt 1970, p. 138).

To sum up, the suggestion that people utilize a Chomskyan deep structure (1965 version) when they recall, comprehend or produce sentences seems unlikely, but the hypothesis has not been truly disconfirmed, and at the moment it is not clear how to do this.

The linguistic archive

We have now come to the conclusion that 1965-style transformations are irrelevant to sentence processing, and that deep structure is not necessarily relevant. The few clues we have are consistent with the deep structure hypothesis – but we can think up alternative explanations.

We are coming round to the view that a classic (1965) transformational grammar represents a kind of archive which sits in the brain ready for consultation, but is possibly only partially consulted in the course of a conversation. Perhaps it could be likened to other types of knowledge, such as the knowledge that four times three is the same as six times two. This information is mentally stored, but is not necessarily directly used when checking to see if the milk bill is correct.

Of course, the information may be represented in the brain in a rather different way from that suggested in a transformational grammar. But once again we are not in a position to *disprove* the transformational model. Until we *have* disproved it, we may say that a transformational grammar (1965-style) represents a linguistic archive which encapsulates a speaker's latent knowledge of her language.

We are *not* assuming a clean break between language knowledge and language usage. In practice the two overlap to a quite considerable extent, and the extent of the overlap varies from sentence to sentence.

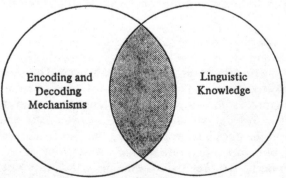

Let us take a simple example:

AUNT AGATHA WAS RUN OVER LAST THURSDAY.

A short passive of this type is generally simpler and quicker to comprehend than a full passive such as

AUNT AGATHA WAS RUN DOWN BY SOMEONE (OR SOMETHING) LAST THURSDAY.

It therefore seems quite unnecessary to suppose that, in order to understand the sentence, a hearer has to recover a Chomsky-like deep structure which includes the agent SOMEONE (or SOMETHING):

SOMEONE (or SOMETHING) RAN OVER AUNT AGATHA LAST THURSDAY.

Instead, he may not pay attention to the agent, he may be too busy thinking about Aunt Agatha. However, if he *did* spend rather longer pondering about the sentence, he could recover not only the agent SOMEONE (or SOMETHING) which the 'classic' deep structure suggests, but much more information in addition (Watt 1970). He could suggest that Aunt Agatha was run over by SOMETHING, rather than SOMEONE, and that this something was probably a MOVING VEHICLE. He obtained all this information from his knowledge of the lexical item RUN OVER – but it is optional whether he uses it or not when he comprehends the sentence.

And RUN OVER is not an isolated example. Other verbs from which a person could also extract a considerable amount of information if necessary are DEFLOWER and GORE. In

MARIGOLD WAS DEFLOWERED

he knows that SOMEONE deflowered Marigold, and that the deflowerer was likely to be male and human (Watt 1970). Similarly, in the sentence

CHARLIE WAS GORED

he can assume that the gorer was male and bovine. This information is *potentially* recoverable, though it *need* not be recovered.

In other words, someone who knows a language has an enormous amount of knowledge which she *could* use when she encodes or decodes, but she does not have to. Or rather, she usually has to use some of it, but often only a rather small proportion.

Another perhaps more obvious example is the sentence:

PALE PEOPLE EAT PINK PILLS.

It is quite unlikely that anyone recovers the full (1965) deep structure when she decodes or encodes this sentence, which is something like:

PEOPLE WHO ARE PALE EAT PILLS WHICH ARE PINK.

There is no doubt that speakers of English *can* relate PINK PILLS to PILLS WHICH ARE PINK – but there is no need for them to do so when they produce or hear this sentence. However, there may be other occasions when speakers *do* need to utilize rather more knowledge in their interpretation of a sentence which starts out in a similar fashion:

DROWNING HEFFALUMPS CAN CAUSE A TERRIBLE COMMOTION.

Here, the hearer might well subconsciously have to query, 'Are we dealing with heffalumps which are drowning, or someone who is drowning heffalumps?' And he might even put his query into words.

This again suggests that a 'classic' transformational grammar represents a linguistic archive whose contents are available for use when a person processes a sentence. In principle, someone could, if he wanted to, recover *all* the knowledge stored in connection with a sentence when he decodes or encodes it. This may be what Chomsky meant when he wrote that:

the generative grammar represents the information concerning sentence structure that is available, in principle, to one who has acquired a language. It indicates how, ideally . . . he would understand a sentence. [CHOMSKY 1963, p. 326]

The word 'ideally' may mean perfect understanding of the sentence as far as is possible within the limits of grammatical knowledge. Of course, in practice, no one has the time or the need to unravel every sentence in this way. Most people make a quick decision about the sentences they hear, and do not consider all the ramifications. In Bever's words, they rely on 'perceptual strategies' or short cuts, rather than on full utilization of 'epistemological structures' or beliefs about language structure (Bever 1970, p. 281).

But it would be a mistake to assume that 'epistemological structures' are an optional extra. A person who could not detect ambiguities, who could not make judgements of grammaticality and who could not link up related sentences would only 'know' their language in a very limited way. There is no clear-cut line between knowing *how* to utter and comprehend sentences, and knowing *that* these sentences are grammatical and how they are related to other sentences. Humans do not behave like spiders, who can weave webs without any conscious knowledge about their skill. Humans need knowledge about their language in order to function properly as articulate mammals. As far as language is concerned, the distinction between knowing *how* (as in knowing how to walk) and knowing *that* (as in knowing that the world is round) is a fuzzy one, because the two types of knowledge overlap.

Let us summarize what we have just said. We have concluded that a transformational grammar, in its classic form, incorporates mainly 'archival knowledge' or 'epistemological structures' – a set of beliefs or intuitions about one's language which may not necessarily be recoverable at a conscious level. These beliefs are not merely optional extras, they are an essential part of anyone's ability to speak and understand a language.

We need to ask a further question about these 'epistemological structures', and that is, how are they acquired? Do children learn how to use language, then later build up full knowledge about it, as Bever suggests (1970)? Or do the two learning processes go on simultaneously? This question has been studied by three psychologists from the University of Pennsylvania (Gleitman, Gleitman and Shipley 1972). They concluded that the process of learning how to speak was intertwined with that of acquiring beliefs about one's language. Both types of knowledge progress simultaneously, though the latter develops considerably more slowly. Even 2-year-olds have *some* notion of grammaticality, though this is rather shaky. And children's judgements about their language remain shaky even when they can speak fluently. It is between the ages of 5 and 8 that children start to have intuitions about their language that parallel those of an adult. Let us illustrate these points.

The fact that even quite young children have some beliefs about their language is shown by 2-year-old Allison, who judged the sequence

*BALL ME THE THROW

to be 'silly', and corrected it to

THROW ME THE BALL.

Similarly, 2-year-old Sarah amended

SONG ME A SING

to

SING ME A SONG.

However, Sarah's judgements were not consistently reliable, since she found

WASH THE DISHES

an odd sentence, and corrected it to

WASH THE DISHES(!)

It was easier to elicit responses from the older children, and the results were more clear cut. For example, when seven children between the ages of 5 and 8 were asked whether the sentence

I AM KNOWING YOUR SISTER

sounded 'sensible' or 'silly', the 5- and 6-year-olds found nothing wrong with it, but the 7- and 8-year-olds disapproved of it, though they could not always say why it was odd. The following is the response given by 7-year-old Claire:

R (Researcher): How about this one: I AM KNOWING YOUR SISTER
C (Claire): No. I KNOW YOUR SISTER
R: Why not I AM KNOWING YOUR SISTER? You can say I AM
   EATING YOUR DINNER.
C: It's different! (*shouting*) You say different sentences in different ways. Otherwise it doesn't make sense!

But for other sentences, Claire not only gave adult judgements concerning grammaticality, she also gave an adult-type reason:

R: How about this one: BOY IS AT THE DOOR.
C: If his name is BOY. You should – the kid is named John, see? JOHN
   IS AT THE DOOR or A BOY IS AT THE DOOR.

The researchers note:

The ability to reflect upon language dramatically increases with age. The older children were better not only in noting deviance but also in explaining where the deviance lies. [GLEITMAN, GLEITMAN AND SHIPLEY 1972, p. 160]

Spontaneous repairs – cases in which a child corrects itself without prompting – provide an alternative way of looking at children's awareness of language structure (Karmiloff-Smith 1986). Younger children often provide unnecessary repairs, as in

YOU PUT THE CHURCH – THE TINY LITTLE CHURCH INTO THE TIN.

Since only one church was involved, this alteration by a 4-year-old was not essential. Slightly older children tend to correct themselves if their original speech could lead to misunderstanding:

LEND ME THE BALL – THE GREEN BALL.

This repair by a 5-year-old was important, because there were several different colour balls around. However, the most sophisticated repairs are those which are inessential for getting across the right message, yet show a deep understanding of the linguistic system:

AND THEN FORTUNATELY THE GIRL – A GIRL OFFERS THE DOG A BONE.

Since there was only one girl in the story, this 6-year-old need not have changed *the* to *a*. But since no girl had yet appeared in the story, the change reflected a realization that it would have been correct to use *the* only if a girl had previously been mentioned.

Repairs, then, reflect a deepening awareness of the linguistic system. First, children can correctly use constructions, but cannot repair their mistakes. At a later stage, they begin to use repairs, sometimes sophisticated ones. Finally, they are able to explain various linguistic points.

Psycholinguistics without linguistics?

We can now summarize the conclusions we have reached in this chapter. We have been examining the relationship between language knowledge (as 'captured' by the classic version of transformational grammar) to the way in which we produce and comprehend sentences. In the first section we noted that transformations were irrelevant to the way in which we encode and decode. In the second section, we saw that the hypothesis that we recover a classic Chomsky-like deep structure when we comprehend a sentence has not been disproved, but is on the whole unlikely. In the final section we concluded that a 1965 transformational grammar represents a person's linguistic archive – a store of knowledge about language that is only partially utilized in the course of conversations. This archive develops simultaneously with, though rather more slowly than, the ability to speak and comprehend sentences.

Chomsky's latest ideas, however, have not been discussed. This is largely because they have not been tested by psychologists, for two reasons. First, many of them have turned away from transformational grammar in disappointment. As one notes: 'By the mid 1970s there remained no unequivocal evidence that transformational grammars provided a model of either the rules or representations that listeners and speakers use during comprehension. As a result, psycho-linguistics largely severed its ties with linguistics' (Tanenhaus 1988, p. 11). Secondly, Chomsky's latest ideas are mostly too imprecise and abstract to test.

Does this mean that psycholinguists can safely ignore Chomsky in the future? Should they either turn to other linguistic theories (Chapter 12) or give up linguistics altogether?

In order to answer this point, let us briefly consider the relationship of language knowledge to usage in a 'principles and parameters' (1986-style) system. Perhaps a cooking analogy might make this clearer, since it can illustrate the various levels of knowledge that might be involved.

Take chocolate mousse. Even a child might make a perfect mousse by following instructions, without any understanding of what she was doing, or what a mousse should look like. In language, this is equivalent to a young child who can talk, but has as yet little awareness of linguistic structure. Chomsky, as we have seen, has never regarded this 'how to do it' level as being his concern.

The next level involves a notion of what a proper mousse should look like, as well as a growing understanding of how a chocolate mousse relates in its composition to other mousses, such as salmon mousse or lemon mousse. In language, this is the level at which a person can reliably judge what is, and what is not a well-formed sentence. It is also the level at which sentences such as IT IS EASY TO HANDLE FLAMINGOS and FLAMINGOS ARE EASY TO HANDLE can be judged to be paraphrases of one another. This is the type of knowledge encapsulated in the classic version of a transformational grammar.

But there is a final, more basic level. This is the discovery that there are only a few fundamental principles underlying the whole of cooking. For example, trapping gas particles within food is the way to make it large in volume and light, a process found in mousse and buns. Or heating causes liquid to evaporate, and the remaining molecules to cling together, as in fried eggs or fudge. These principles are so general, and apply to such a wide range of foods, that they are unlikely to become apparent to the average cook, although she may underlyingly 'know' them, as she prepares food. In relation to language, this basic level is the one Chomsky is aiming at: a few simple principles which will show how the whole thing works.

Such a grandiose aim, if achieved, would be of great importance to psycholinguists. At the moment, it is unclear how one might test Chomsky's fluctuating and somewhat vague proposals (as we have already noted). He himself has likened linguistic theories to those put forward by physicists to account for why the sun's light gets converted into heat (Chomsky 1978, p. 202). Scientists cannot send a probe into the sun, so they have to make the best guess they can from the light emitted at the sun's outermost layers. Linguists cannot as yet identify grammar in the brain, so similar guesses have to be made.

Such theory-building is a valid enterprise. Speculation has led to great steps forward in some areas of science. It would therefore be foolish of psycholinguists to ignore it. Meanwhile, it makes sense for them to push ahead, finding out independently how humans understand and produce speech. These are the topics of the next two chapters.

10 The case of the missing fingerprint
How do we understand speech?

'It seems very pretty,' Alice said, 'but it's rather hard to understand.' You see, she didn't like to confess, even to herself, that she couldn't make it out at all. 'Somehow it seems to fill my head with ideas – only I don't know exactly what they are!'

LEWIS CARROLL
Through the Looking Glass

'Sentence comprehension is like riding a bicycle – a feat far easier performed than described' (Cutler 1976, p. 134). This feat is the topic of this chapter.

First, however, we should consider whether there might be a link between speech comprehension ('decoding') and production ('encoding'). It would be simpler for psycholinguists if they were directly related. However, there is no reason to assume this is so, any more than we should presume that the same muscles are used in sucking and blowing. We must therefore allow for four possibilities:

1 Encoding and decoding are totally different.
2 Decoding is encoding in reverse.
3 Decoding is the same as encoding: that is, decoders reconstruct the message for themselves in the same way as they would construct it if they were speakers.
4 Decoding and encoding are partially the same, and partially different.

This range of options means that we must deal with comprehension and production separately. We shall begin with speech understanding, because this has been more intensively studied.

How should we set about this? One useful way is to note down utterances which hearers find difficult to comprehend, and then find out why. Let us give some examples.

A card pinned to the door of a Bayswater flat said: 'Milkman, please stop milk until July 3. If you do not see this, THE WOMAN WHO HAS THE FLAT ON THE GROUND FLOOR'S SISTER will tell you.' It possibly took the milkman some time to realize who was supposed to be telling him about the milk. Yet there is nothing actually *wrong* with this sentence grammatically. It just takes a long time to process.

A similar example is

THE PIG PUSHED IN FRONT OF THE PIGLETS ATE ALL THE FOOD.

Again, there is nothing really wrong with this sentence. Compare:

THE GIRL PUSHED IN FRONT OF THE BUS ESCAPED WITH MINOR INJURIES.

A more extreme example is:

THE CAT THE DOG THE MAN THE BABY TRIPPED UP BIT SCRATCHED COLLAPSED

(The baby tripped up the man, the man bit the dog, the dog scratched the cat, the cat collapsed).

This is an exceptionally difficult sentence to cope with. Some people find it impossible. But, again, there is nothing tangibly *wrong* with it grammatically. Somehow or other, it is just too complex to be dealt with easily.

If we can satisfactorily account for why these sentences are difficult to understand, we shall have discovered quite a lot about decoding mechanisms.

Ambiguous sentences provide an alternative approach. Consider the following report of a millionaire's activities in the London *Sunday Times*:

His problems began on April 30th this year in Cannes when he left his summer apartment in his white Rolls-Royce and drove a friend to the Monte Carlo branch of an American bank.

No wonder he had problems, if he tried to put his apartment into his car. Judging from the syntax, this is the most likely interpretation. But was anybody genuinely led 'up the garden path' by this sentence, perhaps for a fraction of a second? Or did they use their common sense to realize immediately that even a millionaire's car would not be big enough for his villa? Or did they subconsciously consider both possibilities, then plump for the most plausible one? The solution to this problem would tell us a lot about the way people comprehend sentences.

Broadly speaking, a hearer is likely to reject a possible interpretation, or find a sentence hard to comprehend if:

1 It goes against their expectations.
2 It goes beyond certain 'psychological' limits.

Let us consider each of these. But we will first of all show that decoding is not the simple matter it was once thought to be. People do not passively 'register' the sentences uttered by a speaker. Instead they hear what they *expect* to hear. They actively reconstruct both the sounds and syntax of an utterance in accordance with their expectations.

Hearing what we expect to hear

Until relatively recently, psycholinguists assumed that the process of understanding or decoding speech was a simple one. The hearer was envisaged, metaphorically, as a secretary sitting at a typewriter taking down a dictation. She mentally 'typed out' the sounds she heard one by one, then 'read off' the words formed by them. Or, taking another metaphor, the hearer was envisaged as a detective solving a crime by matching fingerprints to known criminals. All the detective had to do was match a fingerprint found on the scene of the crime against one on his files, and see who it belonged to. Just as no two people's fingerprints are the same, so each sound was regarded as having a unique acoustic pattern.

Unfortunately, this simple picture turns out to be wrong. A series of experiments conducted by phoneticians and psycholinguists have disproved the 'passive secretary' or 'fingerprints' approach. There are a number of problems.

First of all, it is clear that hearers cannot 'take down' or 'match' sounds one by one. Apart from anything else, the speed of utterance makes this an impossible task. If we assume an average of four sounds per English word, and a speed of five words a second, we are expecting the ear and brain to cope with around twenty sounds a second. But humans cannot process this number of separate signals in that time – it is just too many (Liberman *et al.* 1967).

A second reason why the 'passive secretary' or 'fingerprint' approach does not work is that there is no fixed acoustic representation of, say, a T, parallel to the fixed typewriter symbol T. The acoustic traces left by sounds are quite unlike the fingerprints left by criminals. In actual speech, each sound varies considerably depending on what comes before and after it. The T in TOP differs from the T in STOP or the T in BOTTLE. In addition, a sound varies from speaker to speaker to a quite surprising extent. So direct 'copy-typing' or 'matching' of each sound is impossible. If it were feasible, cheap machines which could do this would long ago have flooded the market and made audio-typists an irrelevant luxury.

A third, related problem is that sounds are acoustically on a continuum: B gradually shades into D which in turn shades into G. There is no definite borderline between acoustically similar sounds, just as it is not always possible to distinguish between a flower vase and a mug, or a bush and a tree (Liberman *et al*. 1957).

These findings indicate that there is no sure way in which a human can 'fingerprint' a sound or match it to a mental 'typewriter symbol', because the acoustic patterns of sounds are not fixed and distinct. And even if they were, people would not have time to identify each one positively. The information extracted from the sound waves forms 'no more than a rough guide to the sense of the message, a kind of scaffolding upon which the listener constructs or reconstructs the sentences' (Fry 1970, p. 31).

In interpreting speech sounds, hearers are like detectives who find that solving a crime is not a simple case of matching fingerprints to criminals. Instead, they find a situation where 'a given type of clue might have been left by any of a number of criminals or where a given criminal might have left any of a number of different types of clue' (Fodor, Bever and Garrett 1974, p. 301). What they are faced with is 'more like the array of disparate data from which Sherlock Holmes deduces the identity of the criminal'. In such cases, the detectives' background information must come into play.

In other words, deciphering the sounds of speech is an *active* not a passive process. Hearers have to compute *actively* the possible phonetic message by using their background knowledge of the language. This is perhaps not so astonishing. We have plenty of other evidence for the active nature of this process. We all know how difficult it is to hear the exact sounds of a foreign word. This is because we are so busy imposing on it what we expect to hear, in terms of our own language habits, that we fail to notice certain novel features.

However, it is not only a person's expectation of sound patterns that influences what she hears, but perhaps to an even greater extent, her expectation of syntactic and semantic patterns. We cannot yet be completely sure how we disentangle these, since 'almost every aspect of sentence recognition remains unsettled despite the experimental attention that the problem has recently received' (Fodor, Bever and Garrett 1974, p. 374). But one overall fact seems clear. When someone hears a sentence, she often latches on to outline clues, and 'jumps to conclusions' about what she is hearing. An analogy might make this clearer. Suppose someone found a large foot sticking out from under her bed one night. She would be likely to shriek 'There's a man under my bed', because past experience has led her to believe that large feet are usually attached to male human beings. Instead of just reporting the actual situation. 'There is a foot sticking out from under the bed', she has jumped to the conclusion that this foot belongs to a man, and this man is lying under the bed. The evidence suggests that we make similar 'informed guesses' about the material we hear.

The kind of guesses a person makes depends very much on what she expects to hear. So this is the next question we must tackle. What kind of expectations do people bring to the task of sentence comprehension? And what kind of clues do they look for? One of the first people to work on this was Tom Bever, a psychologist at Columbia University, New York. The next section is based to a large extent on suggestions made by him (1970).

Informed guesses

Hearers approach the sentences of English with at least four basic assumptions, according to Bever (1970). Guided by their expecta-tions, they devise rules of thumb or 'strategies' for dealing with what they hear. Let us briefly consider these assumptions and linked strategies. Although we shall be labelling them 'first', 'second', 'third' and 'fourth', this is not meant to refer to the order in which they are used, since all four may be working simultaneously.

Assumption 1 'Every sentence consists of one or more sentoids or sentence-like chunks, and each sentoid normally includes a noun-phrase followed by a verb, optionally followed by another noun-phrase.' That is, every sentence will either be a simple one such as

DO YOU LIKE CURRY?
TADPOLES TURN INTO FROGS
DON'T TOUCH THAT WIRE

or it will be a 'complex' one containing more than one sentence-like structure or sentoid. For example, the sentence

IT IS NOT SURPRISING THAT THE FACT THAT PETER SINGS IN HIS
  BATH UPSETS THE LANDLADY

contains three sentoids:

IT IS NOT SURPRISING

THAT THE FACT UPSETS THE LANDLADY

THAT PETER SINGS IN HIS BATH.

Within a sentence, each sentoid normally contains either a noun phrase–verb sequence such as

THE LARGE GORILLA GROWLED

or a noun phrase–verb–noun phrase sequence such as

COWS CHEW THE CUD.

The strategy or working principle which follows from assumption 1 seems to be: 'Divide each sentence up into sentoids by looking for noun phrase–verb (–noun phrase) sequences.' This is sometimes referred to as the *canonical sentoid* strategy, since noun phrase–verb–noun phrase is the 'canonical' or standard form of an English sentence. It is clear that we need such a strategy when we distinguish sentoids, since there are often no acoustic clues to help us divide a sentence up. We noted in Chapter 1 that subjects could not possibly have been using acoustic information when they correctly divided into two clauses the sentence:

IN ORDER TO CATCH HIS TRAIN/GEORGE DROVE FURIOUSLY TO THE STATION.

Fodor, Garrett and Bever note:

An early stage in the perceptual analysis of linguistic material is the identification of the sentoids of which the input sentence is composed. By hypothesis, each such sentoid will consist of a subject NP and a verb which may or may not have an object. [FODOR, BEVER AND GARRETT 1974, p. 344]

A clear confirmation of this strategy comes when people are presented with a sentence such as

LLOYD KICKED THE BALL KICKED IT

which was said in a football commentary. Most people deny that it is possible, claiming it must be

LLOYD KICKED THE BALL THEN KICKED IT AGAIN.

But it is a well-formed English sentence, as shown by the similar one

LLOYD THROWN THE BALL KICKED IT.

People just cannot think of the interpretation 'to whom the ball was kicked', the canonical sentoid strategy is too strong. And similar examples abound in the literature, the most famous being:

THE HORSE RACED PAST THE BARN FELL.

A common comment about this one is: 'I can't understand it because I don't know the word "barnfell".' The alternative interpretation of RACED as 'was raced' is rarely considered.

Further confirmation of this strategy comes from so-called 'centre embeddings' – sentences which have a Chinese box-like structure, one lying inside the other. The following is a double centre embedding – one sentence is inside another which is inside yet another.

THE MAN THE GIRL THE BOY MET BELIEVED LAUGHED.

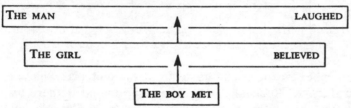

(The man laughed; the girl believed the man; the boy met the girl.) Blumenthal tested to see what happened when sentences of this type were memorized (1966). He noted that subjects tended to recall them as noun–verb sequences:

THE MAN, THE GIRL AND THE BOY MET, BELIEVED AND LAUGHED.

Their immediate reaction to being presented with an unusual sentence was to utilize the canonical sentoid strategy even though it was, strictly speaking, irrelevant. In a later experiment, Bever found to his surprise that subjects imposed an NP–V–NP sequence on sentences of this type *even after practice*. He comments, 'the NVN sequence is so compelling that it may be described as a 'linguistic illusion' which training cannot readily overcome' (Bever 1970, p. 295).

The canonical sentoid strategy seems to start young. Bever notes that by around the age of 2, children are already looking out for noun–verb sequences – though they tend to assume that the first noun goes with the first verb, and interpret

THE DOG THAT JUMPED FELL

as

THE DOG JUMPED.

Assumption 2 'In a noun phrase–verb–noun phrase sequence, the first noun is usually the actor and the second the object.' That is, an English sentence normally has the word order actor–action–object with the person doing the action coming first as in

GIRAFFES EAT LEAVES
DIOGENES BOUGHT A BARREL.

The strategy which stems from assumption 2, seems to be as follows: 'Interpret an NP–V–NP sequence as actor–action–object unless you have strong indications to the contrary.'

NP	V	NP
|	|	|
actor	action	object
|	|	|
PENGUINS	EAT	FISH

A number of experiments have shown that sentences which do not have the actor first take longer to comprehend if there are no semantic clues. The best known of these is Slobin's 'picture verification' experiment (1966a). He showed subjects pictures, and also ready them out a sentence. Then he timed how long it took them to say whether the two matched. He found that passives such as

THE CAT WAS CHASED BY THE DOG

took longer to verify than the corresponding active

THE DOG CHASED THE CAT.

Another picture verification experiment showed that actor–action–object structures are comprehended more quickly than other structures which would fit the NP–V–NP sequence (Mehler and Carey 1968):

THEY	ARE KIDNAPPING	BABIES
|	|	|
actor	action	object

was verified more quickly than

THEY	ARE	NOURISHING LUNCHES
subject	copula	complement

Assumption 3 'When a complex sentence is composed of a main clause and one or more subordinate clauses, the main clause usually comes first.' That is, it is more usual to find a sentence such as

NERO FIDDLED [WHILE ROME BURNED]

than

[WHILE ROME BURNED] NERO FIDDLED.

Similarly,

PETRONELLA EXPECTED [THAT PERICLES WOULD SCRUB THE FLOOR]

is considerably more likely than

*[THAT PERICLES WOULD SCRUB THE FLOOR] PETRONELLA EXPECTED.

   The strategy which follows from assumption 3 seems to be, 'Interpret the first clause as the main clause unless you have clear indications to the contrary.' The existence of this strategy accounts for the correct interpretation of

IT WAS OBVIOUS HE WAS DRUNK FROM THE WAY HE STAGGERED ACROSS THE ROAD.

Here, the subordinate clause is not marked in any way, but the hearer automatically assumes that it comes after the main clause. This strategy also partly accounts for the difficulty of

THE ELEPHANT SQUEEZED INTO A TELEPHONE BOOTH COLLAPSED.

Until she comes across the unexpected word COLLAPSED at the end of the sentence the hearer probably assumes that THE ELEPHANT SQUEEZED . . . was the beginning of the main clause. Further evidence in support of this strategy is the fact that sentences in which the subordinate clause occurs first are relatively hard to memorize. Subjects remembered

HE TOOTED THE HORN BEFORE HE SWIPED THE CABBAGES

more accurately than

AFTER HE TOOTED THE HORN HE SWIPED THE CABBAGES.

[CLARK AND CLARK 1968]

Assumption 4 'Sentences usually make sense.' That is, people generally say things that are sensible. They utter sequences such as

HAVE YOU DONE THE WASHING UP?
THE TRAIN GOES AT EIGHT O'CLOCK

rather than

HAPPINESS SHOOTS LLAMAS
THE HONEY SPREAD MOTHER WITH A KNIFE.

The strategy attached to this assumption is the most powerful of all – though from the linguistic point of view, it is the least satisfactory because it is so vague. It says: 'Use your knowledge of the world to pick the most likely interpretation of the sentence you are hearing.' In certain circumstances this can override all other strategies, and reverse well-attested aspects of language behaviour. For example, under normal circumstances people find it much easier to remember sentences that are superficially grammatical than random strings of words. It is considerably easier to learn the apparently grammatical

THE YIGS WUR VUMLY RIXING HUM IN JEGEST MIV

than the shorter string

THE YIG WUR VUM RIX HUM IN JEG MIV. [EPSTEIN 1961]

But this well-attested result can be *reversed* if the subjects are presented with semantically strange grammatical sentences and ungrammatical strings of words which appear to make sense. Subjects remember more words from strings such as:

NEIGHBOURS SLEEPING NOISY WAKE PARTIES
DETER DRIVERS ACCIDENTS FATAL CARELESS

than they do from sentences such as:

RAPID BOUQUETS DETER SUDDEN NEIGHBOURS
PINK ACCIDENTS CAUSE SLEEPING STORMS. [MARKS AND MILLER 1964].

This expectation that the world will make sense is brought into play in decoding. In the picture verification experiment mentioned above, Slobin (1966a) found that a sentence such as

THE CHEESE WAS EATEN BY THE MOUSE

(where the passive is 'irreversible' since cheeses do not eat mice) was understood as quickly as the active – though normally, passive sentences take longer.

So far, then, we have listed a number of assumptions which hearers have about English, and suggested a number of so-called 'perceptual strategies' which they give rise to:

1 Divide each sentence up into sentoids by looking for NP–V (–NP) sequences ('canonical sentoid strategy').
2 Interpret an NP–V–NP sequence as actor–action–object.
3 Interpret the first clause as the main clause.
4 Use your knowledge of the world to pick the most likely interpretation.

Even quite odd sentences seem easy to understand if they fit in with the strategies:

THE KANGAROO SQUEEZED THE ORANGE AND THE KOOKABURRA ATE THE PIPS.

But sentences which do not fulfil the hearer's expectations are more difficult to comprehend. Each of the following go against one of the four basic strategies. The sentences can be understood reasonably easily, but they need marginally more attention from the hearer:

AFTER RUSHING ACROSS THE FIELD THE BULL TOSSED HARRY
THE VAN WAS HIT BY THE BUS, AND THE CAR WAS RAMMED BY A TAXI
THE POSTMAN BIT THE DOG, AND THE BABY SCRATCHED THE CAT.

When a sentence goes against more than one strategy the effect is rather worse:

THE SHARK PUSHED THROUGH THE SEAWEED WAS ATTACKED BY A TADPOLE.

The sentence is neither ungrammatical, nor incomprehensible. It just seems clumsy and strange, and would possibly cause a hearer to say: 'I'm sorry, I didn't get that. Could you repeat it?'
    It is an interesting fact that speakers tend to avoid sentences which go against perceptual strategies to too great an extent. People just do not *say* things such as:

THE POODLE WALKED RAPIDLY UP THE MOUNTAIN COLLAPSED
JOAN GAVE JUNE A PRESENT ON SATURDAY AND JANE ON SUNDAY.

Strictly speaking, these sentences are not ungrammatical, just odd and unacceptable. Compare the syntactically similar sentences:

THE RAG DOLL WASHED IN THE WASHING MACHINE FELL TO PIECES
MAX GAVE HIS DOG A BATH YESTERDAY AND HIS CAT LAST WEEK.

However, since the 'sensible' sentences above are interpretable *only* because the speaker is able to use the imprecise strategy 4 ('Use your knowledge of the world to pick the most likely interpretation'), sentences of this type *may* be in the process of being eliminated from the English language – since perceptual needs can often influence linguistic rules. To quote Bever: 'The syntax of a language is partly moulded by grammatical responses to behavioural constraints' (1970, p. 321).

Obviously, the four strategies noted so far are not the only ones we use when we decode. Bever's paper has triggered a search for others, particularly ones which might apply to a wider range of languages than his first three (e.g. Kimball 1973; Gruber *et al.* 1978). Let us therefore outline two which might have a broader application, and partially encapsulate the 'canonical sentoid' strategy (Frazier and Rayner 1982, 1988).

The first of these says: 'Assume you are dealing with a simple structure, unless you have evidence to the contrary'. This has been called the 'Principle of Minimal Attachment', because each word is attached to the existing structure with the minimum amount of extra elaboration. On hearing the word PARADED in a sentence such as

THE LION PARADED THROUGH THE TOWN ESCAPED

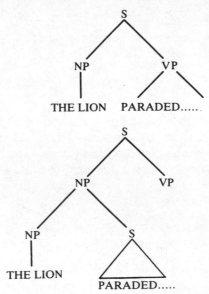

it is far simpler to set up a simple NP VP structure, than one which involves the added complexity of an extra sentence inserted after THE LION.

The second says: 'Try and associate any new item with the phrase currently being processed'. This has been called the 'Principle of Late Closure', because the previous phrase is held open, waiting for new additions, until there is strong evidence that it is complete. In a sentence such as

FIONA DISCOVERED ON MONDAY THE PENGUIN HAD HURT ITS FOOT

it is more natural to assume that ON MONDAY goes with the previous verb DISCOVERED, even though it would be equally plausible from the meaning point of view to assume that Monday was the day on which the penguin injured itself.

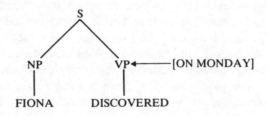

Both these strategies would explain why

THE MAN THE GIRL THE BOY MET BELIEVED LAUGHED

was so readily interpreted as 'The man, the boy, and the girl, all met, believed and laughed' (p. 209). This interpretation involves a much simpler structure than the 'correct' centre-embedded version, and tacking each new person introduced onto the previous one fits in with Late Closure.

As we have seen, the notion of strategies works well. There is plenty of proof that we impose our expectations on to what we hear, so at first sight there is no more to be said. All we need to do, it might seem, is to continue adding to our list of strategies until we have enough to cover the whole of language, and then try to divide them up into strategies that relate only to a single language, such as English, strategies that apply to a whole group of languages, such as those which have the basic word order subject–verb0object, and thirdly, strategies that are universal.

However, when we consider the situation in detail, the notion of strategies raises some problems. Above all, language is enormously complex. Hardly any sentences are as straightforward as:

MARY LIKES STRAWBERRIES

or even

SEBASTIAN DISCOVERED THAT THE GORILLA HAD ESCAPED.

Many of them are considerably more complicated. For example, anyone who listens to the news is likely to hear sentences such as:

BRITISH RAIL EXPECTS THE TRIBUNAL TO RECOMMEND THAT THE DRIVERS SHOULD RETAIN THEIR EXISTING WORKING AGREEMENT, ALTHOUGH THIS WILL BE MODIFIED TO ALLOW SOME VARIATION WHEN THE MANAGEMENT REQUESTS IT.

How many strategies are involved in a sentence like this? Obviously, many more than the few we have discussed. Perhaps twenty? Or a hundred? And supposing there are a hundred, what order do people apply them in? When faced with the problem of organizing dozens of strategies into a coherent model of comprehension, some psycholinguists have argued firstly, that the task is impossible. Secondly, that the whole notion of strategy is meaningless in relation to these longer sentences. Strategies become vague devices of immense power which provide very little concrete information about sentence processing. As one psycholinguist commented: 'One wonders what couldn't be accomplished with an armful of strategies' (Gough 1971, p. 269).

The notion of strategies therefore solves some problems, but raises others. Strategies cannot be totally replaced, but they need to be held in check and supplemented by some more precise procedures. Let us go on to consider how researchers have tried to instill more orderliness into models of comprehension.

Filling in the gaps

As a reaction against the chaos of strategies, a number of researchers have turned towards the neatness and orderly behaviour of computers. Perhaps they could programme a computer so that it would be an 'automatic parser', that is, a machine which could unaided identify the syntactic role of each word, and show how they all fit together. Such machines move from one end of the sentence to the other, dealing with each group of words in turn, checking them internally against an internal grammar which contains information about the structure of English sentences. This is sometimes called a 'left-to-right' model. Perhaps, it has been suggested, humans comprehend speech in this systematic, machine-like way.

Of course, when faced with a simple sentence such as:

PETRONELLA SAW A GHOST

there is hardly any difference between a model which says 'Assume you are dealing with an NP–V–NP structure' (strategy model), and one which says 'Work your way through the sentence looking first for a noun phrase, then for a verb, then another noun phrase' (left-to-right) model). But the difference becomes apparent when we look at how to deal with questions.

Suppose we have a sentence which begins with the words:

WHICH ELEPHANT . . .?

This sentence could end in a number of different ways. We could say:

WHICH ELEPHANT CAN DANCE THE POLKA?
WHICH ELEPHANT SHALL I BUY?
WHICH ELEPHANT SHALL I GIVE BUNS TO?

In the first sentence, the elephant is the subject of the verb, the one who is dancing the polka; in the second, the elephant is the object, the thing being bought; in the third, it is the indirect object, the animal to whom something is being given.

A dedicated strategy model would suggest that hearers start guessing immediately about the role of the word elephant, based on their expectations of the role elephants usually play in sentences. A left–to–right model, on the other hand, suggests that if hearers encounter a group of words which does not immediately fit into the straightforward NP–V–NP pattern, they do not make any rash guesses, they wait and see. They mentally store the words WHICH ELEPHANT in their memory until they have heard enough of the rest of the sentence to enable them to interpret it reliably. For example, in the case of WHICH ELEPHANT SHALL I BUY? they would wait until after the word BUY, since they know that the verb BUY usually has an object, the thing which is bought. They then mentally insert the stored phrase WHICH ELEPHANT into the gap where the object is usually found:

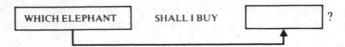

Similarly, in the sentence WHICH ELEPHANT SHALL I GIVE THESE BUNS TO? the hearers would store the words WHICH ELEPHANT until after the word TO. They would know that the word TO must normally be accompanied by a noun, so they would insert the stored phrase into the gap after TO:

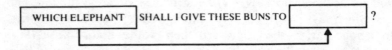

Although there is likely to be some overlap between strategies and gap-filling models, the difference of viewpoint between extreme versions of them is profound. An out-and-out strategy model makes use of any kind of information which can help one to jump to conclusions. Anything and everything is pulled in simultaneously: world knowledge, particular words used, as well as information about language structure. An out-and-out gap-filling model, on the other hand, deals primarily with syntax. The syntactic structures are assumed to have priority over other types of information, and work independently of them. They uphold the notion of language 'modules' put forward by Chomsky (Chapter 5), in which different aspects of language knowledge are perceived to be relatively separate.

Let us now consider the evidence for human gap-filling. How could we possibly find out if hearers do this or not? Two American psychologists, Eric Wanner and Michael Maratsos, have tried to test this theory (Wanner and Maratsos 1978). They point out that if their theory is correct, holding a phrase such as WHICH ELEPHANT in one's mind is likely to take up memory space. Therefore they devised an additional memory test which had to be carried out while the sentence was being processed. They suggested that subjects would find the additional test harder to cope with if there was a phrase such as WHICH ELEPHANT being held in abeyance.

Let us look at their experiment. They used pairs of sentences which contained relative clauses (clauses beginning with words such as WHO, WHICH, THAT). For example:

THE WITCH WHO DESPISED SORCERERS FRIGHTENED LITTLE
CHILDREN
THE WITCH WHOM SORCERERS DESPISED FRIGHTENED LITTLE
CHILDREN.

Relative clauses are similar to questions in that the word beginning
with WH is brought forward (in this case to the front of the clause it
occurs in), no doubt about its role in the sentence. In the first of the
two sentences above, the word WHO is at the front of its clause. But
since it is the subject of the verb DESPISED, it is in its normal position
before the verb. In the second sentence, however, WHOM is the object
of DESPISED. In this case, moving it to the front of the clause has taken
it out of an object's normal place after the verb.

Wanner and Maratsos predicted that the first sentence would be
relatively easy to process, since the word WHO did not have to be held
in one's memory for any length of time. But the second should be
harder because subjects have to remember the word WHOM until they
reach a place where it will fit, in this case after the verb DESPISED.
They therefore flashed up each sentence word by word on to a
television screen. In the middle of the relative clause they stopped,
and gave subjects a list of five names which they had to memorize,
such as JOHN, GEORGE, PETER, PAUL, HENRY.

THE WITCH WHO DESPISED | PAUL | SORCERERS FRIGHTENED LITTLE CHILDREN
  | HENRY |
  | JOHN ETC |

THE WITCH WHOM SORCERERS | BARBARA | DESPISED FRIGHTENED LITTLE CHILDREN
  | MARY |
  | ANNE ETC |

They then continued with the rest of the sentence. After this, subjects
were tested both on their comprehension of the sentences, and on
their memory for the names. As expected, subjects not only found
the second sentence harder to comprehend, but they also made more
mistakes with the names.

It seems, then, that Wanner and Maratsos had proved their point.
But this experiment has some problems in its design. Firstly, it asked
subjects to read, not comprehend aurally. Secondly, the word WHOM

has a slightly old-fashioned flavour which makes the second sentence seem odder than the first. Thirdly, any sentence with altered word order may be more difficult to process, whether or not a word such as WHOM is being held in one's memory.

Wanner and Maratsos, therefore, repeated the experiment with pairs of sentences which contained the same relative pronoun, THAT. In both, subjects had to hold THAT in their memory for some time, though for longer in the second than in the first. For example:

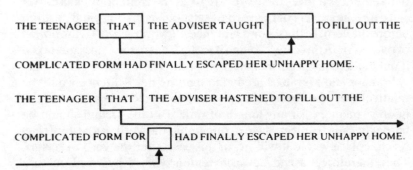

Once again, Wanner and Maratsos found that the second sentence was harder to cope with than the first, both in comprehension and in the memory task, a result which supported their theory. But once again, there are problems. As before, the sentences were read by subjects, not comprehended aurally. And secondly, the pairs of sentences in the second experiment seem rather unnatural, which may have affected the way subjects dealt with them: unnatural sentences may be dealt with in unnatural ways. So we must be cautious about the interpretation of these experiments. They are consistent with a gap-filling model, but there may be other explanations for the difficulty of the second sentence in each pair.

Can we find any other evidence to support a gap-filling model? One indirect piece of evidence is the impossibility of comprehending sentences in which we find so-called 'intersecting dependencies', that is, sentences in which there is more than one gap to be filled, and where there is a pattern HOLD (in memory) A – HOLD B – GAP A – GAP B: (Fodor 1978, 1979):

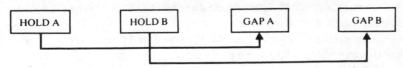

Take the perfectly normal (though unlikely) sentence:

IT IS DIFFICULT TO BREED HIPPOPOTAMUSES IN PONDS.

It is also quite possible to say:

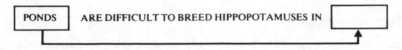

(with the word POND moved to the front) or

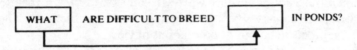

(with the word WHAT replacing HIPPOPOTAMUSES, and moved to the front).

But suppose we combine these two sentences. We get:

WHAT ARE PONDS DIFFICULT TO BREED IN?

which is very odd, and sounds as if we are trying to breed ponds inside the hippopotamuses, rather than vice versa. The problem seems to be due to the pattern of intersecting HOLDS and GAPS:

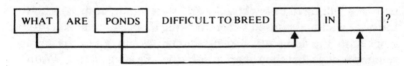

Note that a similar sentence, in which the HOLDS and GAPS lie inside one another (are *nested*, in linguistic terminology) rather than cutting across one another, presents no problems:

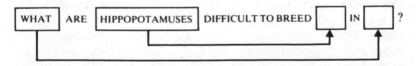

If people have to hold words in their memory until they find gaps to fit them in, this is just the kind of phenomenon we would expect, that one would have problems of interpretation when the HOLDS and GAPS get interleaved, and cannot easily be sorted out.

This provides encouraging support for the gap-filling model.

However, we should note that this is not the only possible explanation for the HIPPOPOTAMUS andPOND puzzle, and other linguists have put forward alternative suggestions (e.g. Chomsky 1978, 1980).

Hares or tortoises?

A left-to-right model is superficially very simple. But it raises a number of fundamental problems about how the rightwards movement takes place. Is the mechanism an impetuous hare, which tries to make a decision about each word as it comes to it? Or is it a cautious tortoise, which pauses before assigning words to structures? There are arguments in favour of both points of view.

A hare-type system is going to be faster than a tortoise-type one – provided the hare makes no mistakes. It will whizz through a straightforward sentence such as

THE YOUNG DUCK SWAM ACROSS THE POND.

But it would have problems with

THE YOUNG DUCK OUT OF THE WASHING UP.

Here, the hare is likely to have made a mistake, and interpreted THE YOUNG DUCK as a noun phrase. It will have been led 'up the garden path', so will have to backtrack, and start again. In this case, the tortoise, who had paused before making a decision, is likely to be quicker in the long run. So do humans keep going back, and reinterpreting what they hear, as some people suggest (e.g. Wanner and Maratsos 1978)? Or do they pause and wait for the next word before making a decision (e.g. Marcus 1980)? A third possibility is that humans make a provisional decision, but keep likely alternatives in their mind, so that they can switch over to these if necessary (Carlson and Tanenhaus 1988). This type of system would be better than that used by either the backtracking hare, or the sluggish tortoise. This compromise solution may be the correct one. According to recent research, the human mind is capable of much more simultaneous computation than had previously been assumed.

The hare–tortoise problem crops up again in gap-filling (Fodor 1978, 1979; Stowe 1988). When a phrase is being held in memory, prior to finding a place for it, a hare jumps into the first available gap, whereas a tortoise holds back until it's sure the gap is the right one. Consider:

THE PHILOSOPHER I SQUEEZED INTO A BARREL FAINTED
THE PHILOSOPHER I SQUEEZED INTO A BARREL WITH FAINTED.

SQUEEZED is a verb which can take an object, so a hare would hastily push THE PHILOSOPHER in after SQUEEZED. This would work well with the first sentence. But in the second, the hare would have to backtrack after hearing the word WITH, since the sentence is, in essence,

I SQUEEZED MYSELF INTO A BARREL WITH THE PHILOSOPHER.

The tortoise, on the other hand, would take a long time to comprehend the first sentence, being unwilling to put THE PHILOSOPHER into the first available gap. But it would win out in the second, when it would not need to backtrack.

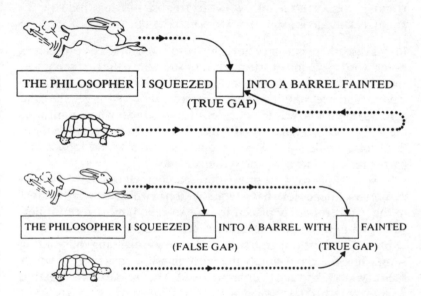

A compromise solution would take the overall context and lexical items into account. Then the hare or tortoise question would be irrelevant, since the hearer would use common sense to fill the gap. For example, in a sentence such as

THE DOG I WALKED ROUND THE SQUARE BARKED CONTINUOUSLY

the listener would probably drop THE DOG into the gap after WALKED, because it's quite common to hear the phrase 'to walk the dog'. But if the sentence had been

THE PROFESSOR I WALKED ROUND THE SQUARE WITH TALKED
  CONTINUOUSLY

the listener would not assume that THE PROFESSOR went into the gap
after WALKED, and would wait for a later gap, on the grounds that it
would be somewhat unusual to walk a professor round the square –
though still possible, if he had got drunk at a party. However,
researchers who argue that syntax has priority over other aspects of
comprehension do not accept this compromise, and claim the hare–
tortoise problem must be resolved.

Another variant of the gap-filling problem occurs when there are
two possible items which could fill one gap. This happens with
sentences such as

THERE IS THE ARTIST MABEL WANTED TO POSE IN THE NUDE FOR
THERE IS THE ARTIST MABEL WANTED TO POSE IN THE NUDE.

In this case, there is a gap where the word TO occurs. The problem is
which word to put into it, THE ARTIST or MABEL? In the first sentence,
MABEL is planning to do the posing, so she goes into the gap. In the
second sentence, MABEL wants THE ARTIST to pose, so he goes into the
gap. But there is no way to tell definitively who goes where until after
the word NUDE. A hare would make a snap-judgement at the time.
A tortoise would wait. A compromise solution would look at the
particular words involved, and then decide.

So what happens? One group of researchers claims to have found
definitive evidence for a hare-type solution in which the word nearest
to the gap is routinely placed in it (a so-called 'most recent filler'
strategy), in this case MABEL (Frazier, Clifton and Randall 1983).
Other researchers disagree with this strategy, claiming that putting
MABEL into the gap is simply the most plausible structure for words
such as WANT (Ford and Dalrymple 1988). They argue that a structure
such as I WANT TO EAT BEANS is more usual than one such as I WANT
HERBERT TO EAT BEANS.

To an outsider, it may seem pointless to argue about so apparently
trivial a point. But the implications are considerable. If a hare-type
solution is valid, then the various aspects of the comprehension
mechanism work relatively independently. The syntax does not get
interleaved fully with word meanings and context until after a provisional syntactic analysis has been made (Ferreira and Clifton 1986;
Frazier 1988). And independent syntactic procedures would indicate
that we are dealing with a separate syntactic module within the mind.

If, on the other hand, the particular words used and general common sense are involved, then the various strands are integrated all the way through (Crain and Steedman, 1985; Marslen-Wilson and Tyler 1980).

Ambiguous sentences would also be treated somewhat differently in the two approaches. Consider:

HUGO RESCUED THE OWL WITH A BROKEN WING
HUGO RESCUED THE OWL WITH A LONG LADDER.

A syntactic 'modular parsing' approach would deal with these in one of two ways. Either it would prefer one way of putting the phrases together, suggesting that the hearer would inevitably be 'garden-pathed' for one of these sentences. Or it would consider both possibilities, then at a later stage consult the lexicon and context to decide which was the most plausible. But an integrated approach would suggest that the syntax, the lexical items and the general context are all being used all the time. At no time would the syntax be dealt with independently. This issue is still unsolved.

So far, the priority of syntax is still unproven, apart from the clear working of the 'canonical sentoid' strategy. Some of the other results which have suggested that syntax overrides everything are based on written language, utilizing somewhat strange sentences. Syntax may well have extra significance in hard to process sentences, when more attention may be given to the constructions used. We may be dealing with a situation parallel to that which is described by the notice posted up in a London launderette:

WHEN ALL ELSE FAILS, READ THE INSTRUCTIONS.

Let us now assess the value of left-to-right models. These may be right in assuming that speakers work through sentences in a principled way, rather than just throwing together a bunch of strategies. But we have very little notion about the detailed mechanisms involved, such as when to make decisions, how to recognize gaps, how to decide which words to put into which gap, and how to deal with alternative possibilities. Above all, we do not know how syntax, word meaning, and general context are combined together.

Furthermore, left-to-right models as simulated on computers have one critical weakness. They cannot cope with ill-formed, but comprehensible sentences, such as:

I HAVE MUCH PROBLEM IN MAKING TO WORK YOUR TELEPHONE.

They therefore need to be integrated with strategy models which can make guesses about imperfect utterances, and which in turn take account the meaning of particular words. Let us therefore move on to consider the role of lexical items.

The role of lexical items

Two greyhounds were trying to get to the races, according to a popular 'shaggy-dog' story. But they were unable to get on their train, because they were pushed back by hundreds of Pekingese dogs rushing round the station. The greyhounds complained to a railway porter who shook his head and said: 'You've got to expect that in peak hour'.

Most people eventually realize the pun of PEAK and PEKE (short for Pekingese dog), and groan accordingly. But stories like this raise a serious issue, that of how people find the meaning of the words they hear. English has numerous homonyms – different words which sound the same – such as HARE/HAIR, BANK (financial institution and river bank) and so on. How do hearers cope with them? In the PEAK/PEKE joke we have two possibilities. Either one meaning of the sound sequence occurred to the hearer, then the other. Or both popped up simultaneously. A similar question is raised by the homonyms found in everyday speech. Does a hearer activate one of these two meanings, perhaps the most plausible one, then go back for the other if the first doesn't work? Or are both meanings briefly considered, then the unwanted one discarded? In brief, are word meanings activated *serially*, or in *parallel*?

Surprisingly, hearers probably consider multiple meanings, though often subconsciously. When subjects were asked to check for the presence of a given sound in a sentence ('Press a button if you come to a word starting with B'), a procedure known as 'phoneme-monitoring', an ambiguous word slowed them down even when they claimed not to have noticed the ambiguity (Foss 1970). Dor example, they responded more slowly to the B in a sentence such as

THE SEAMEN STARTED TO DRILL BEFORE THEY WERE ORDERED TO
  DO SO

(drill holes or take part in a life-boat drill?), than in

THE SEAMEN STARTED TO MARCH BEFORE THEY WERE ORDERED
  TO DO SO.

Furthermore, even irrelevant meanings are considered, according to more recent research. In one now famous experiment (Swinney 1979), passages containing homonyms were read out to subjects. For example,

THE MAN FOUND SEVERAL SPIDERS, ROACHES AND OTHER BUGS IN THE CORNER OF THE ROOM.

Here BUGS clearly referred to insects, though in another context, BUGS could be electronic listening devices. Just after the ambiguous word, the experimenter flashed a sequence of letters up onto a screen, and asked if they formed a word or not (a so-called 'lexical decision task'). He found that subjects responded fastest to words which were related to *either* meaning of the ambiguous word. They said 'Yes' faster to ANT and SPY than they did to SEW. And this was not just due to some accidental experimental effect, because other people have come to the same conclusion (e.g. Tanenhaus *et al.* 1979, Seidenberg *et al.* 1982, Kinoshita 1986).

More surprising still, perhaps, is that subjects reacted similarly even with a homonym such as ROSE which involves two different parts of speech, a noun (the flower) and a verb (past tense of RISE). They were played four sentences, which included the words

THEY BOUGHT A ROSE
THEY BOUGHT A SHIRT
THEY ALL ROSE
THEY ALL STOOD.

The subjects responded fastest to a lexical decision about the word FLOWER following *either* type of ROSE, both the noun and the verb (Seidenberg *et al.* 1982).

Humans therefore momentarily flash up *all* meanings of an ambiguous word, automatically, and without effort: 'Automatic processes are extremely rapid, they are sealed off from awareness and not subject to strategic control, and they do not draw on processing resources' (Tanenhaus *et al.* 1985, p. 367).

But the implications of this finding go well beyond dealing with homonyms. Many words are temporarily ambiguous. In British English, BASKET, BARN, BARGAIN, BAR, BATH all sound the same to begin with. So perhaps humans automatically flash up numerous possible candidates as they hear a word, then narrow it down to the most likely one. Many researchers now think this is what happens, though the narrowing down process is still unclear (Aitchison 1987a).

It appears to be a 'veiled controlled process', in that it is neither automatic, nor consciously carried out. 'Veiled controlled processes are opaque to consciousness, faster than conscious controlled processes, and they make fewer demands on limited processing resources' (Tanenhaus *et al.* 1985, p. 368). Somehow, a 'winner' pops up after the sound pattern has been considered alongside the overall context, the syntax and the frequency of use of the word.

Much more is going on, then, than we consciously realize. Humans are like computers in that the limited amount of information appearing on the screen at any one time gives no indication of the multiple processes which have whizzed through in its inner workings. But they are unlike most computers in that these processes are happening in parallel, rather than one after the other. Computers which can deal with things in parallel like human brains are still in their infancy.

But exactly how much parallel processing is going on in humans? Verbs are a particular area of controversy. Do humans activate in parallel *all* structures that can occur with them? Let us consider this matter.

Versatile verbs

'They've a temper some of them – particularly verbs, they're the proudest – adjectives you can do anything with, but not verbs'. This comment by Humpty Dumpty to Alice in Lewis Carroll's *Through the Looking Glass* reflects a feeling shared by many psycholinguists that verbs are more complicated than other parts of speech. They may provide the 'key' to the sentence by imposing a structure on it.

The effect of verbs has been a major issue for at least twenty years. Fodor, Garrett and Bever (1968) suggested that when someone hears a sentence, they pay particular attention to the verb. The moment they hear it, they look up the entry for this verb in a mental dictionary. The dictionary will contain a list of the possible constructions associated with that verb. For example,

```
KICK    + NP   HE KICKED THE BALL
EXPECT  + NP   HE EXPECTED A LETTER
        + TO   HE EXPECTED TO ARRIVE AT SIX O'CLOCK
        + THAT HE EXPECTED THAT HE WOULD BE LATE.
```

If Fodor, Garrett and Bever are correct in their claim, then sentences containing verbs which give no choice of construction should be easier to process than those which contain 'versatile verbs' – verbs associated with multiple constructions. In the case of a verb such as KICK, the hearer only has a simple lexical entry to check. But in the case of a verb such as EXPECT, they mentally activate each of the possible constructions before picking on the correct one. This suggestion is sometimes known as the 'verbal complexity hypothesis'.

Several psycholinguists have tried to test this theory – though so far the results have been inconclusive. Fodor, Garrett and Bever (1968) tried to test it in two ways. Firstly, they gave undergraduates pairs of sentences which were identical except for the verb. A single construction verb was placed in one sentence (e.g. MAIL), and a multiple construction verb in the other (e.g. EXPECT).

THE LETTER THE SECRETARY THE MANAGER EMPLOYED MAILED WAS
    LATE
THE LETTER THE SECRETARY THE MANAGER EMPLOYED EXPECTED WAS
    LATE.

They then asked the students to paraphrase each sentence. The result was that the sentences with the single construction verbs were marginally (but not significantly) easier to paraphrase than those with the multiple construction verbs. The second experiment was more encouraging. Once again, the experimenters used pairs of sentences. As before, each pair differed only in that one had a single construction verb, and the other a multiple construction one:

THE LETTER WHICH THE SECRETARY MAILED WAS LATE
THE LETTER WHICH THE SECRETARY EXPECTED WAS LATE.

Fodor, Garrett and Bever jumbled up the words in each, and then asked the students to unscramble them. They found what they had hoped to find – that it was much easier to sort out the single construction verb sentences. But both these experiments have been criticized. The problem is that they do not test comprehension directly: they assess the difficulty of a task which occurs *after* the sentence has been originally processed. This led another psychologist to test single versus multiple construction verbs while comprehension was actually in progress (Hakes 1971). He asked subjects to check for the presence of a given sound in a sentence ('Press a button if you come to a word starting with B' – so-called 'phoneme monitoring'). To his surprise, he found that the type of verb did not seem to affect the subjects' performance of this task. He had expected that 'versatile verbs' would be more difficult to cope with, and so would distract the hearer's attention from the sound he had been asked to report. So either the verbal complexity hypothesis is wrong, or phoneme monitoring is ineffective in this case, as some people suggest (e.g. Seidenberg *et al*. 1982).

More recently, researchers have checked on the difficulty of versatile verbs via a lexical decision task – asking subjects to decide whether a sequence of letters such as DOG or GLIT flashed up on a screen is a word or not. Supposedly, reaction times to this task will be slower if it is presented just after subjects have heard a versatile verb. One group of researchers who tried this did not find the predicted effect (Clifton, Frazier and Connine 1984). They concluded that hearers had no extra difficulty provided that the verb was followed by its preferred construction. For example, I THINK THAT . . . (e.g. I THINK THAT MAVIS IS A FOOL) would cause less trouble than I THINK AS . . . (e.g. I THINK AS I WALK TO WORK). In other words, hearers may activate in advance one favoured construction for a given verb, but there is no need for them to activate mentally all possible constructions associated with it. If only one favoured construction is activated per verb, then 'versatile verbs' are no more difficult to deal with than non-versatile ones, except when an odd or unexpected option is chosen.

This conclusion is supported by the work of some other researchers (e.g. Ford, Bresnan and Kaplan 1982). Consider the sentence:

THE PERSON WHO COOKS DUCKS OUT OF WASHING THE DISHES.

At first, we expect the word DUCKS to be the object of the word COOKS. But since we need a main verb, we are forced to revise our interpretation to:

THE PERSON [WHO COOKS] DUCKS OUT OF WASHING THE DISHES.

Our knowledge of the verb COOKS led us astray, since it is often, though not necessarily, followed by the thing which is cooked.

However, another group of researchers *did* find that a versatile verb caused problems, though in a somewhat unexpected way. The number of different constructions following a verb did not matter particularly. Instead, difficulties arose with verbs where it was not immediately obvious who did what to whom (Shapiro, Zurif and Grimshaw 1987). Consider the sentence:

SHELDON SENT DEBBIE THE LETTER.

This type of sentence took up extra processing time because people were not at first sure whether Debbie or something else was being sent.

On balance, versatile verbs do not cause the problems they were once expected to cause. Listeners may be mentally prepared for a variety of constructions, but this does not seem to delay processing, unless there is some additional difficulty, such as an unusual construction, or problems in deciding who did what to whom. Perhaps a hearer is like a car-driver, driving behind a bus. She has certain expectations about what the bus in front is likely to do. It can go straight on, turn left or turn right, and she is ready to respond appropriately to any of these. But she might be taken by surprise if the bus reversed, or rose in the air. Similarly, perhaps versatile verbs are a problem only if they spring a surprise on the hearer.

Further difficulties

So far, the factors we have discussed which affect comprehension have all been linguistic ones. But sentences may also be difficult to Comprehend for general psychological reasons. Understanding speech may use abilities which relate to other aspects of human behaviour, such as visual perception and mathematical skills. In the next few pages we will discuss some aspects of sentence processing which involve more than specific linguistic abilities, though we must bear in mind that it is not always easy to separate linguistic factors out from general cognitive ones, and researchers frequently disagree about which is which.

Let us begin by considering the amount of material which can be processed at any one time. Clearly, there is a limit on this. We know from numerous other areas of human behaviour that there is only a certain amount that a human being can cope with simultaneously, whether he is trying to remember things or is solving a problem. So a sentence that is long or involved will be difficult. Take length. It is often hard on a journey to follow the route directions of a passer-by. People tend to say things like: 'Take the third turning on the left past the fourth pub just before the supermarket next door to the church.' Apart from anything else, this sentence is just too long to be retained in the memory. Before the speaker gets to the end, the hearer is likely to have forgotten the first part.

However, length alone is not particularly important. What matters is the interaction of length with structure. Early research suggested that listeners prefer to deal with the speech they hear sentoid by sentoid. As soon as one sentoid has been decoded, hearers possibly forget the syntax, and remove the gist of what has been said to another memory space (Fodor, Bever and Garrett 1974, p. 339). This seemed to be supported by a number of psycholinguistic experiments. For example, in one experiment, subjects were asked to report as soon as they heard a 'click' which occurred during the sentence (Abrams and Bever 1969). They reacted more quickly to clicks coming at the beginning of sentoids than they did to clicks placed at the end. This suggests that the hearer's mind is cluttered up with information towards the end of a sentoid, leaving little spare attention for noticing clicks. As soon as the sentoid is complete, a person 'wipes the slate clean', and starts afresh.

Recent research suggests that this view is somewhat oversimplified (Flores d'Arcais and Shreuder 1983; Flores d'Arcais 1988). Sentoids are cleared away only if their contents appear to be no longer needed. Speakers are able to retain sentoids in their memory to a greater or lesser extent, if they sense that this will help future processing.

But the overall conclusion is clear. Humans have limited immediate memory space and processing ability. Therefore they clear away sections of speech as soon as they have dealt with them, preferably sentoid by sentoid. This would explain not only why unusually long sentoids are difficult (as in the direction-finding example given earlier), but also, perhaps, why sentences which cannot easily be divided into sentoids are a problem. For example,

THIS IS THE BUS THAT THE CAR THAT THE PROFESSOR THAT THE
   GIRL KISSED DROVE HIT

is more difficult than

THIS IS THE GIRL THAT KISSED THE PROFESSOR THAT DROVE THE CAR
   THAT HIT THE BUS

even though the second sentence has exactly the same number of words and almost the same meaning. Part of the trouble with the first is that you have to carry almost all of it unanalysed in your head. You have to wait until the end of the verb HIT that goes with CAR before you can divide it into sentoids:

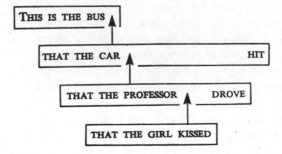

However, in dealing with sentences which cannot easily be divided into sentoids like the one above, it is not only the memory load, but also the difficulty of processing three sentoids simultaneously which causes problems. Three are not impossible (as some people have suggested, e.g. Kimball 1973) because we can (after some thought) compose sentences such as:

THE NEWBORN CROCODILE [WHICH THE KEEPER [YOU WERE TALKING TO THIS AFTERNOON] LOOKS AFTER] IS BEING MOVED TO ANOTHER ZOO.

But in general it is unusual to find more than two sentoids being coped with easily (and two are more difficult than one). It seems to be a fact about human nature that a person can only deal with a limited number of things at one time.

This leads us on to another difficulty, which overlaps with the simultaneous processing problem – that of interruptions. An interrupted structure is only slightly more difficult to process than an uninterrupted one, providing there are clear indications that you are dealing with an interruption. For example, the following sentence has a seventeen-word interruption:

THE GIRL [WHOM CUTHBERT KISSED SO ENTHUSIASTICALLY AT THE PARTY LAST NIGHT WHEN HE THOUGHT NO ONE WAS LOOKING] IS MY SISTER.

It is not particularly difficult to understand because the hearer knows (from the opening sequence THE GIRL WHOM . . .) that he is still waiting for the main verb. However, if there are no indications that an interruption is in progress, the sentence immediately increases in difficulty and oddness:

CUTHBERT PHONED THE GIRL [WHOM HE KISSED SO ENTHUSIASTICALLY AT THE PARTY LAST NIGHT WHEN HE THOUGHT NO ONE WAS LOOKING] UP.

Here UP goes with PHONED, but the hearer has already 'closed off' that branch on his mental tree. He has not left it 'open' and ready for additional material:

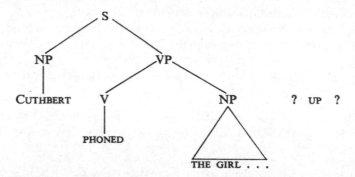

A fourth general difficulty concerns compression of information. Humans need thinking space to let things 'sink in', and they comprehend things best if they are presented only with a small amount of new information at one time. This is why Longfellow's poem *The Song of Hiawatha* is so easy to follow. Each line repeats some information from the previous one, so there is only a small amount of new material in each one:

> By the shores of Gitche Gumee,
> By the shining Big-Sea-Water,
> Stood the wigwam of Nokomis,
> Daughter of the Moon, Nokomis.
> Dark behind it rose the forest,
> Rose the black and gloomy pine-trees,
> Rose the firs with cones upon them;
> Bright before it beat the water,
> Beat the clear and sunny water,
> Beat the shining Big-Sea-Water.

This slow dropping of information contrasts strikingly with the over-compressed:

THIS IS THE BUS THAT THE CAR THAT THE PROFESSOR THAT THE GIRL
   KISSED DROVE HIT.

A further difficulty involves the repetition of items and structures. It is difficult to process a sentence which contains the same word twice, or more than one instance of the same type of structure, especially if the similar constructions are one inside the other. For example:

THIS IS THE BUS [THAT THE VAN [THAT THE CAR HIT] HIT]

with the repeated word HIT is more difficult than

THIS IS THE BUS [THAT THE VAN [THAT THE CAR HIT] COLLIDED WITH].

And the sentence above, which has a so-called relative clause inside another relative clause, is more difficult than a relative clause inside a different type of clause:

I EXPECT [THAT THE BUS [WHICH HIT THE VAN] IS DAMAGED].

In fact, it is so difficult to process one type of clause inside another similar one, that at least one linguist has suggested excluding such sentences from a grammar altogether. But this is not a workable suggestion, because it would also exclude perfectly good sentences such as:

THE OCTOPUS [WHICH THE FISHERMAN [YOU WERE TALKING TO] HAD CAUGHT] LOOKED QUITE REVOLTING.

This is a relative clause inside another relative clause.

Another difficulty, which seems to be partly a general psychological one, and partly a linguistic one, is the difficulty of backward processing (Grosu 1974). In English we normally move forwards when we process sentences. For example, it is easy to comprehend:

MARY, PETER AND PRISCILLA PLAY THE FLUTE, THE PIANO AND THE GUITAR RESPECTIVELY.

In this, the order of the people and the instruments they play moves from left to right:

```
1       2        3         1       2       3
MARY  PETER  PRISCILLA  −  FLUTE  PIANO  GUITAR.
```

It is considerably more difficult to understand

MARY, PETER AND PRISCILLA PLAY THE GUITAR, THE PIANO AND THE FLUTE REVERSELY.

Here, the instruments are given backwards, and you have to reverse the order in which they occur before you can sort out who is playing what:

```
1       2        3         3       2       1
MARY  PETER  PRISCILLA  −  GUITAR  PIANO  FLUTE.
```

The same kind of reversal occurs in the sentence:

THE CAR THAT THE PROFESSOR THAT THE GIRL KISSED DROVE CRASHED.

```
1       2        3         3       2       1
CAR  PROFESSOR  GIRL  −  KISSED  DROVE  CRASHED.
```

Backward processing (and compression) may also be why it is difficult to understand

MY AUNT'S EMPLOYER'S SON'S UMBRELLA'S COLOUR IS YELLOW

compared with the left-to-right uncompressed sentence

THE COLOUR OF THE UMBRELLA OF THE SON OF THE EMPLOYER OF
MY AUNT IS YELLOW

– though alternative explanations are possible (Yngve 1961; Miller and Chomsky 1963; Frazier and Rayner 1988).

Another partly linguistic, partly psychological factor which increases comprehension difficulty is the deletion of surface 'markers'. These are items which help to identify the various constructions. The fewer clues available for recognizing a structure, the more difficult it will be to identify. This is true whether we are dealing with a sentence in a language, or a partly hidden object in front of our eyes. Just as a picture of a face which lacks a nose may take longer to recognize than one with eyes, nose and mouth all complete, so a sentence with a word seemingly missing will take longer to comprehend (Fodor, Garrett and Bever 1968; Hakes 1971; Fodor, Bever and Garrett 1974). For example:

THE CROW THE FOX FLATTERED LOST ITS CHEESE

is more difficult than

THE CROW WHICH THE FOX FLATTERED LOST ITS CHEESE.

In the second sentence WHICH is retained, enabling speakers to note more quickly that they are dealing with a relative clause. Similarly,

SEBASTIAN NOTICED THE BURGLAR HAD LEFT FOOTPRINTS

takes longer to comprehend than

SEBASTIAN NOTICED THAT THE BURGLAR HAD LEFT FOOTPRINTS.

Here, the word THAT gives an immediate indication to the hearer that he is dealing with a so-called 'complement structure'.

Yet another factor which straddles the gap between psychological and linguistic difficulties is the presence of a negative. In general, negative sentences take longer to comprehend than affirmative ones. However, within negative sentences there are some trange discrepancies which relate to the hearer's expectations about his world. For example, it is easier and quicker to negate an expected fact than an unexpected one: it takes less time to comprehend the sentence

THE TRAIN WAS NOT LATE THIS MORNING

if you had *expected* the train to be late. If the train was normally on time, the same sentence would take longer to process. Similarly,

A WHALE IS NOT A FISH and A SPIDER IS NOT AN INSECT

are simpler, and take less time to understand, than

A WHALE IS NOT A BIRD and A SPIDER IS NOT A MAMMAL

because hearers had *expected* the whale to be a fish and the spider an insect (Wason 1965).

Let us now summarize this section. We have listed a number of factors which can make a sentence more difficult to understand. We noted that short-term memory space is limited, that there seems to be a constraint on the number of sentoids that can be processed simultaneously, that unmarked interruptions are difficult to deal with, and so is a sentence which contains too much compressed information. We saw that repetition of items and structures causes problems, and so does backward processing. The deletion of surface clues slows down syntax recognition, and negatives delay sentence processing.

The ground floor's sister

Let us now look again at the three sentences that seemed so difficult at the beginning. The first was a note to the milkman: 'Milkman, please stop milk until July 3. If you do not see this, THE WOMAN WHO HAS THE FLAT ON THE GROUND FLOOR'S SISTER will tell you.' The primary difficulty in this sentence is the presence of an unmarked interruption. The hearer has already mentally closed off the branch in the structure ending with the word WOMAN. Suddenly she is presented with the phrases 's SISTER which she is unable to fit in. In addition, there are several subsidiary problems. The intertwined sentoids are relatively long, and the information is compressed.

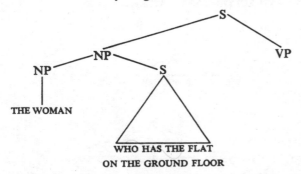

The second sentence

THE PIG PUSHED IN FRONT OF THE PIGLETS ATE ALL THE FOOD

is difficult because it goes against the hearer's linguistic expectations. He assumes that the first noun will go with the first verb in an NP–VP (actor–action) sequence as part of the main clause. So he understandably makes the wrong guesses when he hears the words THE PIG PUSHED . . ., especially as his knowledge of the world tells him that pigs are not usually pushed, they generally do the pushing.

But the difficulty of decoding the sentences above is trivial compared with that of:

THE CAT [THE DOG [THE MAN [THE BABY TRIPPED UP] BIT] SCRATCHED] COLLAPSED.

(The baby tripped up the man, the man bit the dog, the dog scratched the cat, the cat collapsed.)

This sentence is about as difficult as any sentence could possibly be. It goes against the speaker's basic linguistic expectations. The canonical sentoid strategy does not work, because the sentence is not in the form NP–VP–NP, and the objects CAT, DOG, MAN come before the actors DOG, MAN, BABY. From the point of view of meaning the sentence seems topsy-turvy: people do not expect dogs to scratch

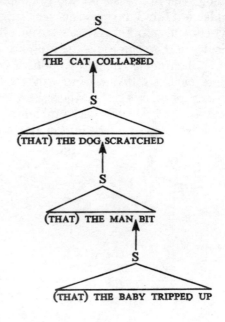

cats and men to bite dogs. It also involves most of the psychological difficulties we discussed. It puts an intolerable strain on short-term memory, it requires the simultaneous processing of three sentoids inside one another, it requires some degree of backward processing, and the word THAT has been omitted, which means that clues to the structure are missing. It is no wonder that most people, when faced with it, say: 'Sorry, it's just not English' – even though, strictly speaking, no grammatical rule has been broken.

Of course, a great deal of work still needs to be done before we fully understand what is happening when we comprehend speech. But, as we have seen, there are a number of ways in which we can usefully approach the problem. Firstly, we can build up a list of basic assumptions that speakers make about their language, and note the linked strategies which hearers utilize when they decode sentences. Secondly, we can carry out experiments which will help us to assess the relative merits of strategy and gap-filling models. Thirdly, we can explore the role of the lexicon. Fourthly, we can work on discovering the general psychological difficulties which affect speech processing. A next step is to integrate all these various strands into a coherent model of speech comprehension.

The story so far

Strategies are too powerful, so left-to-right models became fashionable. These gave too much priority to syntax, so the lexicon became a centre of attention. Theories of comprehension appear to bounce from one extreme to another.

But this would be an over-pessimistic view. The work done in the past twenty years has highlighted some key issues. First, the relationship between strategies and left-to-right models needs to be clarified, since both guesswork and systematic procedures are involved in understanding speech. The weakness of strategies is that they are an unprincipled mish-mash. The major weakness of left-to-right models is that they cannot cope with ill-formed sentences. They also have problems in picking the correct interpretation in ambiguous sentences. Somehow, both types of model have to be combined.

A second issue is the link between syntax and the lexicon. 'Top down' processing, in which humans set up expectations about overall structure, has to be combined with 'bottom up' processing, in which people gather particular words together and try to make sense of them. A few researchers have started to explore this question (e.g. Frazier and Fodor 1978; Marcus 1980). But no satisfactory solution has yet emerged.

Another issue is the extent to which syntax and the lexicon represent separate modules or components within the language system. If so, one would predict that each of them would be dealt with separately and then integrated. If not, one would expect them to be interlinked all the way along. We now know that multiple word possibilities are subconsciously considered, an automatic and independent process which is characteristic of a 'module'. The same thing might, or might not be true of syntax.

A further issue is how general background information is combined with the linguistic facets of a sentence. The tricky and voluminous question of how humans represent the world they live in has not been examined in this book. Johnson-Laird (1983) provides a useful overview. This whole issue of amalgamation clearly needs to be considered in more depth.

Resolving these problems might seem impossible, considering the conflicting views of psycholinguists. But certain facts are becoming clear. Above all, the human mind is an amazingly powerful machine, capable of multiple parallel processing. The major question of the future is how it manages to pull everything together in a manageable whole, instead of getting lost in the umpteen possibilities which are inherent in the data.

Let us now turn to the topic of speech production. As we shall see, this presents us with even more problems than comprehension.

11 The Cheshire Cat's grin
How do we plan and produce speech?

'I wish you wouldn't keep appearing and vanishing so suddenly,'
said Alice. 'You make one quite giddy.'

'All right,' said the Cat; and this time it vanished quite slowly,
beginning with the end of the tail, and ending with the grin, which
remained some time after the rest of it had gone.

'Well! I've often seen a cat without a grin,' thought Alice; 'but
a grin without a cat! It's the most curious thing I ever saw in all my
life!'

LEWIS CARROLL
Alice in Wonderland

It is tantalizingly difficult to observe how anyone actually plans and
produces speech. When somebody utters a sentence, we have very
little idea how long it actually took to plan it, and what processes were
involved. It is equally hard to devise experiments to test what is going
on. There are relatively few reported in psycholinguistic journals,
compared with the thousands available on speech comprehension.
Consequently, we shall be very tentative over any conclusions we
draw. As Fodor, Bever and Garrett comment: 'Practically anything
that one can say about speech production must be considered
speculative, even by the standards current in psycholinguistics'
(Fodor, Bever and Garrett 1974, p. 434).

Clues to what is happening are infuriatingly elusive. In fact, there
seems to be only one situation in which we can actually catch a
speaker as he mentally prepares an utterance, and that is when
someone is trying to recall a forgotten name. The name is often on
'the tip of his tongue', but he cannot quite remember it. His mind is
not completely blank as far as the word is concerned. A teasing and
seemingly uncatchable wraith of it remains. He is left with a 'kind of
disembodied presence, a grin without the Cheshire Cat' (Brown
1970, p. 234).

'Repairs' – situations when speakers correct themselves – are
sometimes proposed as an extra source of information, as in:

FERDINAND CRASHED THE CAR ON MONDAY, SORRY, ON TUESDAY.

But in repairs there is a relatively long time-lag between making a mistake and correcting it. Mostly, speakers behave as if they are listening to another speaker: 'Controlling one's own speech is like attending to somebody else's talk' (Levelt 1983, pp. 96–7). So repairs do not shed very much light on the original planning process.

We therefore have to rely on indirect evidence. This is of two main types. First of all, we can look at the pauses in spontaneous speech. The object of this is to try to detect patterns in the pausing which may give us clues as to when speech is planned. Secondly, we can examine speech errors, both the slips of the tongue found in the conversation of normal people (e.g. HAP-SLAPPILY for 'slap-happily', CAN-TANKEROUS for 'contentious'), and the more severe disturbances of dysphasics – people whose speech is impaired due to some type of brain damage (e.g. TARIB for 'rabbit', RABBIT for 'apple'). Hopefully, breakdown of the normal patterns may give us vital information about the way we plan and produce what we say.

Pauses

It may seem rather paradoxical to investigate speech by studying non-speech. But the idea is not as irrelevant as it appears at first sight. Around 40 to 50 per cent of an average spontaneous utterance consists of silence, although to hearers the proportion does not seem as high because they are too busy listening to what is being said.

The pauses in speech are of two main types: *breathing* pauses and *hesitation* pauses of the er . . . um variety. The first type are relatively easy to cope with. There are relatively few of them (partly because we slow down our rate of breathing when we speak), and they account for only about 5 per cent of the gaps in speech. They tend to come at grammatical boundaries, although they do not necessarily do so (Henderson *et al.* 1965).

Hesitation pauses are more promising. There are more of them, and they do not have any obvious physical purpose comparable to that of filling one's lungs with air. Normally they account for one-third to one-half of the time taken up in talking. Speech in which such pausing does not occur is 'inferior' speech (Jackson 1932). Either it has been rehearsed beforehand, or the speaker is merely stringing together a number of standard phrases she habitually repeats, as when the mother of the 7-year-old who threw a stone through my window rattled off at top speed, 'I do apologize, he's never done anything like that before, I can't think what came over him, he's such a good quiet little boy usually, I'm quite flabbergasted'. Unfortunately, we tend to over-value fluent, glib speakers who may not be thinking what they are saying, and often condemn a hesitant or stammering speaker who may be thinking very hard.

Hesitation pauses are rather difficult to measure, because a long-drawn-out word such as WE. . . ELL, INFA. . . ACT may be substituted for a pause. This type of measurement problem may account for the extraordinary differences of view found among psycholinguists who have done research on this topic. The basic argument is about *where* exactly the pauses occur. One researcher claims that hesitations occur mainly after the first word in the clause or sentoid (Boomer 1965). But other psycholinguists, whose experiments seem equally convincing, find pauses mainly before important lexical items (Goldman-Eisler 1964; Butterworth 1980b). It seems impossible, from just reading about their experiments, to judge who is right.

But in spite of this seemingly radical disagreement we can glean one important piece of information. *All* researchers agree that speakers do not normally pause between clauses, they pause *inside* them. This means that there is overlapping in the planning and production of clauses. That is, instead of a simple sentence

Plan	*Utter*	*Plan*	*Utter*
clause A	clause A	clause B	clause B

we must set up a more complicated model:

Plan clause A	*Plan* clause B	
	Utter clause A	*Utter* clause B

In other words, it is quite clear that we do not cope with speech one clause at a time. We begin to plan the next clause while still uttering the present one.

Armed with this vital piece of information, we can now attempt to elaborate the picture by looking at the evidence from speech errors.

Speech errors: the nature of the evidence

Linguists are interested in speech errors because they hope that language in a broken-down state may be more revealing than language which is working perfectly. It is possible that speech is like an ordinary household electrical system, which is composed of several relatively independent circuits. We cannot discover very much about these circuits when all the lamps and sockets are working perfectly. But if a mouse gnaws through a cable in the kitchen, and fuses one circuit, then we can immediately discover which lamps and sockets are linked together under normal working conditions. In the same way, it might be possible to find selective impairment of different aspects of speech.

The errors we shall be dealing with are, firstly, slips of the tongue, and, secondly, the speech of dysphasics – people with some more serious type of speech disturbance. Because the evidence is rather unusual, let us consider its nature a little more fully.

Everybody's tongue slips now and again, most often when the tongue's owner is tired, a bit drunk, or rather nervous. So errors of this type are common enough to be called normal. However, if you mention the topic of slips of the tongue to a group of people at least one of them is likely to smirk knowingly and say 'Ah yes, tongue slips are sexual in origin, aren't they?' This fairly popular misconception has arisen because Sigmund Freud, the great Viennese psychologist, wrote a paper suggesting that words sometimes slipped out from a person's subconscious thoughts, which in his view were often concerned with sex. For example, he quotes the case of a woman who said her cottage was situated ON THE HILL-THIGH (BERGLENDE) instead of 'on the hillside' (Berglehne), after she had been trying to recall a childhood incident in which 'part of her body had been grasped by a prying and lascivious hand' (Freud 1901). In fact, this type of example occurs only in a relatively small number of tongue slips (Ellis 1980). It is true, possibly, that a percentage of girls have the embarrassing experience of sinking rapturously into, say, Archibald's arms while inadvertently murmuring 'Darling Algernon'. It is also perhaps true that anyone talking about a sex-linked subject may get embarrassed and stumble over his words, like the anthropology professor, who, red to the ears with confusion, talked about a PLENIS-BEEDING CEREMONY (penis-bleeding ceremony) in New Guinea. But otherwise there seems little to support the sexual origin myth. Perhaps one might add that people tend to notice and remember sexual slips more than any other type. During the anthropology lecture mentioned above, almost everybody heard and memorized the PLENIS-BEEDING example. But few people afterwards, when questioned, had heard the lecturer say, YAM'S BOOK ON YOUNG-

GROWING (Young's book on yam-growing). So laying aside the sex myth, we may say that slips of the tongue tell us more about the way a person plans and produces speech than about his or her sexual fantasies.

Dysphasia is rather different from slips of the tongue, in that it is far from 'normal'. The name *dysphasia* comes from a Greek word which means 'bad speech', and so is used to mean 'impaired speech' – though in the USA the term *aphasia*, which means literally 'without speech', is the more usual term for speech disorders.

Dysphasia covers an enormous range of speech problems. At one end of the range we find people who can only say a single word such as O DEAR, O DEAR, O DEAR, or more usually, a swear word such as DAMN, DAMN, DAMN. One unproved theory is that people who have had a severe stroke sometimes find their speech 'petrified' into the word they were uttering as the stroke occurred. At the other end of the scale are people with only occasional word-finding difficulties – it is not always clear where true dysphasia ends and normal slips of the tongue begin. The fact that one merges into the other means that we can examine both types of error together in our search for clues about the planning and production of speech (Ellis 1985).

The typology of dysphasia (attempts to classify dysphasia into different kinds of disturbance) is a confused and controversial topic, and is beyond the scope of this book. Here we shall look at examples of name-finding difficulties, which is perhaps the most widespread of all dysphasic symptoms. Although it affects some patients more than others, it is usually present to some degree in most types of speech disturbance. A vivid description of this problem occurs in Kingsley Amis's novel *Ending Up* (1974). The fictional dysphasic is a retired university teacher, Professor George Zeyer, who had a stroke five months previously:

'Well, anyway, to start with he must have a, a, thing, you know, you go about in it, it's got, er, they turn round. A very expensive one, you can be sure. You drive it, or someone else does in his case. Probably gold, gold on the outside. Like that other chap. A bar – no. And probably a gold, er, going to sleep on it. And the same in his . . . When he washes himself. If he ever does, of course. And eating off a gold – eating off it, you know. Not to speak of a private, um, uses it whenever he wants to go anywhere special, to one of those other places down there to see his pals. Engine. No. With a fellow to fly it for him. A plate. No, but you know what I mean. And the point is it's all because of us. Without us he'd be nothing, would he? But for us he'd still be living in his, ooh, made out of . . . with a black woman bringing him, off the – growing there, you know. And the swine's supposed to be some sort of hero. Father of his people and all that. A plane, a private plane, that's it.'

It was not that George was out of his mind, merely that his stroke had afflicted him, not only with hemiplegia, but also with that condition in which the sufferer finds it difficult to remember nouns, common terms, the names of familiar objects. George was otherwise fluent and accurate and responded normally to other's speech. His fluency was especially notable; he was very good at not pausing at moments when a sympathetic hearer could have supplied the elusive word. Doctors, including Dr Mainwaring, had stated that the defect might clear up altogether in time, or might stay as it was, and that there was nothing to be done about it.

Of course, not every dysphasic is as fluent as George. And sometimes a patient is in the disqueiting situation of thinking she has found the right word – only to discover to her dismay, when she utters it, that it is the wrong one. A description of this unnerving experience occurs in Nabokov's *Pale Fire*:

> She still could speak. She paused and groped and found
> What seemed at first a serviceable sound,
> But from adjacent cells imposters took
> The place of words she needed, and her look
> Spelt imploration as she sought in vain
> To reason with the monsters in her brain.

Perhaps the following two extracts will give a clearer picture of the problem. They are taken from tape-recordings of a severely dysphasic patient in her seventies who had had a stroke two months earlier.

The patient (P) has been uttering the word RHUBARB, apparently because she is worried about her garden which is going to rack and ruin while she is in hospital. The therapist (T) tries to comfort her then says:

T: NOW THEN, WHAT'S THIS A PICTURE OF? (showing a picture of an apple).
P: RA-RA-RABBIT.
T: NO, NOT A RABBIT. IT'S A KIND OF FRUIT.
P: FRUIT.
T: WHAT KIND OF FRUIT IS IT?
P: O THIS IS A LOVELY RABBIT.
T: NOT A RABBIT, NO. IT'S AN APPLE.
P: APPLE, YES.

T: CAN YOU NAME ANY OTHER PIECES OF FRUIT? WHAT OTHER KINDS
  OF FRUIT WOULD YOU HAVE IN A DISH WITH AN APPLE?
P: BEGINNING WITH AN A?
T: NO, NOT NECESSARILY.
P: O WELL, RHUBARB.
T: PERHAPS, YES.
P: OR RHUBARB.

In the second extract, the same type of phenomenon occurs, but
in a different context.

T: WHAT'S THIS BOY DOING? (showing a picture of a boy swimming).
P: O HE'S IN THE SEA.
T: YES.
P: DRIVING . . . DRIVING. IT'S NOT VERY DEEP. HE'S DRIVING WITH HIS
  FEET, HIS LEGS. DRIVING. WELL DRIVING, ER DIVING.
T: IN FACT HE'S . . .
P: SWIMMING.
T: GOOD, WHAT ABOUT THIS ONE? (showing a picture of a boy climbing
  over a wall).
P: DRIVING, ON A . . . ON A WALL.
T: HE'S WHAT?
P: DR . . . DRIVING, HE'S CLIMBING ON A WALL.

Most of the mistakes in these passages represent an extension of
the selection problems seen in ordinary slips of the tongue. That is,
the same kind of mistakes occur as in normal speech, but they occur
more often and seem less obvious.

Broadly speaking, we may categorize speech errors into two basic
types. First, we have those in which a wrong item (or items) is chosen,
where something has gone wrong with the *selection* process. For
example,

DID YOU REMEMBER TO BUY SOME TOOTHACHE? (Did you remember
  to buy some toothpaste?)

Such errors are generally classified as 'slips of the tongue', though
more accurately they are 'slips of the brain'.

Secondly, we find errors in which the correct choice of word has
been made, but the utterance has been faultily assembled as in

SOMEONE'S BEEN WRITENING THREAT LETTERS (Someone's been
  writing threatening letters).

Let us look at these two categories, *selection errors* and *assemblage errors* more carefully, and attempt to subdivide them.

Errors in which wrong items have been chosen are most commonly whole word errors. There are three main types: *semantic errors* (or similar meaning errors), *malapropisms* (or similar sound errors) and *blends*.

So-called *semantic* or *similar meaning* errors are fairly common. In fact, they are so usual that they often pass unnoticed. We are talking about naming errors in which the speaker gets the general 'semantic field' right, but uses the wrong word, as in

DO YOU HAVE ANY ARTICHOKES? I'M SORRY, I MEAN AUBERGINES.

This kind of mistake often affects pairs of words. People say LEFT when they mean 'right', UP when they mean 'down', and EARLY instead of 'late', as in

IT'S SIX O'CLOCK. WON'T THAT BE TOO EARLY TO BUY BREAD?

Mistakes like this occur repeatedly in the speech of some dysphasics, and in its extreme form the general condition is sometimes rather pompously labelled 'conceptual agrammatism' (Goodglass 1968). Such patients repeatedly confuse words like YESTERDAY, TODAY and TOMORROW. They seem able to find names connected with the general area they are talking about, but unable to pinpoint particular words within it, so that a 'garden roller' is likely to be called a LAWN MOWER, a 'spade' may be called a FORK, and a 'rake' may be called a HOE. A mistake like this occurred in one of the dysphasic passages quoted above: the patient said DIVING when she meant 'swimming'. At other times, a patient may use a paraphrase such as WATER COMPARTMENT for 'drinking trough', or HORSE HUT for 'stable'.

The second type of word selection error, so-called *malapropisms* occur when a person confuses a word with another, similar sounding one. The name comes from Mrs Malaprop, a character in Richard Sheridan's play *The Rivals*, who continually confused words which sounded alike, as in

SHE'S AS HEADSTRONG AS AN ALLEGORY ON THE BANKS OF THE NILE
(She's as headstrong as an alligator on the banks of the Nile).

and

A NICE DERANGEMENT OF EPITAPHS (A nice arrangement of epithets).

Not only in Sheridan's play, but in real life also, the results are sometimes hilarious, as when a lady lecturer claimed that

YOU KEEP NEWBORN CHICKS WARM IN AN INCINERATOR (You keep newborn chicks warm in an incubator).

Equally funny was a man's statement that he had NUBILE TOES instead of 'mobile' ones.

So far, we have mentioned selection errors connected with meaning, and selection errors connected with the sound of the word. But it would be a mistake to assume that we can easily place mistakes into one or the other category. Often the two overlap. Although children's mistakes are usually purely phonetic ones, as in

MUSSOLINI PUDDING (semolina pudding)
NAUGHTY STORY CAR PARK (multi-storey car park),

the majority of adult ones have some type of semantic as well as phonetic link. The malapropism INCINERATOR for 'incubator' is a case in point, since in addition to the phonetic similarity both words are connected with the idea of heat. Another example is the statement

YOU GO UNDER A RUNWAY BRIDGE (You go under a railway bridge),

where, in addition to the similar sounds, both words describe a track for a means of transport. Yet another example is the error

COMPENSATION PRIZE (consolation prize).

However, the semantic connection does not always have to be between the two words that are being confused. Sometimes the intruding idea comes in from the surrounding context, as in the statement

LEARNING TO SPEAK IS NOT THE SAME THING AS LEARNING TO TALK (Learning to speak is not the same thing as learning to walk).

Another example of this type of confusion was uttered by a nervous male involved in a discussion on BBC's *Woman's Hour* about a cat who never seemed to sleep, because it was perpetually chasing mice. He said:

HOW MANY SHEEP DOES THE CAT HAVE IN ITS HOUSE THEN? I'M SORRY, I MEAN MICE, NOT SHEEP.

The speaker correctly remembered that he was talking about an animal of some kind, but the animal had somehow become contaminated by the sound of the word SLEEP, resulting in SHEEP! He may also have been influenced by the fact that humans reputedly count sheep jumping over fences in order to get to sleep.

The third type of selection error, so-called *blends*, are an extension and variation of semantic errors. They are fairly rare, and occur when two words are 'blended' together to form one new one. For example,

NOT IN THE SLEAST

contains a mixture of 'slightest and least'. And

PLEASE EXPLAND THAT

is a mixture of 'explain and expand'. A rather more bizzare example of a blend occurs in the first passage of dysphasic speech quoted on p. 246. The patient had been talking about RHUBARB, and was trying to think of the word APPLE. What came out was a mixture of the two, RABBIT! Such mixes are also known as *contaminations* since the two words involved 'contaminate' one another. Often, in this kind of mistake, both the items chosen are equally appropriate. It is just that the speaker seems to have accidentally picked two together – or rather failed to choose between two equally appropriate words in time. She has not so much picked the wrong word, as not decided which of the right ones she needed.

Sometimes two items are intentionally blended together in order to create a new word. Lewis Carroll makes Humpty Dumpty explain in *Alice Through the Looking Glass* that SLITHY means 'lithe and slimy', commenting, 'You see, it's like a portmanteau – there are two meanings packed up into one word' – though Lewis Carroll's made-up words may not be as intentional as they appear. Apparently, he suffered from severe migraine attacks, and many of his strange neologisms are uncannily like the kind of temporary dysphasia produced by some migraine sufferers (Livesley 1972). Perhaps better examples of intentional blends are SMOG from 'smoke and fog', and BRUNCH from 'breakfast and lunch'. There are sometimes interesting parallels of this type to be spotted between slips of the tongue and language change.

Let us now turn to *assemblage errors* – errors in which the correct word choice has been made, but the items chosen have been faultily assembled. There are three main types: transpositions, anticipations and repetitions, which may affect words, syllables or sounds.

Transpositions are not, on the whole, very common (Cohen 1966; Nooteboom 1969). Whole words can switch places, as in

DON'T BUY A CAR WITH ITS TAIL IN THE ENGINE (Don't buy a car with its engine in the tail)

I CAN'T HELP THE CAT IF IT'S DELUDED (I can't help it if the cat's deluded)

and so can syllables:

I'D LIKE A VIENEL SCHNITZER (I'd like a Viener Schnitzel).

But perhaps the best known are the sound transpositions known as spoonerisms. These are named after a real-life person, the Reverend William A. Spooner, who was Dean and Warden of New College, Oxford, around the turn of the century. Reputedly, he often transposed the initial sounds of words, resulting in preposterous sentences, such as

THE CAT POPPED ON ITS DRAWERS (The cat dropped on its paws)
YOU HAVE HISSED ALL MY MYSTERY LECTURES (You have missed all my history lectures)
YOU HAVE TASTED THE WHOLE WORM (You have wasted the whole term).

However, there is something distinctly odd about these original spoonerisms. One suspects that the utterances of the Reverend Spooner were carefully prepared for posterity, probably by his students (Augarde 1984). The odd features are that they always make sense, they affect only initial sounds, and there is no discernible phonetic reason for the transposed sounds. In real life, spoonerisms do not usually make sense, as in

TILVER SILLER (Silver tiller).

They can affect non-initial sounds, as in

A COP OF CUFFEE (A cup of coffee).

And they frequently occur between phonetically similar sounds, as in

LEAK WINK (weak link).

Anticipations, particularly sound anticipations, are the most widespread type of assemblage error (Cohen 1966; Nooteboom 1969). Here, a speaker anticipates what he is going to say by bringing in an item too early. Note that it is not always possible to distinguish between anticipations and potential transpositions if the speaker stops himself half-way through, after realizing his error. This may partially account for the high recorded proportion of anticipations compared with transpositions. For example, the following could be a prematurely cut off transposition:

I WANT YOU TO TELL MILLICENT . . . I MEAN, I WANT YOU TO TELL MARY
WHAT MILLICENT SAID.

But the following sound anticipations are clearly just simple
anticipations. A participant in a television discussion referred, much
to his embarrassment, to:

THE WORST GERMAN CHANCELLOR (The West German Chancellor).

Here he had anticipated the vowel in GERMAN. The same thing
happened to the man, who interrupting over-eagerly, begged to
make

AN IMPOITANT POINT (an important point).

Repetitions (or *perseverations*) are rather rarer than anticipations,
though commoner than transpositions. We find repeated words, as
in:

A: ISN'T IT COLD? MORE LIKE A SUNDAY IN FEBRUARY.
B: IT'S NOT TOO BAD – MORE LIKE A FEBRUARY IN MARCH I'D SAY.
    (It's not too bad – more like a Sunday in March).

An example of a repeated sound occurred when someone referred
to:

THE BOOK BY CHOMSKY AND CHALLE (Chomsky and Halle)

– perhaps an indication of the mesmerizing effect of Chomsky on a
number of linguists! Repetitions are relatively unusual because
normal people have a very effective 'wipe the slate clean' mechanism.
As soon as they have uttered a word, the phonetic form no longer
remains to clutter up the mind. This is perhaps the greatest single
difference between ordinary people and dysphasics, who often, to
their frustration and despair, repeatedly repeat sounds and words
from the sentence before. A dysphasic had been shown a picture of
an apple. After some prompting, she said the word APPLE. She was
then shown a picture of a blue ball. When asked what it was, she
replied without hesitation APPLE. The therapist pointed out that she
was confusing the new object with the previous one. 'Of course, how
stupid of me', replied the patient. 'This one's an APPLE. No, no, I
didn't mean that, I mean APPLE!' A similar example occurs in the
dialogue on p. 247 where the patient keeps repeating the word RHUBARB.
We have now outlined the main types of selection and assemblage errors:

Selection Errors	*Assemblage Errors*
Semantic errors	Transpositions
Malapropisms	Anticipations
Blends	Repetitions

Planning and producing utterances

What (if anything) can we learn from this seemingly strange array of errors? In fact, quite a lot. First of all, we can suggest what the units of planning are – in other words, the size of chunk we prepare in advance ready for utterance. Secondly, we can look at the process of word selection. Thirdly, we can make hypotheses as to how words and syntax are planned and assembled.

The unit of planning

The unit of planning appears to be what is sometimes called a *tone group* or *phonemic clause* – a short stretch of speech spoken with a single intonation contour. For example,

WHAT TIME IS IT?
DEBORAH BOUGHT SOME SNAILS
MAX TOOK A BATH/BEFORE HE WENT TO THE PARTY.

Note, by the way, that a so-called *phonemic* clause (or tone group) should not be confused with a *syntactic* clause (or sentoid). The two quite often coincide, but do not necessarily do so. For example,

I WANT TO BUY SOME BUNS

is a single phonemic clause, though it is regarded in transformational grammar as containing two underlying syntactic clauses. In this chapter the word *clause* refers to a phonemic clause, unless otherwise stated.

The main reason for confidently asserting that the tone group is the unit of planning is that slips of the tongue usually occur within a single tone group. For example:

WE'LL GO TO TAXI IN A CHOMSKY (We'll go to Chomsky in a taxi)
WE FORGED THIS CONGRESS . . . CONTRACT IN OUR OWN CONGRESSES
(We forged this contract in our own congresses).

This strongly suggests that each tone group is planned and executed as a whole. If larger units were prepared, we would expect to find frequent contamination between clauses. As it is, such interference is rare, so much so that Boomer and Laver (1968) regard it as a tongue slip 'law' that 'The target and the origin of a tongue-slip are both located in the same tone-group' (with 'law' to be understood in a statistical rather than in an absolute sense).

On the rare occasions when this 'law' is broken, whole *words* slip into the preceding clause, rather than sound segments. That is, words can cross clause boundaries, whereas sounds generally do not. For example:

WHEN YOU BUY THE LAUNDRY . . . (When you take the laundry, please buy me some cigarettes)
WHEN YOU TAKE THE ROSES OUT, ADMIRE . . . (When you take the garbage out, admire the roses)
EXTINGUISH YOUR SEATBELTS . . . (Extinguish your cigarettes and fasten your seatbelts).

Compare these with the following sound transpositions and anticipations, which all occur within the same clause:

SHE WROTE ME A YETTER . . . (letter yesterday)
twapter chelve (chapter twelve)
A COP OF CUFFEE (a cup of coffee)
DOG WAS . . . (Doug was a doctor).

This phenomenon indicates that key words are thought out while the preceding clause is being uttered – whereas the detailed organizations of a tone group are left till later.

Word selection

Moving on therefore to word selection, our most direct information comes from the 'tip of the tongue' (TOT) experiment (Brown and McNeill 1966). Less direct evidence comes from selection errors.

The TOT experiment was a simple one. The researchers assembled a group of students, and read them out definitions of relatively uncommon words. For example, when the 'target' word was SEXTANT, the students heard the definition: 'A navigational instrument used in measuring angular distances, especially the altitude of sun, moon and stars at sea'. Some of the students recognized the right word immediately. But others went into a TOT ('tip of the tongue') state. They felt they were on the verge of getting the word, but not quite there. In this state the researchers asked them to fill in a questionnaire about their mental search. To their surprise, they found that the students could provide quite a lot of information about the elusive missing name. Sometimes the information was semantic, and sometimes it was phonetic. For example, in response to the definition of SEXTANT, several students provided the similar meaning words ASTROLABE, COMPASS and PROTRACTOR. Others remembered that it had two syllables and began with an s, and made guesses such as SECANT, SEXTON, and SEXTET.

Semantically, this suggests similar meaning words are linked together in the mind. We probably activate a number of them, before pinpointing one in particular (Baars 1980, Aitchison 1987). When errors occur we have been insufficiently precise in locating the exact one needed – as with YESTERDAY instead of 'tomorrow,' SHIRT instead of 'blouse,' and (another example from the TOT experiment) BARGE, HOUSEBOAT, JUNK instead of 'sampan'.

Phonetically, we find a similar picture. People seem to activate several similar sounding words, before narrowing down the field to one. Malapropisms such as COMPETENCE for 'confidence' and NATIVE APE for 'naked ape' suggest that people look for words with certain outline characteristics, such as similar initial consonant and number of syllables before they finally select one (Fay and Cutler 1977). Adults give higher priority to the initial consonant than to the number of syllables, so that they often produce malapropisms such as CONDESCENDING for 'condensing', and SEGREGATED for 'serrated'. Children, on the other hand, seem to pay extra attention to the number of syllables, and produce comparatively more malapropisms with a wrong initial consonant, as in ICE CREAM TOILET for 'ice cream cornet' (cornet = cone), MISTAKE CAR for 'estate car', LEPRECHAUN for 'unicorn' (Aitchison and Straf 1981). Of course, the situation is not quite as straightforward as suggested above, because a number of other factors play a role in memory, such as the presence of a rhyming suffix, as in PERISCOPE for 'stethoscope', PORCUPINE for 'concubine'. As with all psycholinguistic phenomena, there are a large number of intertwined variables to be considered.

The exact mechanisms involved when words are selected is unclear. We probably start with the 'idea of a word', then only later fit it to a phonetic form. This is shown by cases when we cannot remember a key word, even though it is clearly 'there' in some sense:

HE TOOK A LOT OF. . . WHAT'S THE WORD I WANT? ER . . . PERSUASION.

But in fluent speech, selecting the meaning and fitting on the sounds are processes which overlap. People probably begin to find possible phonetic forms while they are still finalizing their choice of word. This is shown by slips in which the word uttered has some meaning and some sound similarity to the target, as in HE WAS IN THE NEXT TRAIN COMPONENT (compartment).

A 'spreading activation' or 'interactive activation' theory is supported by some recent research (Motley 1985, Aitchison 1987). In this model, activation of similar words spreads out and diffuses in a chain reaction. If someone was trying to say MONDAY, all the days of the week would be strongly activated, which would in turn activate the months of the year, though less strongly. Each meaning would stimulate a sound pattern which in turn would rouse further sound patterns. So the 'idea' of MONDAY might trigger MONDAY, MAYDAY or MIDDAY. SATURDAY and SUNDAY would trigger each other, and so on. The task of the speaker is not only to select the word she wants, but to suppress the ones she does not require. Dysphasics in particular seem to have problems over this, since they let through a far wider range of inappropriate words than normal speakers do, though there is usually some link with the target, as in DRIVING for 'swimming', caused by DRIVING for 'diving' and DIVING for 'swimming'.

The final selection process is not yet understood. But the general picture is clear. Words which are relevant both in sound and meaning get more and more excited. Finally, one wins out over the others. A 'monitoring device' may be a further requirement, a final check once the word has been chosen that it is indeed the right one.

Planning and assemblage

Let us now consider how the words and syntax are planned and assembled. We can divide this into two main stages: firstly, *outline planning*, which begins while the previous clause is being uttered. Secondly, *detailed planning*, which takes place while the clause is actually in progress. Outline planning means the choice of key words, syntax and intonation pattern, whereas detailed planning involves the fitting together of previously chosen words and syntax.

We know that outline planning includes the choice of intonation pattern, because errors which occur within the tone group (the unit of planning) do not normally disrupt the intonation pattern, as in:

TAKE THE FREEZES OUT OF THE STEAKER.

We are now faced with a tricky and much disputed question: which comes first, the words or the syntactic pattern? Those who argue that the words come first point out quite simply that 'key' words determine the choice of syntax, and by 'key' words they mean above all nouns, verbs and sometimes adjectives. Clearly, verbs influence the choice of syntax more than the nouns – but the noun may, in some cases, influence the choice of verb.

Those who suggest that the syntax comes first put forward an equally strong argument. They note that when a speaker makes a word selection error, she almost always picks a wrong word belonging to the same word class as the target word. That is, nouns are confused with other nouns, verbs with other verbs, and adjectives with other adjectives. Even dysphasic speech, which is often quite garbled, tends to follow this pattern (though exceptions do occur). People say UP instead of 'down', JELLY instead of 'blancmange', TRANSLATION instead of 'transformation'. But there is no reason for parts of speech to cling together like this. Why shouldn't verbs and nouns get confused? The fictional Mrs Malaprop gets her word classes confused much of the time, which is why many of her malapropisms are implausible. She says things such as:

YOU WILL PROMISE TO FORGET THIS FELLOW – TO ILLITERATE HIM, I
    SAY, QUITE FROM YOUR MEMORY (You will promise . . . to obliterate
    him . . . from your memory).

But in real life, it is extremely unusual to find adjective–verb confusions of the ILLITERATE for 'obliterate' type uttered by Mrs Malaprop. Even malapropisms uttered by children generally follow this similar word-class pattern:

YOU TAKE AN ANTELOPE IF YOU SWALLOW POISON (You take an
    antidote if you swallow poison)
I'M LEARNING TO PLAY THE ELBOW (I'm learning to play the oboe).

According to the 'syntax first' supporters, the most likely explanation for this phenomenon is that the syntax has already been chosen, and the words are then slotted in: 'Unless the syntactic structure is already constructed, word selection would not be constrained to proper word classes' (Fromkin 1973, p. 30). 'The very fact that a mistakenly selected word always or nearly always belongs to the same word class as the intended word indicates that the grammatical structure of the phrase under construction imposes imperative restrictions on the selection of words' (Nooteboom 1969, p. 130).

How are we to solve this controversy between the 'words first' and 'syntax first' supporters? Who is right? Possibly both sides, to some extent. On the one hand, it is unlikely that the key word advocates are entirely correct. There is no evidence that we assemble *all* the key words, and then bind them together with joining words. On the other hand, it is quite impossible to plan the syntax with no idea of the lexical items which are going to be used. For example, the syntax of

JOHN CLAIMED TO BE ABLE TO EAT A LIVE FROG

must depend to some extent on the word CLAIM, since other words with a similar meaning take a different construction. We cannot say

*JOHN ASSERTED TO BE ABLE TO EAT A LIVE FROG

or

*JOHN DECLARED TO BE ABLE TO EAT A LIVE FROG.

We possibly start by picking perhaps *one* key verb or noun, and then build the syntax around it. Later we slot other words into the remaining gaps.

If one key word triggers off the syntax, then we must assume that words in storage are clearly marked with their word class or part of speech (e.g. noun, verb) as well as with information about the constructions they can enter into. For example:

EAT	VERB
	NP – EAT – NP

We are, therefore, hypothesizing that when people plan utterances they mentally set up syntactic trees which are built around selected key words:

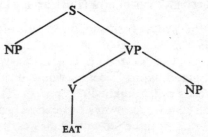

A key word can be used in planning before it has acquired its phonetic form. This is indicated by slips of the tongue such as

WHEN IS IT GOING TO BE RECOVERED BY?

In this sentence the syntax was picked for 'mend', but the phonetic form activated was RECOVERED. The 'word idea' here is not just an intangible 'concept', but a definite and firmly packaged lexical item. It includes both an understanding of what is being referred to and a firm word class label (verb), as well as information about the syntactic configurations it can enter into.

By the detailed planning stage, we assume that the major lexical and syntactic choices have already been made. The items chosen now have to be correctly assembled. This involves at least two types of manoeuvre: on the one hand, lexical items have to be put into their correct slots in the sentence. This has been wrongly carried out in

IT'S BAD TO HAVE TOO MUCH BLOOD IN THE ALCOHOL STREAM (It's bad to have too much alcohol in the blood stream)
A FIFTY-POUND DOG OF BAG FOOD (A fifty-pound bag of dog food).

The slotting in of lexical items must also include the slotting in of negatives, since these can get disturbed as in

IT'S THE KIND OF FURNITURE I NEVER SAID I'D HAVE (It's the kind of furniture I said I'd never have)
I DISREGARD THIS AS PRECISE (I regard this as imprecise).

The second type of detailed planning involves adding on word endings in the appropriate place. This has been done incorrectly in:

SHE WASH UPPED THE DISHES (She washed up the dishes)
SHE COME BACKS TOMORROW (She comes back tomorrow)
HE BECAME MENTALIER UNHEALTHY (He became mentally unhealthier).

However, we can say rather more about the assemblage of words and endings than the vague comment that they are 'slotted together'. We noted in Chapter 3 that speakers seem to have an internal neural 'pacemaker' – a biological 'beat' which helps them to integrate and organize their utterances, and that this pacemaker may utilize the syllable as a basic unit. If we look more carefully, we find that syllables are organized into *feet* – a foot being a unit which includes a 'strong' or stressed syllable. And we see that feet are organized into tone groups. In other words, we have a hierarchy of rhythmic units: tone groups made up of feet, and feet made up of syllables:

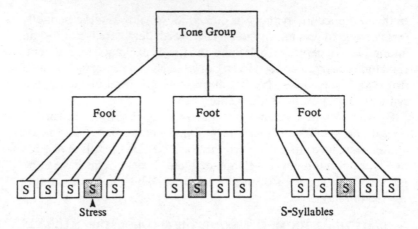

So within each tone group an utterance is planned foot by foot. This is indicated by the fact that transposed words are normally similarly stressed, and occupy similar places in their respective feet. For example:

HE FOUND A WÍFE FOR HIS JÓB (He found a job for his wife)
THE QUÁKE CAUSED: EXTENSIVE VÁLLEY: IN THE DÁMAGE (The quake caused extensive damage in the valley).

Within each foot, the stressed or 'tonic' word may be activated first, since tonic words are statistically more likely to be involved in tongue slips than unstressed ones (Boomer and Laver 1968). Moreover, the importance of the syllable as a 'psychologically real' unit is shown by the fact that tongue slips 'obey a structural law with regard to syllable place' (Boomer and Laver 1968, p. 7). That is, the initial sound of a syllable will affect another initial sound, a final sound will affect another final, and vowels affect vowels, as in:

JAWFULLY LOINED (lawfully joined)
HASS OR GRASH (hash or grass)
BUD BEGS (bed bugs).

According to one theory, sound misplacements like those above occur because a 'scan-copying' mechanism has gone wrong (Shattuck-Hufnagel 1979). Supposedly, words already selected for utterance are kept chalked up on a mental blackboard, waiting to be used. A scanning device copies each word segment across into its correct place, then wipes it off the blackboard. In an error such as LOWING THE MORN (mowing the lawn) the L in LAWN was mistakenly copied across to the beginning of the wrong word, and wiped away. The remaining M was then copied onto the only available word-beginning. In a repetition error, such as CHEW CHEW (two) TABLETS, the speaker forgot to wipe CH off the board after copying it.

As in CHEW CHEW, misplaced segments end up forming real though inappropriate words more often than one would expect from chance (Motley 1985). HOLED AND SEALED (soled and heeled), BEEF NEEDLE (noodle) SOUP, MORE THAN YOUR WIFE'S (life's) WORTH are further examples of this tendency. This is further evidence of the existence of a monitoring device which double-checks the final result to see if it is plausible. An overhasty check has perhaps allowed these real words through.

The general picture of speech production is of practised behaviour performed in a great hurry, such a hurry that the speaker does not have time to check the details in full. Just as in the comprehension of speech, a listener employs perceptual strategies (short cuts which enable him to jump to conclusions about what he is hearing), so in the production of speech, production strategies are possibly utilized. A speaker does not have time to check each segment of the word in detail, but possibly relies on a monitoring device to stop the utterance of too many inappropriate words. If, however, a word happens to be superficially plausible, it is likely to pass the monitoring device and be uttered.

Let us recapitulate: at the outline planning stage, the key words, syntax, and intonation of the tone group as a whole are set up. At the detailed planning stage, words and endings are slotted in foot by foot, with the stressed word in each foot possibly activated first. Finally, the remaining unstressed syllables are assembled.

Where does all this leave us? Still fairly much in the dark, compared with what we need to know. There are still enormous gaps in our knowledge, and much of what we have said is hypothetical. We have realized that, for every clause uttered, a human speaker must be carrying out a number of complex overlapping tasks. The question of how all this can be fitted into a coherent linguistic model is still to be solved. Perhaps, as an epilogue to the problems of speech planning and production, we can quote the words of a character in Oscar Wilde's play *The Importance of Being Earnest*, who commented that 'Truth is never pure, and rarely simple.'

12 Banker's clerk or hippopotamus?
The future of psycholinguistics

He thought he saw a Banker's Clerk
Descending from a bus:
He looked again, and found it was
A Hippopotamus.

LEWIS CARROLL
Sylvie and Bruno

Psycholinguistics is, as this book has shown, a field of study riddled with controversies. Frequently, apparently simple data can be interpreted in totally different ways. The psycholinguist often finds that he is in the same situation as the Lewis Carroll character who is not sure whether he is looking at a banker's clerk or a hippopotamus.

In this general situation, it would be over-optimistic to predict the future of the subject with any confidence. However, certain lines of inquiry are beginning to emerge as important, some of which are mentioned or foreshadowed in this book. Perhaps a useful way to introduce them is to outline briefly the conclusions we have reached so far, and show the issues which arise from them.

General conclusions

As we noted in the Introduction, three psycholinguistic topics can be singled out as particularly important: the acquisition question, the relationship of linguistic knowledge to language use, and the comprehension and production of speech – and these areas were the principal concern of this book.

We introduced the topic of acquisition by outlining the 'nature–nurture' controversy. Is language a 'natural' phenomenon such as walking or sexual activity? Or is it a skill which we learn, such as knitting? We saw that Skinner's attempts to explain language as purely learned behaviour turn out to be a dismal failure. The claim that the antics of rats can explain language is without foundation. Not only are animal experiments irrelevant to language acquisition, but language itself, on closer examination, is infinitely more complex than one might imagine. This, we saw, leaves us with a problem. If psychologists are unable to explain the acquisition of language by means of simple learning theories, how is it that humans become proficient at talking in such a relatively short period of time? One possible solution has been proposed by Chomsky: he suggests that a person's ability to speak is innate rather than learned – that the human species is 'pre-programmed' for language. This is the possibility that we examined in the next few chapters.

In Chapter 2 we looked at human language beside animal communication. We noted that, as far as we could tell, the human race is the only species which possesses language. Although a number of animal communication systems share some features of human language, no animal communication system possesses them all. And when we looked at the attempts made to teach a simplified language system to apes, we saw that their achievements in this sphere do not seem particularly impressive compared with those of human children. The apes seem capable of learning a language-like system, but they do not seem predisposed to learn it. In brief, the results of the animal experiments suggest that language in humans is an innately programmed activity.

In Chapters 3 and 4 we examined the biological evidence. We noted that the brain, as well as the teeth, tongue and vocal cords, seem to have been adapted to the needs of speech. We also pointed out that talking requires the synchronization of so many different operations that it seems likely that humans are innately 'set' to cope with this task. We also noted that language has all the hallmarks of biologically triggered behaviour. It emerges when the individual reaches a certain level of maturation, then develops at its own natural pace, following a more or less standard sequence of 'milestones'. And direct teaching and intensive practice appear to have relatively little effect. We therefore came to the firm conclusion that there was biological evidence for innate language ability.

Our next step was to try and find out exactly what is innate. In Chapter 5, therefore, we outlined the views of Chomsky. First, we described his 'classic' (1965) views, in which he suggested that every child is born equipped with a Language Acquisition Device, which contained a hypothesis-maker, a set of language universals, and an evaluation procedure which supposedly picked out the best possible grammar for the child. We then explained that he had abandoned these early views largely because the evaluation procedure had proved impossible to specify. Consequently, he had failed to solve the 'learnability' problem, how children acquire a full grammar on the basis of the scanty evidence they are exposed to.

Next, we moved on to his more recent 'principles and parameters' viewpoint (1986). Here, the learnability problem is solved by the assumption that children are guided somewhat more rigidly by their innate programme. He now assumes that children are born with a two-tier system – a set of language principles, and a further set of 'parameters', aspects of language which can vary in certain specified ways. The child has to observe the language he or she is exposed to, and 'set switches' in one direction or another. The language faculty is perceived to be a separate 'module' or component in the mind, independent of general cognitive abilities.

In Chapters 6 and 7 we looked at language acquisition in the light of Chomsky's proposals. In Chapter 6, we noted that children's speech is not just a random amalgam of badly copied adult utterances. Children seem to be instinctively aware that language is rule-governed, and to be devising their own rules to account for the data they hear. However, in the early stages the rules did not seem to be necessarily linguistic ones. Children might just be applying their general intelligence.

In Chapter 7 we considered three alternative possibilities. Either children contain highly specific linguistic information, which requires minimal exposure to activate, as Chomsky suggests. Or children solve the puzzle of language by using their general intelligence. Or they are equipped with an innate language processing device.

Chomsky's proposals were not borne out. Although children have some outline clues about language, in that they are predisposed to look for hierarchical structure and structure-dependent operations, they seem unaware that language might be organized on two levels, a 'deep' level and a 'surface' one. They do not seem to know about universal constraints at an early age, and there was no sign of 'switch-setting'.

However, there seems to be much more than general intelligence at work, aided by helpful parents and a desire to satisfy everyday needs. There is no clear-cut link between parental input and children's output. Children's progress cannot be explained by assuming that they talk to get what they want. Furthermore, there are several cases in the literature – Marta, Chelsea and Genie in particular – where there is an enormous discrepancy between linguistic and general cognitive abilities.

Children seem to be equipped with an innate linguistic puzzle-solving device. They appear to extract language from the jumble of speech they hear going on around them by following a set of inbuilt 'operating principles'. In other words, they have relatively little advance knowledge about the actual *form* of language, but seem instead to have a remarkable ability for processing linguistic data. We are still a long way from specifying exactly how the operating principles work. And we do not know how children backtrack in order to correct their wrong assumptions. This is still quite puzzling, since they seem to be impervious to corrections by other people.

We may summarize the contents of Chapters 1 to 7 by saying that we found strong evidence in favour of the suggestion that a human's ability to talk is innate. However, when it came to discovering exactly *what* is innate, we ran into difficulties. Chomsky's assertion that children are endowed with a highly structured Universal Grammar seems over-optimistic. His proposals are not borne out by the evidence. We preferred, instead, the suggestion that children have an inbuilt ability for *processing* linguistic data – an ability which seems to be partly separate from general cognitive abilities. But we do not yet understand the mechanisms underlying the language processor.

In the rest of the book, we turned to the language of adults. Chapters 8 and 9 were devoted to the relationship between language knowledge as specified in a transformational grammar and language use. In Chapter 8 we first explained just why someone might want to propose a transformational grammar in the first place, and outlined some of the steps by which Chomsky arrived at his classic (1965) version. We then described some of the problems which cropped up with transformations, and showed how in attempting to solve them Chomsky moved on to a somewhat different version, one which deals with a far deeper, more abstract type of knowledge.

In Chapter 9 we described the various attempts by psycholinguists in the 1960s and 1970s to test whether a classic transformational grammar was of any relevance in the comprehension and production of speech. We concluded, as they did, that transformations were certainly not used in speech processing, and that the notion that hearers recover a Chomsky-like deep structure was somewhat unlikely, though had not been conclusively disproved. We decided that a classic transformational grammar represented a 'linguistic archive' which contained knowledge about language, such as which sentences are paraphrases of one another. It was not directly used in speech comprehension, though was available for consultation if necessary. We further noted that Chomsky's most recent model was even less likely to be of direct use to speakers and hearers. But it would be foolish of psycholinguists to ignore his views entirely. He was seeking for fundamental principles of language which, if found, would profoundly affect our understanding of how people cope with speech.

Having concluded that a transformational grammar is no help in explaining how a person actually *uses* language, we then turned to our final topic: what exactly *does* happen when someone comprehends or produces an utterance?

Chapter 10 dealt with the process of comprehension. We noted that, to a surprising extent, people hear what they expect to hear. They look for certain clues when they are decoding, and if they find them, they jump to conclusions about what the speaker is saying. In other words, people utilize perceptual strategies or short cuts in the comprehension of speech. Sentences are difficult to understand if the perceptual strategies do not work, or if they involve other more general difficulties, such as backward processing. However, strategies alone could not fully explain how we comprehend sentences, they were too haphazard and too powerful. So we considered an orderly left-to-right model. This worked well, particularly when dealing with complicated sentences. Such a model holds items in memory until it reaches a gap in the structure where they fit. But numerous queries remain concerning the gap-filling mechanism. Furthermore, it is unclear how strategies and gap-filling models interweave, as they seem to do. And the relationship between syntax and the lexicon in left-to-right models is still obscure, particularly as recognizing words turns out to be a more complex process than had previously been supposed. Numerous possible candidates are automatically activated, and the suppression of unwanted words is as important as the recognition of one wanted one.

In Chapter 11 we turned to speech production. This proved to be a highly complex process in which each clause is partially planned while the previous one is being uttered. Key words, outline syntax and intonation are possibly planned first, then the remaining words and endings are slotted into the correct place. The organization and integration of the various parts of the clause depend on a rhythmic principle. Selecting words involves activating numerous possible ones, then narrowing down the choice to the required one.

Let us now summarize our conclusions concerning the three topics we investigated.

First, *something* specific to language is innate, even though we are not entirely sure what this something consists of. Language cannot be explained simply as an offshoot of general intelligence, even though we undoubtedly make use of general cognitive abilities when we speak, in a way as yet undefined.

Secondly, we realized that transformational grammar is relatively little use in explaining *how* we comprehend and produce utterances. The link between language knowledge, as represented in a transformational grammar, and language use is tenuous. However, Chomsky is seeking to specify potentially important principles underlying language, so should not be ignored.

Thirdly, we realize that comprehension and production are far more complex processes than most people have assumed. They involve a considerable amount of parallel processing, and the suppression of unwanted alternatives turns out to be as important as the selection of particular words and structures.

Where do we go from here?

Future prospects

Cooperation between disciplines is possibly the key to future progress in psycholinguistics. The necessity of a link between linguistics and psychology is obvious. But collaboration is also needed between psycholinguists and those involved in ethology, neurology and artificial intelligence.

Let us look at each of the three main areas dealt with in this book and see how collaborative efforts might solve some of the major problems – and in some cases are beginning to do so already.

The acquisition problem is likely to be helped by a growing understanding of 'guided learning' (Gould and Marler 1987). Instinct was once thought to be diametrically opposed to learning. Insects such as bees were assumed to be pre-programmed with instincts, but more complex animals were thought to rely mainly on learning. But this is turning out to be a false dichotomy. Insects need to learn quite a lot, though this learning is innately guided. Bees, for example, seem to be innately disposed to learn about the various types of flowers, since 'it would be impossible to equip each bee at birth with a field guide to all the flowers it might visit' (Gould and Marler 1987, p. 62). And the apparently free-range learning of higher animals is turning out to be innately guided. They are pre-programmed to 'tune in' to particular aspects of the environment. Innately guided learning is the 'key' to human language, which is why children find it easier to learn to talk than to cope with the apparently much simpler tasks of learning to add and subtract. A fuller knowledge of this phenomenon in the animal world is likely to advance our understanding of it in humans.

Research into other systems within the mind, such as the visual system, are also likely to promote our understanding of language, in two ways. First, it can help us deal with the question of maturation within humans. Are other human abilities immediately available to babies? Or is there a slow tadpole to frog progression, with infants behaving fairly differently from adults? The range of answers might help us to understand how language is likely to be dealt with.

Second, we can gain insights into the tricky question of modularity. Many people now agree that the mind has a 'modular structure', that is, it consists of a number of relatively separate 'modules' or components, each with its own function. However, no-one can agree on the exact nature of these modules. Are they biologically programmed entities which remain separate throughout life (e.g. Fodor 1983, 1985)? Are they independent entities at birth, but gradually link up and interact as humans mature (e.g. Gardner 1983, 1985)? Or is the mind relatively unified at first, with separate modules developing in the course of time: 'Modules are not born; they are made' (Bates *et al*. 1988, p. 284)? Or are they a combination of these possibilities: 'Modularity should not be solely restricted to innate givens; modularity can also arise developmentally as the *product* of constructive processes' (Karmiloff-Smith 1986, p. 142)? A deeper understanding of all modular systems would be of advantage for language.

Modularity is also important for the second major topic of this book, *the relationship of language knowledge to language usage*. Most people agree that there are modules within modules. But there are some radical disagreements as to how many sub-modules are likely to exist within the language faculty, and how they work (e.g. Fodor 1983, 1985; Bates *et al*. 1988). According to Fodor, 'informational encapsulation is an essential property of modular systems' (Fodor 1985, p. 3). The information in a module is 'encapsulated' within it, in the sense that it works independently of other modules. For example, in word recognition, the automatic activation of all words which fit the sound pattern is typical of a modularized system, because it does not take into account the syntax or context. And some psycholinguists have argued for 'modular parsing', in that the comprehension of sentences is claimed to start with the blind application of syntactic rules (Chapter 10). These modules clearly involve knowledge, yet they are identified via their usage. We therefore need to know how many modules there are, how they interact with each other, and how they link up with non-modularized capacities such as thinking before we can solve the knowledge–usage problem.

A further way of sorting out the knowledge and usage problem is to explore the psychological validity of other models of grammar, apart from Chomsky's. Both 'generalized phrase structure grammar' (GPSG) (Gazdar *et al*. 1985) and 'lexical-functional grammar' (Bresnan 1982) propose grammars in which the divide between linguistic structures and the processes which utilize them are much closer. There is now a growing body of work which attempts to test these models.

The interweaving of world knowledge with linguistic knowledge is already being studied by pragmatics, the branch of linguistics which looks at how people actually use speech in real-life situations. If you are asked 'Do you know the time?', why are you likely to say 'Seven o'clock' and not simply 'Yes'? Or if someone said: The film's at eight. Can we trust Penelope's car?', the assumption one makes is that Penelope has a car which might break down, which might make us miss the film. How did we come to this conclusion, when there are in theory numerous other deductions we could have made from these sentences? Possible insights into how we pick the most relevant interpretation are already under discussion (e.g. Sperber and Wilson 1986), and will further clarify the knowledge–usage issue.

A major problem in sorting out issues of *comprehension and production* has been the relative feebleness of digital computers. Computers have been the major metaphor for human language processes for the past ten years at least, yet 'there is a fundamental flaw in the assumption that speech perception is carried out in a processor that looks at all like a digital computer' (Elman and McClelland 1984). Recently, however, more powerful, parallel processing computers have come into being. And processing models are being devised which take the human brain as its inspiration: 'We wish to replace the "computer metaphor" as a model of the mind with the "brain metaphor" as a model of the mind' (Rumelhart *et al*. 1986, p. 75).

These new models take into account the fact that in most human tasks a number of different pieces of information must be kept in the mind at once. Intuitively, each aspect of the situation influences all the other aspects, and is in turn influenced by them. The pioneers in this field note: 'To articulate these intuitions, we and others have turned to a class of models we call *Parallel Distributed Processing* (PDP) models. These models assume that information processing takes place through the interactions of a large number of simple processing elements called units, each sending excitatory and inhibitory signals to other units' (McClelland *et al.* 1986). In brief, the units themselves are very simple, metaphorically somewhat like brain cells. They are distributed in various locations. The power and interest of the system is their interconnections, so that this type of theory is also known as 'connectionism'.

To take a well-known example (McClelland *et al.* 1986), suppose in reading one came across a word whose second letter could be either P or R because the bottom half has been covered with an ink blot (SPOT/SROT). P and R would be activated by the top half, but then R would be suppressed because when possible lexical items are considered, there is no word *SROT. Information about each letter form, and about each lexical item, is possibly stored in a separate place, but all this is linked up and considered in parallel.

The physiological flavour of this model exerts a great appeal, and 'connectionism is in a state of explosive development' (Johnson-Laird 1988, p. 193). As yet, it has been applied only to fragments of language processing and learning (McClelland and Rumelhart 1986), as briefly mentioned in Chapters 7 and 10. So far, its main importance in language processing has been to emphasize the fact that suppression is at least as important as selection. Its application to language learning is more controversial, though it has been welcomed by some as a theory which 'fundamentally recasts our methods of investigating and thinking about large tracts of the map of learning' (Sampson 1987, p. 871). It will undoubtedly be a major influence on psycholinguistics in the next few years, especially as it claims to be able to handle the integration of world knowledge into speech processes.

To summarize, we have pinpointed several ways in which insights from different disciplines are likely to move psycholinguistics forwards in the near future with regard to the topics examined in this book.

Overall, then, the next few years are likely to be marked by interdisciplinary co-operation. A quarter of a century ago, psycho-linguistics was a new, fringe discipline, like a small spring or a seedling, compared to the more mature areas of the subject. Now, it can be viewed as a wide river, which is gathering increasing momentum as other streams feed into it. Or we can perhaps envisage it as a flourishing tree, whose branches shoot out in all directions, and which is likely to get taller and stronger still. Exactly how the subject will develop is uncertain. Psycholinguistics is a field of study likely to spring surprises on researchers. A seemingly dead and forgotten area may suddenly spring into life. A living and on-going subject 'is constantly sprouting new leaves on old wood, and sometimes quite suddenly the bush is ablaze with blossom of a novel shade' (A. L. Lloyd).

Notes and suggestions for further reading

This section contains outline suggestions for further reading. I have kept these to a minimum, since the books recommended will give further references if these are needed. I have also drawn attention to certain over-simplifications or biases in the book which might mislead the beginning student.

Introduction

The distinction drawn here between psychological and linguistic psycholinguistics is perhaps over-simplified. Psychological psycholinguists are sometimes divided into experimental psychologists and developmental psychologists. The latter often bridge the gap between psychologists and linguists, utilizing both natural data and the results of experiments – as in the work of Roger Brown and Dan Slobin.

For those who wish to acquaint themselves with linguistics there are numerous elementary textbooks. The following are fairly widely used as introductions to the subject (full details are given in the list of references at the end of this book): Aitchison (1987), Akmajian, Demers and Harnish (1984), Fromkin and Rodman (1988), Yule (1985). For more specific information on transformational-generative grammar, Brown (1984) and Newmeyer (1987) contain clear accounts of the changes which have taken place in Chomsky's views over the years. Radford (1988), and Van Riemsdijk and Williams (1986) are good coursebooks. Cook (1988) provides a brief survey of his recent ideas. Alternative viewpoints (along-side Chomsky's) are outlined in Horrocks (1987) and Sells (1985).

For surveys of psycholinguistics which deal with some of the topics I have omitted, see Clark and Clark (1977), Ellis and Beattie (1986), Garnham (1985).

Chapter 1

This chapter is based to a large extent on Chomsky's review of Skinner's book *Verbal Behavior* (Chomsky 1959). This article, now a linguistic 'classic' is perhaps still the best starting point for understanding the direction taken by language acquisition studies in the 1960s and early 1970s. Note that Chomsky sometimes in his writings wrongly implies that Skinner typifies the mainstream of current psychological thought, a misleading fallacy (as Sampson 1975, explains).

The viewpoint that language is entirely dependent on general cognitive abilities gained popularity in the 1970s, when it was christened 'the cognitive revolution' by some of its supporters. This movement is well represented by Donaldson (1978), Sampson (1980), Bruner (1974, 1975), and more recently by Bates *et al.* (1988), Bates and MacWhinney (1987).

Chapter 2

Animal communication is looked at in a wider perspective in Griffin (1984). For overviews from the linguistic point of view, see Sebeok (1977), Sebeok and Umiker-Sebeok (1980), Demers (1988). On birdsong, see Nottebohm (1984).

The properties of sign language, and its relationship to spoken language, are discussed in Wilbur (1987) and Padden (1988).

Dingwall (1988) provides a useful summary chart of the various talking apes, who now number more than fifteen. De Luce and Wilder (1983) is a book of papers by various authors which provides a useful survey of the linguistic achievements (or non-achievements) of primates.

With regard to work on the individual apes, the literature is now voluminous, and different papers highlight different aspects of their achievements, so it is difficult to select 'key' papers. In the references below, major books are noted in bold print. Of the 'first generation' apes, Washoe and other chimps taught by her trainers are discussed in B. T. Gardner and R. A. Gardner (1971, 1975, 1980, 1985); R. A. Gardner and B. T. Gardner (1969, 1978, 1984); Fouts (1983); Fouts *et al.* (1982, 1984). Sarah's achievements are in D. Premack (1970, 1971, 1972, 1976); A. J. Premack (1976); Premack and Premack (1974, **1983**).

Of the later apes, Lana and her successors are discussed in Rumbaugh (**1977**), Savage-Rumbaugh and Rumbaugh (1980), Savage-Rumbaugh (**1986**). The gorilla Koko is dealth with in

Patterson (1978, 1980), Patterson and Linden (**1981**). Nim Chimpsky is discussed in Terrace (**1979**, 1979a, 1983).

Chapter 3

This chapter took its inspiration from Lenneberg's pioneering (1967) work, which is still worth reading, though certain sections are now out of date.

Springer and Deutsch (1985) provide a readable introduction to the brain as a whole. Excellent overviews on the location of language in the brain can be found in Caplan (1987, 1988).

Chapter 4

The early part of this chapter is based on Lenneberg (1967), who is now regarded as an insightful pioneer.

The section on the stages of child language is based on Brown (1973) which contains a comprehensive summary of his own work with the 'Harvard children', Adam, Eve and Sarah, in the early stages of language acquisition.

Reich (1986) provides a summary of language development which takes into account a wider range of children. Scovel (1988) discusses the 'critical period' issue.

Chapter 5

This chapter is based primarily on Chomsky (1965) for his 'classical' views on transformational grammar, and on Chomsky (1986) for his more recent ones. See the notes on the Introduction (above) for accounts of Chomsky's work written by others. The pros and cons of Chomsky's viewpoint(s) are discussed in Modgil and Modgil (1987).

Most of the literature on 'learnability' and the 'logical problem' of language acquisition is highly technical. For a useful summary, see Atkinson (1987).

Chapter 6

Bennett-Kastor (1988) discusses how to analyse child language.

Over the early stages of language acquisition, Barrett (1985) contains a range of views on one-word utterances. Aitchison (1987a) gives an outline of the main current theories on early word meaning.

Bloom, Lightbown and Hood (1975), Bowerman (1973), Braine (1976), and Brown (1973) discuss two-word utterances at some length. MacWhinney (1978) gives an account of the acquisition of word endings. Fletcher (1985) provides a detailed account of the development of one child.

Chapter 7

The view expressed in this chapter that neither Chomsky's 'content' claim nor general intelligence can account for language is possibly shared by a majority of child-language researchers, though not by all. Goodluck (1986) argues strongly for Chomsky's viewpoint, and studies by Lust (1983, 1986) are consistent with the notion of 'switch-setting' with regard to the 'principle branching direction' of languages. The general puzzle-solving approach is supported by Bates *et al.* (1988), Bates and MacWhinney (1987), MacWhinney (1987a).

There are several books of readings which contain various views on child language, of which the most wide-ranging are possibly Fletcher and Garman (1986), MacWhinney (1987), Wanner and Gleitman (1982). For work on languages other than English, and the most recent version of Slobin's 'operating principles', see Slobin (1985).

Other instances of children whose intelligence and language fails to match are discussed in Curtiss (1981, 1982, 1988, 1988a).

Speech addressed to children is discussed in Snow and Ferguson (1977), Ferguson (1978), Fernald (1984), Wells and Robinson (1982).

The 'No negative evidence' problem is dealt with at some length in Bowerman (1988).

The description of the 'flowing with the tide' approach is a somewhat oversimplified account of the 'connectionist' or 'parallel distributed processing' (PDP) viewpoint of Rumelhart and McClelland (1987), on which see Chapter 12 in this book.

Chapter 8

As noted in the text, this chapter is based on Chomsky (1957) and (1986). See the notes on the Introduction for more comprehensive accounts of Chomsky's work.

Chapter 9

More detailed coverage of the material in this chapter can be found in Fodor, Bever and Garrett (1974) which, when it was published, was regarded as a definitive account of much of the early research on transformational grammar. However, they do not necessarily share the view of the 'archival' nature of a classic transformational grammar, which was proposed by Watt (1970).

Chapter 10

Speech perception has been somewhat skated over in this chapter. A short introduction can be found in Matthei and Roeper (1983), and more detailed treatment in Lieberman and Blumstein (1988).

The early part of this chapter is based on Bever's pioneering article on 'perceptual strategies' (1970) which is discussed in some depth in Fodor, Bever and Garrett (1974). Wider-based strategies are dealt with in Kimball (1973), Frazier and Rayner (1982, 1988).

'Gap-filling' models are discussed in Wanner and Maratsos (1978), Fodor (1978), Roeper and Matthei (1983). Marcus (1980) is an attempt to provide a full computational model.

Work on word recognition and selection is summarized and discussed in Aitchison (1987a).

There are a number of important recent collections of papers on speech comprehension, though they are not particularly easy to read. Dowty, Karttunen and Zwicky (1985) provide a useful overview of various approaches. King (1983) deals with the topic from the angles of artificial intelligence and theoretical linguistics, and Flores d'Arcais and Jarvella (1983) approach it from a psychology point of view.

Chapter 11

The examples of slips of the tongue in this chapter are mainly from my own collection, supplemented by examples from Fromkin (1973).

Cutler (1988) and Fromkin (1988) discuss the value of speech errors as evidence for speech production. Fromkin (1973), Fromkin (1980), and Cutler (1982) are collections of papers which deal with slips of the tongue.

Butterworth (1980) and (1983) are collections of papers which deal with a variety of issues on speech production. The papers in Allport *et al*. (1987) deal with the relation of perception to production, and of spoken language to written.

The literature on the topic of speech production tends to be split between those who take a serial (events happen in a specified order) view (e.g. Garrett 1988), and those who take a parallel processing view (e.g. Motley 1985). This chapter has tried to combine the two approaches.

On the lexicon, see Aitchison (1987a), Emmorey and Fromkin (1988).

Gardner (1974) is a readable account of brain damage problems in general. Lesser (1978) provides an introduction to the topic of dysphasia (aphasia), Caplan (1987) provides an up-to-date survey. Kean (1985) is a book of readings on the problem of aphasics who lack syntax.

Chapter 12

The predictions in this chapter are based on my own intuitions and discussions with colleagues.

Carston (1988) provides a useful survey of the differences between Chomsky's view of modularity and Fodor's. Tanenhaus *et al*. (1985) have a useful discussion from a psychology point of view.

Johnson-Laird (1988) has a brief introduction to PDP models, and McClelland (1988) promotes and defends them. The major works on PDP are the two volumes by Rumelhart and McClelland (1986), and McClelland and Rumelhart (1986).

The relationship between PDP models and brain physiology is examined in Ballard (1986).

References

Abrams, K., and Bever, T. G. (1969), 'Syntactic structure modifies attention during speech perception and recognition', *Quarterly Journal of Experimental Psychology*, **21**, pp. 280–90

Aitchison, J. (1981), *Language Change: Progress or Decay?* London: Fontana

Aitchison, J. (1987), *Linguistics* (3rd edn), London: Hodder and Stoughton, Teach Yourself Books

Aitchison, J. (1987a), *Words in the Mind: An Introduction to the Mental Lexicon*, Oxford: Basil Blackwell

Aitchison, J. (1988), Review of Hyams (1986) and Roeper and Williams (1987), *Journal of Linguistics* **24**, 527–31

Aitchison, J., and Straf, M. (1981), 'Lexical storage and retrieval: a developing skill?' *Linguistics* **19**, 751–95. Also in Cutler (1982)

Akmajian, A., Demers, R. A., and Harnish, R. M. (1984), *Linguistics: An Introduction to Language and Communication* (2nd edn), Cambridge, Mass: MIT Press

Allport, A., Mackay, D., Prinz, W., and Scheerer, E. (1987), *Language Perception and Production*, New York: Academic Press

Asher, J. and Price, B. (1967), 'The learning strategy of total physical response: some age differences', *Child Development*, **38**, pp. 1220–7

Atkinson, M. (1987), 'Mechanisms for language acquisition: learning, parameter-setting and triggering', *First Language*, **7**, pp. 3–30

Augarde, T. (1984), *The Oxford Guide to Word Games*, Oxford: Oxford University Press

Baars, B. J. (1980), 'The competing plans hypothesis: an heuristic viewpoint on the causes of errors in speech', in Dechert and Raupach (1980)

Ballard, D. H. (1986), 'Cortical connections and parallel processing: structure and function', peer commentary, and author's response, *Behavioral and Brain Sciences*, **9**, pp. 67–90

Bar-Adon, A., and Leopold, W. F. (1971), *Child Language: A Book of Readings*, Englewood Cliffs, NJ: Prentice-Hall

Barrett, M. (1982), 'The holophrastic hypothesis: conceptual and empirical issues', *Cognition* **11**, pp. 47–76

Barrett, M. (1985), *Children's Single-Word Speech*, Chichester: Wiley

Barrett, M. (in press), 'Early language development', in A. Slater and G. Bremner (eds), *Infant Development*, London: Lawrence Erlbaum

Bates, E., Bretherton, I., and Snyder, L. (1988), *From First Words to Grammar: Individual Differences and Dissociable Mechanisms*, Cambridge: Cambridge University Press

Bates, E., and MacWhinney, B. (1987), 'Competition, variation, and language learning', in MacWhinney (1987)

Bellugi, U. (1971), 'Simplification in children's language', in Huxley and Ingram (1971)

Bellugi, U., and Brown, R. (1964), *The Acquisition of Language*, Monograph of the Society for Research in Child Development, no. 29

Bennett-Kastor, T. (1988), *Analyzing Children's Language: Methods and Theories*, Oxford: Basil Blackwell

Berko, J. (1958), 'The child's learning of English morphology', *Word*, **14**, pp. 150–77. Also in Bar-Adon and Leopold (1971)

Bernstein, B. (1972), 'Social class, language and socialisation', in P. P. Giglioli (ed.), *Language and Social Context*, Harmondsworth: Penguin

Bever, T. G. (1970), 'The cognitive basis for linguistic structures', in Hayes (1970)

Bever, T. G. (1981), 'Normal acquisition processes explain the critical period for language learning', in K. C. Diller (ed.), *Individual Differences and Universals in Language Learning Aptitude*, Rowley, Mass: Newbury House

Bever, T. G., Fodor, J. A., and Weksel, W. (1965), 'Theoretical notes on the acquisition of syntax: a critique of "Contextual Generalisation" ', *Psychological Review*, **72**, pp. 467–82

Bever, T. G., Lackner, J. R., and Kirk, R. (1969), 'The underlying structures of sentences are the primary units of immediate speech processing', *Perception and Psychophysics*, **5**, pp. 225–31

Blank, M., Gessner, M., and Esposito, A. (1979), 'Language without communication: a case study', *Journal of Child Language*, **6**, pp. 329–52

Bloch, B., and Trager, G. (1942), *Outline of Linguistic Analysis*, Baltimore: Waverley Press

Bloom, L. (1970), *Language Development: Form and Function in Emerging Grammars*, Cambridge, Mass: MIT Press

Bloom, L. (1973), *One Word at a Time*, The Hague: Mouton

Bloom, L., Lightbown, P., and Hood, L. (1975), *Structure and Variation in Child Language*, Monograph of the Society for Research in Child Development 40.2

Bloom, L., Tackeff, J., and Lahey, M. (1984), 'Learning *to* in complement constructions', *Journal of Child Language*, **11**, pp. 391–406

Blumenthal. A. L. (1966), 'Observations with self-embedded sentences', *Psychonomic Science*, **6**, pp. 453–54

Blumenthal, A. L. (1967), 'Prompted recall of sentences', *Journal of Verbal Learning and Verbal Behavior*, 6, pp. 203–6

Boomer, D. S. (1965), 'Hesitation and grammatical encoding', *Language and Speech*, 8, pp. 148–58. Also in Oldfield and Marshall (1968)

Boomer, D. S., and Laver, J. D. M. (1968), 'Slips of the tongue', *British Journal of Disorders of Communication*, 3, pp. 1–12. Also in Fromkin (1973)

Borer, H., and Wexler, K. (1987), 'The maturation of syntax', in Roeper and Williams (1987)

Bowerman, M. (1973), *Early Syntactic Development*, Cambridge: Cambridge University Press

Bowerman, M. (1985), 'What shapes children's grammars?', in Slobin (1985) vol. 2

Bowerman, M. (1987), 'Commentary: mechanisms of language acquisition', in MacWhinney (1987)

Bowerman, M. (1988), 'The "no negative evidence" problem: how do children avoid constructing an overly general grammar', in Hawkins (1988)

Braine, M. D. S. (1963), 'The ontogeny of English phrase structure: the first phase', *Language*, 39, pp. 1–14. Also in Bar-Adon and Leopold (1971), Ferguson and Slobin (1973)

Braine, M. D. S. (1971), 'The acquisition of language in infant and child', in C. E. Reed (ed.), *The Learning of Language*, New York: Appleton-Century-Crofts

Braine, M. D. S. (1976), *Children's First Word Combinations*, Monograph of the Society for Research in Child Development, 41.1

Bresnan, J. W. (1982), *The Mental Representation of Grammatical Relations*, Cambridge, Mass: MIT Press

Brown, K. (1984), *Linguistics Today*, London: Fontana

Brown, E. R. (1958), *Words and Things*, New York: The Free Press

Brown, R. (1970), *Psycholinguistics: Selected Papers*, New York: The Free Press

Brown, R. (1973), *A First Language*, London: Allen and Unwin

Brown, R., and Bellugi, U. (1964), 'Three processes in the child's acquisition of syntax', in Lenneberg (1964). Also in Brown (1970)

Brown, R., Cazden, C., and Bellugi, U. (1968), 'The child's grammar from I to III', in J. P. Hill (ed.), *Minnesota Symposium on Child Psychology*, vol. II, Minneapolis: University of Minnesota Press. Also in Brown (1970), Ferguson and Slobin (1973)

Brown, R., and Fraser, C. (1964), 'The acquisition of syntax', in Bellugi and Brown (1964)

Brown, R., and McNeill, D. (1966), 'The "Tip of the Tongue" phenomenon', *Journal of Verbal Learning and Verbal Behavior*, 5, pp. 325–37. Also in Brown (1970).

Bruner, J. S. (1974), 'From communication to language: a psychological perspective', *Cognition*, **3**, pp. 255–87

Bruner, J. S. (1975), 'The ontogenesis of speech acts', *Journal of Child Language*, **2**, pp. 1–21

Buffery, A. W. H. (1978), 'Neuropsychological aspects of language development', in Waterson and Snow (1978)

Butterworth, B. (1980), *Language Production*, vol. I, *Speech and Talk*, New York: Academic Press

Butterworth, B. (1980a), 'Evidence from pauses in speech', in Butterworth (1980)

Butterworth, B. (1983), *Language Production*, vol. 2, *Development, Writing and Other Language Processes*, New York: Academic Press

Caplan, D. (1987), *Neurolinguistics and Linguistic Aphasiology: An Introduction*, Cambridge: Cambridge University Press

Caplan, D. (1988), 'The biological basis for language', in Newmeyer (1988), vol. 3

Caplan, D., Lecours, A. R., and Smith, A. (1984), *Biological Perspectives on Language*, Cambridge, Mass: MIT Press

Carlson, G. N., and Tanenhaus, M. K. (1988), 'Thematic roles and language comprehension', in W. Wilkins (ed.), *Syntax and Semantics*, vol. 21: *Thematic Relations*, New York: Academic Press

Carston, R. (1988), 'Language and cognition', in Newmeyer (1988), vol. 3

Cazden, C. (1972), *Child Language and Education*, New York: Holt, Rinehart and Winston

Cheshire, J. (1982), *Variation in an English Dialect: A Sociolinguistic Study*, Cambridge: Cambridge University Press

Chomsky, C. (1969), *The Acquisition of Syntax in Children from 5 to 10*, Cambridge, Mass: MIT Press

Chomsky, N. (1957), *Syntactic Structures*, The Hague: Mouton

Chomsky, N. (1959), Review of Skinner's *Verbal Behavior*, *Language*, **35**, pp. 26–58

Chomsky, N. (1963), 'Formal properties of grammars', in Luce, Bush and Galanter (1963)

Chomsky, N. (1965), *Aspects of the Theory of Syntax*, Cambridge, Mass: MIT Press

Chomsky, N. (1967), 'The formal nature of language', in Lenneberg (1967)

Chomsky, N. (1971), 'Recent contributions to the theory of innate ideas', in J. R. Searle (ed.), *The Philosophy of Language*, Oxford: Oxford University Press

Chomsky, N. (1972), *Language and Mind*, enlarged edition, New York: Harcourt Brace Jovanovich

Chomsky, N. (1972a), *Problems of Knowledge and Freedom*, London: Fontana

Chomsky, N. (1978), 'On the biological basis of language capacities', in Miller and Lenneberg (1978). Also in Chomsky (1980)

Chomsky, N. (1979), *Language and Responsibility*, Sussex: The Harvester Press

Chomsky, N. (1980), *Rules and Representations*, Oxford: Basil Blackwell

Chomsky, N. (1981), *Lectures on Government and Binding*, Dordrecht: Foris

Chomsky, N. (1982), *Some Concepts and Consequences of the Theory of Government and Binding*, Cambridge, Mass: MIT Press

Chomsky, N. (1986), *Knowledge of Language: Its Nature, Origin and Use*, New York: Praeger

Chomsky, N. (1988). *Language and Problems of Knowledge*, Cambridge, Mass: MIT Press

Clark, E. V. (1987), 'The principle of contrast: a constraint on language acquisition', in MacWhinney (1987)

Clark, H. H., and Clark, E. V. (1968), 'Semantic distinctions and memory for complex sentences', *Quarterly Journal of Experimental Psychology*, **20**, pp. 129–38

Clark, H. H., and Clark, E. V. (1977), *Psychology and Language*, New York: Harcourt Brace Jovanovich

Clifton, C., Frazier, L., and Connine, C. (1984), 'Lexical expectations in sentence comprehension', *Journal of Verbal Learning and Verbal Behavior*, **23**, pp. 696–708

Cohen, A. (1966), 'Errors of speech and their implication for understanding the strategy of language users', in Fromkin (1973)

Cook, V. J. (1988), *Chomsky's Universal Grammar*, Oxford: Basil Blackwell

Cooper, W. E., and Walker, E. C. T. (1979), *Sentence Processing*, New York: Lawrence Erlbaum

Crain, S., and Steedman, M. (1985), 'On not being led up the garden path: the use of context by the psychological syntax processor', in Dowty, Karttunen and Zwicky (1985)

Critchley, M. (1970), *Aphasiology*, London: Edward Arnold

Cromer, R. F. (1970), 'Children are nice to understand: surface structure clues for the recovery of a deep structure', *British Journal of Psychology*, **61**, pp. 397–408

Cromer, R. F. (1976), 'Developmental strategies for language', in V. Hamilton and M. D. Vernon (eds), *The Development of Cognitive Processes*, New York: Academic Press

Cross, T. (1977), 'Mothers' speech adjustments: the contribution of selected child listener variables', in Snow and Ferguson (1977)

Cruttenden, A. (1970), 'A phonetic study of babbling', *British Journal of Disorders of Communication*, **5**, pp. 110–17

Curtiss, S. (1977), *Genie: a psycholinguistic study of a modern-day 'wild child'*, New York: Academic Press

Curtiss, S. (1981), 'Dissociations between language and cognition: cases and implications', *Journal of Autism and Developmental Disorders*, 11, pp. 15–30

Curtiss, S. (1982), 'Developmental dissociation of language and cognition', in L. K. Obler and L. Menn (eds), *Exceptional Language and Linguistics*, New York: Academic Press

Curtiss, S. (1988), 'Abnormal language acquisition and the modularity of language', in Newmeyer (1988), vol. 2

Curtiss, S. (1988a), 'Abnormal language acquisition and grammar: evidence for the modularity of language', in Hyman and Li (1988)

Curtiss, S., Fromkin, V., Krashen, S., Rigler, D., and Rigler, M. (1974), 'The linguistic development of Genie', *Language*, 50, pp. 528–54

Cutler, A. (1976), 'Beyond parsing and lexical look-up: an enriched description of auditory sentence comprehension', in Wales and Walker (1976)

Cutler, A. (1982), *Slips of the Tongue and Speech Production*, Berlin: Mouton

Cutler, A. (1988), 'The perfect speech error', in Hyman and Li (1988)

Cutler, A., and Norris, D. (1979), 'Monitoring sentence comprehension', in Cooper and Walker (1979)

de Boysson-Bardies, B., Sagart, L., and Durand, C. (1984), 'Discernible differences in the babbling of infants according to target language', *Journal of Child Language*, 11, pp. 1–15

De Cecco, J. P. (1967), *The Psychology of Thought, Language and Instruction*, New York: Holt, Reinhart and Winston

de Luce, J., and Wilder, H. (eds) (1983), *Language in Primates*, New York: Springer-Verlag

De Reuck, A. V. S., and O'Connor, M. O. (1964), *Disorders of Language*, London: Churchill Livingstone

De Villiers, J. G., and De Villiers, P. A. (1978), *Language Acquisition*, Cambridge, Mass: Harvard University Press

De Villiers, P. A., and De Villiers, J. G. (1979), 'Form and function in the development of sentence negation', *Stanford University Papers and Reports on Child Language Development*, 17, pp. 37–64

Dechert, H. W., and Raupach, M. (1980), *Temporal Variables in Speech*, The Hague: Mouton

Dell, G. (1986), 'A spreading activation theory of retrieval in sentence production', *Psychological Review*, 93, pp. 283–321

Dell, G. S., and Reich, P. A. (1981), 'Stages in sentence production: an analysis of speech error data', *Journal of Verbal Learning and Verbal Behavior*, 20, pp. 611–29

Demers, R. A. (1988), 'Linguistics and animal communication', in Newmeyer (1988), vol. 3

Dennis, M. (1983), 'Syntax in brain-injured children', in Studdert-Kennedy (1983)

Dingwall, W. O. (1971), *A Survey of Linguistic Science*, Maryland: University of Maryland

Dingwall, W. O. (1988), 'The evolution of human communicative behavior', in Newmeyer (1988), vol. 3

Donaldson, M. (1978), *Children's Minds*, London: Fontana/Collins

Dowty, D. R., Karttunen, L., and Zwicky, A. M. (1985), *Natural Language Parsing: Psychological, Computational and Theoretical Perspectives*, Cambridge: Cambridge University Press

Eimas, P. D. (1984), 'Infant competence and the acquisition of language', in Caplan, Lecours and Smith (1984)

Eimas, P. D. (1985), 'The perception of speech in early infancy', *Scientific American*, **252** (1), pp. 34–40

Eimas, P. D., Siqueland, E., Jusczyk, P., and Vigorito, J. (1971), 'Speech perception in infants', *Science*, **171**, pp. 303–6

Ellis, A. W. (1980), 'On the Freudian theory of speech errors', in Fromkin (1980)

Ellis, A. W. (1985), 'The production of spoken words: a cognitive neuropsychological perspective', in A. W. Ellis (ed.), *Progress in the Psychology of Language*, vol. 2. London: Lawrence Erlbaum

Ellis, A. W., and Beattie, G. (1985), *The Psychology of Language and Communication*, London: Weidenfeld and Nicolson

Elman, J., and McClelland, J. L. (1984), 'Speech perception as a cognitive process: the interactive activation model', in N. Lass (ed.), *Speech and Language: Advances in Basic Research and Practice*, vol. 10, New York: Academic Press

Emmorey, K. D., and Fromkin, V. A. (1988), 'The mental lexicon', in Newmeyer (1988), vol. 3

Epstein, W. (1961), 'The influence of syntactical structure on learning', *American Journal of Psychology*, **74**, pp. 80–5

Ervin, S. M. (1964), 'Imitation and structural change in children's language', in Lenneberg (1964)

Ervin-Tripp, S. (1971), 'An overview of theories of grammatical development', in Slobin (1971)

Evans, W. E., and Bastian, J. (1969), 'Marine mammal communication: social and ecological factors', in H. T. Andersen (ed.), *The Biology of Marine Mammals*, New York: Academic Press

Fay, D., and Cutler, A. (1977), 'Malapropisms and the structure of the mental lexicon', *Linguistic Inquiry*, **8**, pp. 505–20

Ferguson, C. A. (1978), 'Talking to children: a search for universals', in J. H. Greenberg, C. A. Ferguson and E. Moravcsik (eds), *Universals of Human Language*, vol. 1, Stanford, Cal: Stanford University Press

Ferguson, C. A., and Slobin, D. I. (1973), *Studies of Child Language Development*, New York: Holt, Reinhart and Winston

Fernald, A. (1984), 'The perceptual and affective salience of mothers' speech to infants', in L. Feagans, C. Garvey, and R. Golinkoff (eds), *The Origins and Growth of Communication*, New Brunswick: Ablex

Ferreira, F. and Clifton, C. (1986), 'The independence of syntactic processing', *Journal of Memory and Language*, **25**, pp. 348–68

Fillenbaum, S. (1971), 'Psycholinguistics', *Annual Review of Psychology*, **22**, pp. 251–308

Fillenbaum, S. (1973), *Syntactic Factors in Memory*, The Hague, Mouton

Fillmore, C. J., Kempler, D., and Wang, W. S-Y. (1979), *Individual Differences in Language Behaviour*, New York: Academic Press

Fletcher, P. (1983), 'Verb-form development: Lexis or grammar?', in C. I. Phew and C. E. Johnson (eds), *Proceedings of the Second International Congress for the Study of Child Language*, vol. 2, Lanham, Md: University Press of America

Fletcher, P. (1985), *A Child's Learning of English*, Oxford: Basil Blackwell

Fletcher, P. and Garman, M. (1986), *Language Acquisition* (2nd edn), Cambridge: Cambridge University Press

Flores d'Arcais, G. B. (1988), 'Language perception', in Newmeyer (1988), vol. 3

Flores d'Arcais, G. B., and Jarvella, R. J. (1983), *The Process of Language Understanding*, Chichester and New York: Wiley

Flores d'Arcais, G. B., and Levelt, W. J. M. (1970), *Advances in Psycholinguistics*, Amsterdam: North Holland

Flores d'Arcais, G. B., and Schreuder, R. (1983), 'The process of language understanding: a few issues in contemporary psycholinguistics', in Flores d'Arcais and Jarvella (1983)

Fodor, J. A. (1966), 'How to learn to talk: some simple ways', in Smith and Miller (1966)

Fodor, J. A. (1983), *The Modularity of Mind*, Cambridge, Mass: MIT Press

Fodor, J. A. (1985), 'Precis of *The Modularity of Mind*', *The Behavioral and Brain Sciences*, **8**, pp. 1–5

Fodor, J. A., Bever, T. G., and Garrett, M. F. (1974), *The Psychology of Language*, New York: McGraw Hill

Fodor, J. A., and Garrett, M. (1966), 'Some reflections on competence and performance', in Lyons and Wales (1966)

Fodor, J. A., and Garrett, M. (1967), 'Some syntactic determinants of sentential complexity', *Perception and Psychophysics*, **2**, pp. 289–96

Fodor, J. A., Garrett, M., and Bever, T. G. (1968), 'Some syntactic determinants of sentential complexity, II: verb structure', *Perception and Psychophysics*, **3**, pp. 453–61

Fodor, J. D. (1978), 'Parsing strategies and constraints on transformations', *Linguistic Inquiry*, 9, pp. 427–73

Fodor, J. D. (1979), 'Superstrategy', in Cooper and Walker (1979)

Fodor, J. D., and Crain, S. (1987), 'Simplicity and generality of rules in language acquisition', in MacWhinney (1987)

Ford, M., Bresnan, J., and Kaplan, R. (1982), 'A competence-based theory of syntactic closure', in Bresnan (1982).

Ford, M., and Dalrymple, M. (1988), 'A note on some psychological evidence and alternative grammars', *Cognition*, 29, pp. 63–73

Foss, D. (1970), 'Some effects of ambiguity upon sentence comprehension', *Journal of Verbal Learning and Verbal Behavior*, 9, pp. 699–706

Fourcin, A. J. (1978), 'Acoustic patterns and speech acquisition', in Waterson and Snow (1978)

Fouts, R. S. (1983), 'Chimpanzee language and elephant tails: a theoretical synthesis', in de Luce and Wilder (1983)

Fouts, R. S., Fouts, D. H., and Schoenfeld, D. (1984), 'Sign language conversational interaction between chimpanzees', *Sign Language Studies* 42, pp. 1–12

Fouts, R. S., Hirsch, A., and Fouts, D. (1982), 'Cultural transmission of a human language in a chimpanzee mother/infant relationship', in H. E. Fitzgerald, J. A. Mullins, and P. Page (eds), *Psychobiological Perspectives: Child Nurturance Series*, vol. 3, New York: Plenum Press

Frazier, L. (1988), 'Grammar and language processing', in Newmeyer (1988), vol. 2

Frazier, L., Clifton, C., and Randall, J. (1983), 'Filling gaps: decision principles and structure in sentence comprehension', *Cognition*, 13, pp. 187–222

Frazier, L., and Fodor, J. D. (1978), 'The sausage machine: a new two stage parsing model', *Cognition*, 6, pp. 291–325

Frazier, L. and Rayner, K. (1982), 'Making and correcting errors during sentence comprehension: eye movements in the analysis of structurally ambiguous sentences', *Cognitive Psychology*, 14, pp. 178–210

Frazier, L., and Rayner, K. (1988), 'Parameterizing the language processing system: left- vs. right-branching within and across languages', in Hawkins (1988)

Freud, S. (1901), 'Slips of the tongue', in Fromkin (1973)

Fromkin, V. A. (1971), 'The non-anomalous nature of anomalous utterances', *Language*, 47, pp. 27–52. Also in Fromkin (1973)

Fromkin, V. A. (1973), *Speech Errors as Linguistic Evidence*, The Hague: Mouton

Fromkin, V. A. (1980), *Errors in Linguistic Performance: Slips of the Tongue, Ear, Pen and Hand*, New York: Academic Press

Fromkin, V. A. (1988), 'Grammatical aspects of speech errors', in Newmeyer (1988), vol. 2

Fromkin, V. A., and Rodman, R. (1988),*An Introduction to Language* (4th edn), New York: Holt, Reinhart and Winston

Fry, D. B. (1970), 'Speech reception and perception', in Lyons (1970)

Gardner, B. T., and Gardner, R. A. (1971), 'Two-way communication with an infant chimpanzee', in A. Schrier and F. Stollnitz (eds), *Behavior of Nonhuman Primates*, vol. 4, New York: Academic Press

Gardner, B. T., and Gardner, R. A. (1975), 'Evidence for sentence constituents in the early utterances of child and chimpanzee', *Journal of Experimental Psychology: General*, **104**, pp. 244–67

Gardner, B. T., and Gardner, R. A. (1980), 'Two comparative psychologists look at language acquisition', in Nelson (1980)

Gardner, B. T., and Gardner, R. A. (1985), 'Signs of intelligence in cross-fostered chimpanzees', *Philosophical Transactions of the Royal Society of London*, **B 308**, pp. 159–76

Gardner, H. (1974), *The Shattered Mind: The Person After Brain Damage*, New York: Knopf

Gardner, H. (1983), *Frames of Mind*, New York: Basic Books

Gardner, H. (1985), 'The centrality of modules', *The Behavioral and Brain Sciences*, **8**, pp. 12–14

Gardner, R. A., and Gardner, B. T. (1969), 'Teaching sign language to a chimpanzee', *Science*, **165**, pp. 664–72

Gardner, R. A., and Gardner, B. T. (1978), 'Comparative psychology and language acquisition', in K. Salzinger and F. Denmark (eds), *Psychology: the State of the Art, Annals of the New York Academy of Sciences*, **309**, pp. 37–76

Gardner, R. A., and Gardner, B. T. (1984), 'A vocabulary test for chimpanzees (Pan troglodytes)', *Journal of Comparative Psychology*, **96**, pp. 381–404

Garnham, A. (1985), *Psycholinguistics: Central Topics*, London: Methuen

Garrett, M. F. (1976), 'Syntactic processes in sentence production', in Wales and Walker (1976)

Garrett, M. F. (1980), 'Levels of processing in sentence production', in Butterworth (1980)

Garrett, M. F. (1980a), 'The limits of accommodation: arguments for independent processing levels in sentence production', in Fromkin (1980)

Garrett, M. F. (1984), 'The organization of processing structure for language production: applications to aphasic speech', in Caplan, Lecours and Smith (1984)

Garrett, M. F. (1988), 'Processes in language production', in Newmeyer (1988), vol. 3

Garrett, M. F., Bever, T., and Fodor, J. A. (1966), 'The active use of grammar in speech perception', *Perception and Psychophysics*, **I**, pp. 30–32

Gazzaniga, M. S. (1970), *The Bisected Brain*, New York: Appleton-Century-Crofts

Gazzaniga, M. S. (1983), 'Right hemisphere language following brain bisection: a 20-year perspective', *American Psychologist*, **38**, pp. 525–49

Gazdar, G., Klein, E., Pullum, G., and Sag, I. (1985), *Generalized Phrase Structure Grammar*, Oxford: Basil Blackwell

Geschwind, N. (1979), 'Specializations of the human brain', *Scientific American*, **241**, (September), pp. 158–71

Gleitman, L. R. (1984), 'Biological predispositions to learn language', in P. Marler and H. S. Terrace (eds), *The Biology of Learning*, Berlin: Springer-Verlag

Gleitman, L. R., Gleitman, H., and Shipley, E. F. (1972), 'The emergence of the child as grammarian', *Cognition*, **1**, pp. 137–64

Gleitman, L. R., Newport, E. L. and Gleitman, H. (1984), 'The current status of the motherese hypothesis', *Journal of Child Language*, **11**, pp. 43–79

Gleitman, L. R., and Wanner, E. (1982), 'Language acquisition: the state of the state of the art', in Wanner and Gleitman (1982)

Goldman-Eisler, F. (1964), 'Hesitation, information and levels of speech production', in De Reuck and O'Connor (1964)

Goldman-Rakic, P. S. (1982), 'Organization of frontal association cortex in normal and experimentally brain-injured primates', in M. A. Arbib, D. Caplan and J. C. Marshall (eds), *Neural Models of Language Processes*, New York: Academic Press

Goodglass, H. (1968), 'Studies on the grammar of aphasics', in Rosenberg and Kaplin (1968)

Goodluck, H. (1986), 'Language acquisition and linguistic theory', in Fletcher and Garman (1986)

Gough, P. B. (1971), 'Experimental Psycholinguistics', in Dingwall (1971)

Gould, J. L., and Marler, P. (1987), 'Learning by instinct', *Scientific American*, **256** (1), pp. 62–73

Griffin, D. R. (1984), *Animal Thinking*, Cambridge, Mass: Harvard University Press

Griffiths, P. (1986), 'Early vocabulary', in Fletcher and Garman (1986)

Grosu, A. (1974), 'On the complexity of center-embedding', Mimeo

Grosu, A. (1974a), 'On self-embedding and double function', *Linguistic Inquiry*, **5**, pp. 464–9

Gruber, E. H., Beardsley, W., and Caramazza, A. (1978), 'Parallel function strategy in pronoun assignment', *Cognition*, **6**, pp. 117–33

Gruber, J. S. (1967), 'Topicalization in child language', *Foundations of Language*, **3**, pp. 37–65

Hakes, D. T. (1971), 'Does verb structure affect sentence comprehension?', *Perception and Psychophysics*, **10**, pp. 229–32

Halle, M., Bresnan, J., and Miller, G. A. (1978), *Linguistic Theory and Psychological Reality*, Cambridge, Mass: MIT Press

Halliday, M. A. K. (1975), *Learning How to Mean*, London: Edward Arnold

Hamburger, H., and Crain, S. (1984), 'Acquisition of cognitive compiling', *Cognition*, **17**, pp. 85–136

Harley, B. (1986), *Age in Second Language Acquisition*, Avon, England: Multilingual Matters

Harris, M., Barrett, M., Jones, D., and Brookes, S. (1988), 'Linguistic input and early word meaning', *Journal of Child Language*, **15**, pp. 77–94

Hatch, E. M. (1983), *Psycholinguistics: A Second Language Perspective*, Rowley, Mass: Newbury House

Hawkins, J. A. (1988), *Explaining Language Universals*, Oxford: Basil Blackwell

Hayes, C. (1951), *The Ape in Our House*, New York: Harper

Hayes, J. R. (1970), *Cognition and the Development of Language*, New York: Wiley

Heath, S. B. (1983), *Ways with Words*, Cambridge: Cambridge University Press

Henderson, A., Goldman-Eisler, F., and Skarbek, A. (1965), 'The common value of pausing time in spontaneous speech', *Quarterly Journal of Experimental Psychology*, **17**, pp. 343–5

Herman, L. M., Richards, D. G., and Wolz, J. P. (1984), 'Comprehension of sentences by bottlenosed dolphins', *Cognition*, **16**, pp. 129–219

Hockett, C. F. (1963), 'The problem of universals in language', in J. H. Greenberg (ed.), *Universals of Language*, Cambridge, Mass: MIT Press

Hockett, C. and Altmann, S. (1968), 'A note on design features', in T. Sebeok (ed.), *Animal Communication: Techniques of Study and Results of Research*, Bloomington: Indiana University Press

Horrocks, G. (1987), *Generative Grammar*, London: Longman

Hurford, J. (1975), 'A child and the English question formation rule', *Journal of Linguistics*, **2**, pp. 299–301

Huxley, R., and Ingram, E. (1971), *Language Acquisition: Models and Methods*, New York: Academic Press

Hyams, N. (1986), *Language Acquisition and the Theory of Parameters*, Dordrecht: Reidel

Hyams, N. (1987), 'The theory of parameters and syntactic development', in Roeper and Williams (1987)

Hyman, L. M., and Li, C. N. (1988), *Language, Speech and Mind*, New York: Routledge

Jackson, H. J. (1932), *Selected Writings*, vol. II, London: Hodder and Stoughton.

Jakobovits, L. A., and Miron, M. S. (1967), *Readings in the Psychology of Language*, Englewood Cliffs, NJ: Prentice-Hall

Jakobson, R. (1962), 'Why "Mama" and "Papa"?', in Bar-Adon and Leopold (1971)

Johnson-Laird, P. N. (1970), 'The perception and memory of sentences', in Lyons (1970)

Johnson-Laird, P. N. (1974), 'Experimental psycholinguistics', *Annual Review of Psychology*, **25**, pp. 135–60

Johnson-Laird, P. N. (1983), *Mental Models*, Cambridge, Mass: Harvard University Press

Johnson-Laird, P. N. (1988), *The Computer and the Mind: An Introduction to Cognitive Science*, London: Fontana

Johnson-Laird, P. N., and Stevenson, R. (1970), 'Memory for syntax', *Nature*, **227**, p. 412

Johnston, J. R., and Slobin, D. I. (1979), 'The development of locative expressions in English, Italian, Serbo-Croatian and Turkish', *Journal of Child Language*, **6**, pp. 529–45

Kachru, B. J., Lees, R. B., Malkiel, Y., Pietrangeli, A., and Saporta, S. (1973), *Issues in Linguistics*, Papers in Honor of Henry and Renee Kahane, Chicago: Illinois University Press

Karmiloff-Smith, A. (1979), *A Functional Approach to Child Language: A Study of Determiners and Reference*, Cambridge: Cambridge University Press

Karmiloff-Smith, A. (1983), 'Language development as a problem-solving process', *Stanford University Papers and Reports on Child Language Development*

Karmiloff-Smith, A. (1986), 'From meta-processes to conscious access: evidence from children's metalinguistic and repair data', *Cognition*, **23**, pp. 95–147

Kean, M.-L. (1985), *Agrammatism*, Orlando, Fla: Academic Press

Keele, S. W. (1987), 'Sequencing and timing in skilled perception and action: an overview', in Allport, Mackay, Prinz, and Scherer (1987)

Keil, F. (1986), 'On the structure-dependent nature of stages of cognitive development', in I. Levin (ed.), *Stage and Structure: Reopening the Debate*, Norwood, NJ: Ablex

Kellogg, W. N., and Kellogg, L. A. (1933), *The Ape and the Child*, New York: McGraw Hill

Kimball, J. (1973), 'Seven principles of surface structure parsing in natural language', *Cognition*, **2**, pp. 15–47

Kimura, D. (1967), 'Functional asymmetry of the brain in dichotic listening', *Cortex*, **3**, pp. 163–78

King, M. (1983), *Parsing Natural Language*, London and New York: Academic Press.

Kinoshita, S. (1986), 'Sentence context effect on lexically ambiguous words: evidence for a postaccess inhibition process', *Memory and Cognition*, **13**, pp. 579–95

Kinsbourne, M. (1975), 'Minor hemisphere language and cerebral maturation' in Lenneberg and Lenneberg (1975)

Kinsbourne, M. and Hiscock, M. (1987), 'Language lateralization and disordered language development', in S. Rosenberg (ed.), *Advances in Applied Psycholinguistics*, vol. 1, Cambridge: Cambridge University Press

Klima, E., and Bellugi, U. (1966), 'Syntactic regularities in the speech of children', in Lyons and Wales (1966), revised version in Bar-Adon and Leopold (1971)

Krashen, S. D. (1973–4), 'Lateralization, language learning, and the critical period: some new evidence', *Language Learning*, **23**, pp. 63–74

Kucsaj II, S. A. (1983), *Crib Speech and Language Play*, New York: Springer-Verlag

Kuhl, P. K. (1987), 'Perception of speech and sound in early infancy', in P. Salapatek and L. Cohen (eds), *Handbook of Infant Perception*, vol. 2, New York: Academic Press

Kuhl, P., and Miller, J. D. (1974), 'Discrimination of speech sounds by the chinchilla: /t/ vs /d/ in CV syllables', *Journal of the Acoustical Society of America*, **56**, series 42 (abstract)

Kuhl, P., and Miller, J. D. (1975), 'Speech perception by the chinchilla: phonetic boundaries for synthetic VOT stimuli', *Journal of the Acoustical Society of America*, **57**, series 49 (abstract)

Lashley, K. S. (1951), 'The problem of serial order in behavior', in L. A. Jefress (ed.), *Cerebral Mechanisms in Behavior*, New York: Wiley, also in Saporta (1961)

Lecours, A. R., Basso, A., Moraschini, S., and Nespoulous, J.-L. (1984), 'Where is the speech area, and who has seen it?', in Caplan, Lecours and Smith (1984)

Lee, V. (1979), *Language Development*, London: Croom Helm and The Open University Press

Lenneberg, E. H. (1964), *New Directions in the Study of Language*, Cambridge, Mass: MIT Press

Lenneberg, E. H. (1967), *Biological Foundations of Language*, New York: Wiley

Lenneberg, E. H., and Lenneberg, E. (1975), *Foundations of Language Development*, vols. 1 and 2, New York: Academic Press

Lesser, R. (1978), *Linguistic Investigations of Aphasia*, London: Edward Arnold

Levelt, W. J. M. (1983), 'Monitoring and self-repair in speech', *Cognition*, **14**, pp. 41–104

Levy, J. (1979), 'Strategies of linguistic processing in human split-brain patients', in Fillmore, Kempler and Wang (1979)

Liberman, A. M., Cooper, F., Shankweiler, D. P., and Studdert-Kennedy, M. (1967), 'Perception of the speech code', *Psychological Review*, **74**, pp. 431–61

Liberman, A. M., Harris, K. S., Hoffman, H. S., and Griffith, B. C. (1957), 'The discrimination of speech sounds within and across phoneme boundaries', *Journal of Experimental Psychology*, **54**, pp. 358–68

Lieberman, P. (1972), *The Speech of Primates*, The Hague: Mouton

Lieberman, P. (1975), *On the Origins of Language*, New York: Macmillan

Lieberman, P. (1984), *The Biology and Evolution of Language*, Cambridge, Mass: Harvard University Press

Lieberman, P., and Blumstein, S. E. (1988), *Speech Physiology, Speech Perception and Acoustic Phonetics*, Cambridge: Cambridge University Press

Livesley, B. (1972), 'The Alice in Wonderland syndrome', *Teach In*, **1**, pp. 770–74

Luce, R. D., Bush, R. R., and Galanter, E. (1963), *Handbook of Mathematical Psychology*, vol. 2, New York: Wiley

Lust, B. (1983), 'On the notion "Principle Branching Direction": a parameter of universal grammar', in Y. Otsu, H. Van Riemsdijk, K. Inoue, A. Kamio, N. Kawasaki (eds), *Studies in Generative Grammar and Language Acquisition*, Tokyo: International Christian University

Lust, B. (1986), *Studies in the Acquisition of Anaphora*, Dordrecht: Reidel

Lyons, J. (1970), *New Horizons in Linguistics*, Harmondsworth: Penguin

Lyons, J. (1981), *Language and Linguistics: An Introduction*, Cambridge: Cambridge University Press

Lyons, J., and Wales, R. J. (1966), *Psycholinguistics Papers*, Edinburgh: Edinburgh University Press

McCawley, J. D. (1988), Review of Chomsky (1986), *Language*, **64**, pp. 355–65

McClelland, J. L. (1988), 'Connectionist models and psychological evidence' *Journal of Memory and Learning*, **27**, pp. 107–23

McClelland, J. L. and Rumelhart, D. E. (1986), *Parallel Distributed Processing: Explorations in the Microstructure of Cognition*, vol. 2: Psychological and Biological Models, Cambridge, Mass: MIT Press

McClelland, J. L., Rumelhart, D. E., and Hinton, G. E. (1986), 'The appeal of parallel distributed processing', in Rumelhart and McClelland (1986)

McNeill, D. (1966), 'Developmental psycholinguistics', in Smith and Miller (1966)

McNeill, D. (1970), *The Acquisition of Language*, New York: Harper and Row

McShane, J. (1979), 'The development of naming', *Linguistics*, **17**, pp. 879–905

McShane, J. (1980), *Learning to Talk*, Cambridge: Cambridge University Press

Mackain, K., Studdert-Kennedy, M., Spieker, S., and Stern, D. (1983), 'Infant intermodal speech perception is a left-hemisphere function', *Science*, **219**, pp. 1347–9

Mackay, D. G. (1987), 'Constraints on theories of sequencing and timing in language perception and production', in Allport, Mackay, Prinz and Scherer (1987)

Mackay, D. G., Allport, A., Prinz, W., and Scherer, E. (1987), 'Relationship and modules within language perception and production: an introduction', in Allport, Mackay, Prinz and Scherer (1987)

Maclay, H. (1973), 'Linguistics and psycholinguistics', in Kachru (1973)

Macnamara, J. (1977), *Language Learning and Thought*, New York: Academic Press

MacWhinney, B. (1978), *The Acquisition of Morphophonology*, Monograph of the Society for Research in Child Development, **43**, pp. 1–2

MacWhinney, B. (1987), *Mechanisms of Language Acquisition*, Hillsdale, New Jersey: Lawrence Erlbaum

MacWhinney, B. (1987a), 'The competition model', in MacWhinney (1987)

Maratsos, M. (1978), 'New models in linguistics and language acquisition', in Halle, Bresnan and Miller (1978)

Maratsos, M. (1982), 'The child's construction of grammatical categories', in Wanner and Gleitman (1982)

Maratsos, M., and Chalkley, M. A. (1980), 'The internal language of children's syntax: the ontogenesis and representation of syntactic categories', in Nelson (1980)

Marcus, M. P. (1980), *A Theory of Syntactic Recognition for Natural Language*, Cambridge, Mass: MIT Press

Marks, L., and Miller, G. (1964), 'The role of semantic and syntactic constraints in the memorization of English sentences', *Journal of Verbal Learning and Verbal Behavior*, **3**, pp. 1–5

Marler, P. (1988), 'Birdsong and neurogenesis', *Nature*, **334**, pp. 106–7

Marshall, J. C. (1970), 'The biology of communication in man and animals', in Lyons (1970)

Marshall, J. C. (1987), Review of Savage-Rumbaugh (1986), *Nature*, **325**, p. 310

Marslen-Wilson, W. D., and Tyler, L. K. (1980), 'The temporal structure of spoken language understanding', *Cognition*, **8**, pp. 1–71

Matthei, E. H. (1981), 'Children's interpretation of sentences containing reciprocals', in Tavakolian (1981)

Matthei, E. and Roeper, T. (1983), *Understanding and Producing Speech*, London: Fontana

294   *The Articulate Mammal*

Mazurkewich, I., and White, L. (1984), 'The acquisition of the dative alternation: unlearning overgeneralizations', *Cognition*, 16, pp. 261–83

Mehler, J. (1963), 'Some effects of grammatical transformations on the recall of English sentences', *Journal of Verbal Learning and Verbal Behavior*, 2, pp. 346–51

Mehler, J., and Carey, P. (1968), 'The interaction of veracity and syntax in the processing of sentences', *Perception and Psychophysics*, 3, pp. 109–11

Mehler, J., Jusczyk, P., Lambertz, G., and Halsted, N. (1988), 'A precursor of language acquisition in young infants', *Cognition*, 29, pp. 143–78

Miles, H. L. (1983), 'Apes and language: the search for communicative competence', in de Luce and Wilder (1983)

Miller, G. A. (1962), 'Some psychological studies of grammar', *American Psychologist*, 1, pp. 748–62, also in Jakobovits and Miron (1967) and De Cecco (1967)

Miller, G. A., and Chomsky, N. (1963), 'Finitary models of language users', in Luce, Bush and Galanter (1963)

Miller, G. A., and Lenneberg, E. (1978), *Psychology and Biology of Language and Thought*, New York: Academic Press

Miller, G. A., and McKean, K. (1964), 'A chronometric study of some relations between sentences', *Quarterly Journal of Experimental Psychology*, 16, pp. 297–308. Also in Oldfield and Marshall (1968)

Miller, W., and Ervin, S. (1964), 'The development of grammar in child language', in Bellugi and Brown (1964)

Milner, B., Branch, C., and Rasmussen, T. (1964), 'Observations on cerebral dominance', in De Reuck and O'Connor (1964). Also in Oldfield and Marshall (1968)

Modgil, S., and Modgil, C. (1987), *Noam Chomsky: Consensus and Controversy*, Philadelphia, Pa: The Falmer Press

Morse, P. A. (1976), 'Speech perception in the human infant and rhesus monkey', in S. Harnad, H. Steklis and J. Lancaster (eds), *Origins and evolution of language and speech, Annals of the New York Academy of Sciences*, vol. 280

Morton, J. (1971), 'What could possibly be innate?', in J. Morton (ed.), *Biological and Social Factors in Psycholinguistics*, London: Logos Press

Moscovitch, M. (1983), 'Stages of processing and hemisphere differences in language in the normal subject', in Studdert-Kennedy (1983)

Motley, M. T. (1985), 'Slips of the tongue', *Scientific American*, 253 (September), pp. 114–19

Nelson, K. (1973), *Structure and strategy in learning to talk*, Monograph of the Society for Research in Child Development, 38, pp. 1–2

Nelson, K. (1980), *Children's Language*, vol. 2, New York: Gardner Press

Newmeyer, F. J. (1986), *Linguistic Theory in America* (2nd edn), New York: Academic Press

Newmeyer, F. J. (1988), *Linguistics: The Cambridge Survey*, vols. 1–4, Cambridge: Cambridge University Press

Newport, E. L., Gleitman, H., and Gleitman, L. R. (1977), 'Mother I'd rather do it myself: the contribution of selected child listener variables', in Snow and Ferguson (1977)

Nishigauchi, T., and Roeper, T. (1987), 'Deductive parameters and the growth of empty categories', in Roeper and Williams (1987)

Nooteboom, S. G. (1969), 'The tongue slips into patterns', in A. G. Sciarone *et al.* (eds), *Nomen: Leyden Studies in Linguistics and Phonetics*, The Hague: Mouton. Also in Fromkin (1973)

Nottebohm, F. (1975), 'A zoologist's view of some language phenomena with particular emphasis on vocal learning', in Lenneberg and Lenneberg (1975), vol. 1

Nottebohm, F. (1984), 'Vocal learning and its possible relation to replaceable synapses and neurons', in Caplan, Lecours and Smith (1984)

O'Grady, W. (1989), 'The transition from optional to required subjects', *Journal of Child Language*

Oldfield, R. C., and Marshall, J. C. (1968), *Language: Selected Readings*, Harmondsworth: Penguin

Osherson, D. N., and Wasow, T. (1976), 'Task specificity and species-specificity in the study of language: a methodological note', *Cognition*, **4**, pp. 203–14

Padden, C. A. (1988), 'Grammatical theory and signed languages', in Newmeyer (1988), vol. 2

Patterson, F. G. (1978), 'The gestures of a gorilla: language acquisition in another pongid', *Brain and Language*, **5**, pp. 72–97

Patterson, F. G. (1980), 'Innovative uses of language by a gorilla: a case study', in Nelson (1980)

Patterson, F. G., and Linden, E. (1981), *The Education of Koko*, New York: Holt, Reinhart and Winston

Peirce, C. S. (1932), *Collected Papers of Charles Sanders Peirce*, vol. 2, edited by C. Hartshorne and P. Weiss, Cambridge, Mass: Harvard University Press

Penfield, W., and Roberts, L. (1959), *Speech and brain mechanisms*, Princeton, NJ: Princeton University Press

Peters, A. M. (1977), 'Language learning strategies: does the whole equal the sum of the parts?', *Language*, **53**, pp. 560–73

Peters, A. M. (1983), *The Units of Language Acquisition*, Cambridge: Cambridge University Press

Petitto, L. A., and Seidenberg, M. S. (1979), 'On the evidence for linguistic abilities in signing apes', *Brain and Language*, **8**, pp. 162–83

Pinker, S. (1984), *Language Learnability and Language Development*, Cambridge, Mass: Harvard University Press

Pinker, S. (1987), 'The bootstrapping problem in language acquisition', in MacWhinney (1987)

Pinker, S., and Prince, A. (1988), 'On language and connectionism: analysis of a parallel distributed processing model of language acquisition', *Cognition*, **28**, pp. 73–193

Premack, A. J. (1976), *Why Chimps Can Read*, New York: Harper and Row

Premack, D. (1970), 'The education of Sarah', *Psychology Today*, **4**, pp. 55–8

Premack, D. (1971), 'Language in chimpanzee?', *Science*, **172**, pp. 808–22

Premack, D. (1972), 'Teaching language to an ape', *Scientific American* (October), pp. 92–9

Premack, D. (1976), *Intelligence in Ape and Man*, Hillsdale, NJ: Lawrence Erlbaum Associates

Premack, D., and Premack, A. J. (1974), 'Teaching visual language to apes and language-deficient persons', in Schiefelbusch and Lloyd (1974)

Premack, D., and Premack, A. J. (1983), *The Mind of an Ape*, New York: Norton

Radford, A. (1988), *Transformational Grammar: A First Course*, Cambridge: Cambridge University Press

Radford, A. (1988a), 'Small children's small clauses', *Transactions of the Philological Society*, **86**, pp. 1–43

Randall, J. (1987), *Indirect Positive Evidence: Overturning Generalizations in Language Acquisition*, Bloomington, Ind: Indiana University Linguistics Club

Reich, P. A. (1986), *Language Development*, Englewood Cliffs, NJ: Prentice-Hall

Richards, D. G., Wolz, J. P., and Herman, L. M. (1984), 'Mimicry of computer-generated sounds and vocal labeling of objects by a bottlenosed dolphin', *Journal of Comparative Psychology*, **98**, pp. 10–28

Ricks, D. M. (1975), 'Vocal communication in pre-verbal normal and autistic children', in N. O'Connor (ed.), *Language, Cognitive Deficits, and Retardation*, London: Butterworth

Roeper, T., and Matthei, E. (1983), *Understanding and Producing Speech*, London: Fontana

Roeper, T., and Williams, E. (1987), *Parameter Setting*, Dordrecht: Reidel

Rosenberg, S., and Koplin, J. H. (1968), *Developments in Applied Psycholinguistics Research*, New York: Macmillan

Rosenfield, D. (1978), 'Some neurological techniques for accessing localization of function', in Walker (1978)

Rumbaugh, D. M. (1977), *Language Learning by a Chimpanzee: The LANA Project*, New York: Academic Press

Rumelhart, D. E., Hinton, G. E., and McClelland, J. L. (1986), 'A general framework for parallel distributed processing', in Rumelhart and McClelland (1986)

Rumelhart, D. E., and McClelland, J. L. (1986), *Parallel Distributed Processing: Explorations in the Microstructure of Cognition*, vol. 1: Foundations, Cambridge, Mass: MIT Press

Rumelhart, D. E., and McClelland, J. L. (1987), 'Learning the past tense of English verbs: implicit rules or parallel distributed processing?', in MacWhinney (1987). Also in McClelland and Rumelhart (1986)

Sachs, J. S. (1967), 'Recognition memory for syntactic and semantic aspects of connected discourse', *Perception and Psychophysics*, 2, pp. 437–42

Sampson, G. (1975), *The Form of Language*, London: Weidenfeld and Nicolson

Sampson, G. (1980), *Making Sense*, Oxford: Oxford University Press

Sampson, G. (1987), Review of Rumelhart and McClelland (1986), Language, 63, pp. 871–86

Saporta, S. (1961), *Psycholinguistics: A Book of Readings*, New York: Holt, Reinhart and Winston

Savage-Rumbaugh, E. S. (1986), *Ape Language: From Conditioned Response to Symbol*, Oxford: Oxford University Press

Savage-Rumbaugh, E., and Rumbaugh, D. M. (1980), 'Language analogue project, phase II: theory and tactics', in Nelson (1980)

Savin, H., and Perchonock, E. (1965), 'Grammatical structure and the immediate recall of English sentences', *Journal of Verbal Learning and Verbal Behavior*, 4, pp. 348–53

Schiefelbusch, R. L., and Lloyd, L. L. (1974), *Language Perspectives – Acquisition, Retardation, and Intervention*, Baltimore: University Park Press

Schlesinger, I. M. (1967), 'A note on the relationship between psychological and linguistic theories', *Foundations of Language*, 3, pp. 397–402

Schlesinger, I. M. (1971), 'Production of utterances and language acquisition', in Slobin (1971)

Scovel, T. (1988), *A Time to Speak: A Psycholinguistic Examination of the Critical Period for Language Acquisition*, Rowley, Mass: Newbury House

Sebeok, T. A. (1977), *How Animals Communicate*, Indiana: Indiana University Press

Sebeok, T. A., and Umiker-Sebeok, J. (1979), *Speaking of Apes: A Critical Anthology of Two-Way Communication with Man*, New York: Plenum

Sebeok, T. A., and Rosenthal, R. (1981), *The Clever Hans Phenomenon: Communication with Horses, Whales, Apes and People*, New York: The New York Academy of Sciences

298   *The Articulate Mammal*

Sebeok, T. A., and Umiker-Sebeok, J. (1980), *What the Speechless Creatures Say*, Bloomington: Indiana University Press

Seidenberg, M. S., Tanenhaus, M. K., Leiman, J. M., and Bienkowski, M. (1982), 'Automatic access of the meaning of ambiguous words in context: some limitations of knowledge-based processing', *Cognitive Psychology*, 14, pp. 481–537

Sells, P. (1985), *Lectures on Contemporary Syntactic Theories*, Stanford, Cal: Stanford University Center for the Study of Language and Information

Seyfarth, R. M., Cheney, D. L., and Marler, P. (1980), 'Monkey responses to three different alarm calls: evidence for predator classification and semantic communication', *Science*, 210, pp. 801–3

Seyfarth, R. M., Cheney, D. L., and Marler, P. (1980a), 'Vervet monkey alarm calls: semantic communication in a free-ranging primate', *Animal Behavior*, 28, pp. 1070–94

Shapiro, L. P., Zurif, E., and Grimshaw, J. (1987), 'Sentence processing and the mental representation of verbs', *Cognition*, 27, pp. 219–46

Shattuck-Hufnagel, S. (1979), 'Speech errors as evidence for a serial-ordering mechanism in sentence production', in Cooper and Walker (1979)

Shatz, M. (1982), 'On mechanisms of language acquisition: can features of the communicative environment account for development?', in Wanner and Gleitman (1982)

Sinclair-de-Zwart, H. (1969), 'Developmental Psycholinguistics', in D. Elkind and J. Flavell (eds), *Studies in Cognitive Development*, Oxford: Oxford University Press

Skinner, B. F. (1957), *Verbal Behavior*, New York: Appleton-Century-Crofts

Slobin, D. I. (1966), 'The acquisition of Russian as a native language', in Smith and Miller (1966)

Slobin, D. I. (1966a), 'Grammatical transformations and sentence comprehension in childhood and adulthood', *Journal of Verbal Learning and Verbal Behavior*, 5, pp. 219–27

Slobin, D. I. (1971), *The Ontogenesis of Grammar*, New York: Academic Press

Slobin, D. I. (1971a), 'On the learning of morphological rules', in Slobin (1971)

Slobin, D. I. (1971b), *Psycholinguistics*, Glenview, Illinois: Scott Foresmann

Slobin, D. I. (1973), 'Cognitive prerequisites for the development of grammar' in Ferguson and Slobin (1973)

Slobin, D. I. (1975), 'On the nature of talk to children', in Lenneberg and Lenneberg (1975)

Slobin, D. I. (1977), 'Language change in childhood and in history', in Macnamara (1977)

Slobin, D. I. (1979), 'The origins of grammatical encoding of events', in W. Deutsch (ed.), *The Child's Construction of Language*, London: Academic Press

Slobin, D. I. (1982), 'Universal and particular in the acquisition of language', in Wanner and Maratsos (1982)

Slobin, D. I. (1985), *The Crosslinguistic Study of Language Acquisition*, vols. 1 and 2, Hillsdale, NJ: Lawrence Erlbaum

Slobin, D. I. (1985a), 'Why study acquisition crosslinguistically?', in Slobin (1985)

Slobin, D. I. (1985b), 'Crosslinguistic evidence for the language-making capacity', in Slobin (1985)

Slobin, D. I., and Welsh, C. A. (1967), 'Elicited imitation as a research tool in developmental psycholinguistics', in Ferguson and Slobin (1973)

Smith, F., and Miller, G. A. (1966), *The Genesis of Language*, Cambridge, Mass: MIT Press

Smith, N. V. (1973), *The Acquisition of Phonology: A Case Study*, Cambridge: Cambridge University Press

Snow, C. E., and Ferguson, C. A. (1977), *Talking to Children: Language Input and Acquisition*, Cambridge: Cambridge University Press

Springer, S. P., and Deutsch, G. (1985), *Left Brain, Right Brain* (rev. edn), New York: Freeman

Stahlke, H. F. W. (1980), 'On asking the question: can apes learn language?', in Nelson (1980)

Stoel-Gammon, C., and Cooper, A. (1984), 'Patterns of early lexical and phonological development', *Journal of Child Language*, 11, pp. 247–71

Struhsaker, T. T. (1967), 'Auditory communication among vervet monkeys (Cercopithecus aethiops)', in S. A. Altmann (ed.), *Social communication among Primates*, Chicago: Chicago University Press

Stowe, L. (1988), *Models of Gap-Location in the Human Language Processor*, Bloomington, Ind: Indiana University Linguistics Club

Studdert-Kennedy, M. (1983), *Psychobiology of Language*, Cambridge, Mass: MIT Press

Swinney, D. (1979), 'Lexical access during sentence comprehension: (Re)consideration of context effects', *Journal of Verbal Learning and Verbal Behavior*, 18, pp. 645–59

Sperber, D., and Wilson, D. (1986), *Relevance: Communication and Cognition*, Oxford: Basil Blackwell

Tanenhaus, M. K. (1988), 'Psycholinguistics: an overview', in Newmeyer (1988), vol. 3

Tanenhaus, M. K., Carlson, G. N., and Seidenberg, M. S. (1985), 'Do listeners compute linguistic representations', in Dowty, Karttunen and Zwicky (1985)

Tanenhaus, M. K., Leiman, K. H., and Seidenberg, M. S. (1979), 'Evidence for multiple stages in the processing of ambiguous words in syntactic contexts', *Journal of Verbal Learning and Verbal Behavior*, **18**, pp. 427–41

Tavakolian, S. L. (1981), *Language Acquisition and Linguistic Theory*, Cambridge, Mass: MIT Press

Terrace, H. S. (1979), *Nim*, New York: Knopf

Terrace, H. S. (1979a), 'How Nim Chimpsky changed my mind', *Psychology Today* (November 1979), pp. 65–76

Terrace, H. S. (1983), 'Apes who "talk": language or projection of language by their teachers?', in de Luce and Wilder (1983)

Terrace, H. S., Petitto, L. A., Sanders, R. J., and Bever T. G. (1980), 'On the grammatical capacity of apes', in Nelson (1980)

Thorpe, W. H. (1961), *Bird Song: The Biology of Vocal Communication and Expression in Birds*, Cambridge: Cambridge University Press

Thorpe, W. H. (1963), *Learning and Instinct in Animals* (2nd edn), London: Methuen

Thorpe, W. H. (1972), 'Vocal communication in birds', in R. A. Hinde (ed.), *Non-Verbal Communication*, Cambridge: Cambridge University Press.

Van Riemsdijk, H., and Williams, E. (1986), *Introduction to the Theory of Grammar*, Cambridge, Mass: MIT Press

Vargha-Khadem, F., O'Gorman, A. M., Watters, G. V. (1985), 'Aphasia and handedness in relation to hemisphere side, age at injury and severity of cerebral lesion during childhood', *Brain*, **8**, pp. 677–96

Vihman, M. M., Macken, M. A., Miller, R., Simmons, H., and Miller, J. (1985), 'From babbling to speech: a re-assessment of the continuity issue', *Language*, **61**, pp. 397–445

von Frisch, K. (1950), *Bees: Their Vision, Chemical Sense and Language*, Ithaca, NY: Cornell University Press

von Frisch, K. (1954), *The Dancing Bees*, London: Methuen

von Frisch, K. (1967), *The Dance and Orientation of Bees*, translated by L. E. Chadwick, Cambridge, Mass: Harvard University Press

Vygotsky, L. S. (1962), *Thought and Language*, Cambridge, Mass: MIT Press

Wales, R. J., and Walker, E. (1976), *New Approaches to Language Mechanisms*, Amsterdam: North Holland

Walker, E. (1978), *Explorations in the Biology of Language*, Sussex: The Harvester Press

Wanner, E. (1974), *On Remembering, Forgetting and Understanding Sentences: A Study of the Deep Structure Hypothesis*, The Hague: Mouton

Wanner, E., and Gleitman, L. R. (1982), *Language Acquisition: The State of the Art*, Cambridge: Cambridge University Press

Wanner, E., and Maratsos, M. (1978), 'An ATN approach to comprehension', in Halle, Bresnan and Miller (1978)

Wason, P. C. (1965), 'The contexts of plausible denial', *Journal of Verbal Learning and Verbal Behavior*, 4, pp. 7–11. Also in Oldfield and Marshall (1968)

Waterson, N., and Snow, C. (1978), *The Development of Communication*, Chichester: John Wiley and Sons

Watt, W. C. (1970), 'On two hypotheses concerning psycholinguistics', in Hayes (1970)

Weir, R. H. (1962), *Language in the Crib*, The Hague: Mouton

Weir, R. H. (1966), 'Some questions on the child's learning of phonology', in Smith and Miller (1966)

Wells, G. (1974), 'Learning to code experience through language', *Journal of Child Language*, 1, pp. 243–69

Wells, G. (1979), 'Learning and using the auxiliary verb in English', in Lee (1979)

Wells, G. (1980), 'Apprenticeship in meaning', in Nelson (1980)

Wells, G. (1982), *Interactive Encounters with Language*, Cambridge: Cambridge University Press

Wells, G. (1986), *The Meaning Makers: Children Learning Language and Using Language to Learn*, London: Hodder and Stoughton

Wells, G., and Robinson, W. P. (1982), 'The role of adult speech in language development', in C. Fraser and K. R. Scherer (eds), *Advances in the Social Psychology of Language*, Cambridge: Cambridge University Press

Wexler, K., and Culicover, P. W. (1980), *Formal Principles of Language Acquisition*, Cambridge, Mass: MIT Press

Wilbur, R. B. (1987), *American Sign Language: Linguistics and Applied Dimensions*, Boston: Little Brown

Wilson, B., and Peters, A. M. (1988), 'What are you cookin' on a hot?', *Language*, 64, pp. 249–73

Yamada, J. (1988), 'The independence of language: evidence from a retarded hyperlinguistic individual', in Hyman and Li (1988)

Yule, G. (1985), *The Study of Language*, Cambridge: Cambridge University Press

Yngve, V. (1961), 'The depth hypothesis', reprinted in F. W. Householder (ed.), *Syntactic Theory I: Structuralist*, Harmondsworth: Penguin (1972)

Zangwill, O. L. (1964), 'Intelligence in aphasia', in De Reuck and O'Connor (1964)

Zangwill, O. L. (1973), 'The neurology of language', in N. Minnis (ed.), *Linguistics at Large*, St Albans: Paladin

Index